D0891410

Discourses
of Ethnicity

Discourses of Ethnicity

Culture and Protest
in Jharkhand

SUSANA B.C. DEVALLE

SAGE PUBLICATIONS
New Delhi/Newbury Park/London

First published in 1992 by
Sage Publications India Pvt Ltd
M-32 Greater Kailash Market I
New Delhi 110 048

Sage Publications Inc   **Sage Publications Ltd**
2455 Teller Road   6 Bonhill Street
Newbury Park, California 91320   London EC2A 4PU

Published by Tejeshwar Singh for Sage Publications India Pvt Ltd, photo-typeset by Jayigee Enterprises, Madras, and printed at Chaman Enterprises, Delhi.

Library of Congress Cataloging-in-Publication Data

Devalle, Susana B. C.
    Discourses of ethnicity : culture and protest in Jharkhand / Susana B.C. Devalle.
        p. cm.
Includes bibliographical references and index (p.   ).
    1. Ethnicity—India—Jharkhand. 2. Jharkhand (India)—Scheduled tribes. 3. Jharkhand (India)—Politics and government. 4. Jharkhand (India)—Social conditions. I. Title.
GN635. I4D474   1992   306′.08′0954—dc20   91-42550

ISBN 81–7036–268–7 (India)
        0–8039–9416–8 (U.S.)

Contents

List of Maps and Charts

Abbreviations

AJSU	All-Jharkhand Students Union
BCKU	Bihar Colliery Kamgar Union
BJP	Bengal Judicial Proceedings
CI	Census of India
Congress(I)	Congress Party
CPI(M)	Communist Party of India (Marxist)
CR	*Calcutta Review*
EPW	*Economic and Political Weekly*
F	*Frontier*
GI	Government of India
HT	*The Hindustan Times*
IE	*Indian Express*
JCC	Jharkhand Co-ordination Committee
JMM	Jharkhand Mukti Morcha
MCC	Marxist Coordination Committee
NR	*The New Republic*
P	*Patriot*
TI	*The Times of India*
TS	*The Statesman*
TT	*The Telegraph*
WBDR	West Bengal District Records, N.S.

Preface

Ethnicity has acquired an important presence in the world today. In the course of the last decades, 'ethnic issues' overflowed the frontiers of established nation-states and emerged as one of the foci of international politics. At the same time, it became evident that there was a high degree of mystification surrounding the concept of ethnicity, and that it had been never fully explained or was taken as a self-explanatory variable in most socio-anthropological approaches to the phenomenon.

The aim of this book is to examine the relationship between historical structure, human experience and social consciousness in the constitution of ethnicity. The argument moves from the universal level of theory to the particular level where the problem under study is examined through the specific case of the adivasis of Bihar's Jharkhand region in India. The discussion also moves from the identification of the most visible aspects of the phenomenon (ethnicity as a language for political expression; overt actions and movements), to other aspects not so visible (class expressed in cultural terms; cultural protest). Stress is put on ethnicity as a process (the sociology of ethnicity), not on the description of fixed ethnic forms (*ethno-graphia*). In this way, the theoretical proposals and the discussion of the Jharkhand case seek to raise relevant points regarding the nature and contents of ethnic phenomena and on cultural dynamics. In locating the objectification of ethnicity within a historical framework, the book discusses basic issues concerning class, culture, social classification, modes of protest and the forging of collective identities among subordinate groups, thus seeking to bridge the theoretical gap between social anthropology and social history, in the hope of contributing towards an interdisciplinary social analysis.

This book was written between 1986 and 1989, and revised in 1990. The discussion of the situation in Jharkhand is based on data collected during fieldwork in India in 1980, 1981, and 1984, on archival documents and statistical materials consulted in England and India, and contemporary reports, documents and newspapers. Discussions with specialists and colleagues in different parts of the world helped greatly to refine the analysis. Additional research on ethnic phenomena in a variety of social contexts also proved valuable in the elaboration of theoretical proposals for the study of the subject and the development of a comparative perspective. Discussions on the ethnic question and indigenous movements held with people belonging to various ethno-national groups have also helped in the comprehension of the problem.

Conventional acknowledgments are inadequate to express how much this book owes to all those who gave it their support, knowledge and infinite patience while in the making. The ideas expressed in this volume are also a product of the privileged position that only some of us enjoy: to observe the social forces that for many others make up the reality they have to live day by day. In using this privilege, I hope to have done justice to what I saw and heard. I owe a great debt to the people in India and particularly in Jharkhand who, showing great tolerance toward yet another 'scientific intruder', paid attention to my queries and helped me understand the realities of their socio–political world.

The final version of this volume is the outcome of innumerable changes, many of them born of the comments and criticisms of colleagues. In the course of this process, Lionel Caplan provided me with enriching comments. The 'hand of history' was always generously extended to me by friends and colleagues, among them, Bipan Chandra and S. Bhattacharya; Harjot S. Oberoi and David Lorenzen carefully read and discussed earlier drafts of the manuscript. I also offer my grateful thanks to Nirmal Sengupta and Jorge Galeano for their helpful comments.

My lasting institutional affiliation with El Colegio de Mexico, and especially with the Centre for Asian and African Studies, provided me with a solid stronghold where I could discuss my ideas, plan fieldwork, and conclude the writing process. While in India, I was fortunate to be associated as a guest scholar with Jawaharlal Nehru University and the Centre for Social Sciences Research (Calcutta), at the invitation of the University Grants

Commission. My especial thanks to Barun De for his help while I was in Calcutta. My stays in India were greatly facilitated by the kindness of Graciela de la Lama, then Mexican Ambassador to India. I am also grateful to the staff of the India Office Library, the University of Minnesota Library, the S.O.A.S. Library at the University of London, the University of Texas at Austin Library, the Menzies Library at the Australian National University, and the Nehru Memorial Museum and Library in New Delhi. This lengthy list of acknowledgments cannot end without mentioning some of the silent partners in this project: Ezequiel de la Rosa, the author of the maps that accompany the text; Elia Aguilar, who patiently typed the bibliography; a host of good friends who brought me back to reality when work threatened to swallow me up; Leslie Falconer for her friendship and her generosity during my stays in London, and my students, who proved to be sharp critics and enthusiastic interlocutors. I end by holding again the 'hand of history': my deep thanks to Harjot S. Oberoi, who provided fertile ground wherein ideas could flourish, for his constant support.

Mexico   SUSANA B. C. DEVALLE
24 March 1991

Introduction

Ethnicity: Metaphors, Realities, Discourses

There exists a scholastic and academic historico–political out-look which sees as real and worthwhile only such movements of revolt that are one hundred per cent conscious.... But reality produces a wealth of the most bizarre combinations. It is up to the theoretician to unravel these in order to discover fresh proof of his theory, to 'translate' into theoretical language the elements of historical life....

Antonio Gramsci, Prison Notebooks

Facing the Problem: The Ethnic Riddle

Ethnicity has not been translated in Jharkhand into a single dis-course.[1] Collective memory appears as an anchor as well as a vast field that could give life to new formulations. Collective identities

---

[1] *Discourse* is used in this study to refer to all kinds of language, including but also extending beyond what is actually written or said, in relation to a social, economic, political and cultural *con-text* (*cum* texto). Discourses are socially and historically conditioned, are purposive and addressed to an interlocutor. A *text* is a discourse's verbal or non-verbal manifestation; it is the *material* moment of the discourse.

do not exist in pure forms but are forged with many interwoven elements that changed in the course of time.

In the political terrain, reality indeed proves to have produced 'a wealth of the most bizarre combinations' (Gramsci 1973: 200). The different uses of ethnicity in the political arena have created confusions in the understanding of ethnic-based movements. This confusion seems to arise from an uncritical evaluation of movements of varied contents and social bases, and from a rather general inability to comprehend the different ways in which protest can be expressed.

Furthermore, it is absolutely essential to locate the problem of ethnicity as a historical problem. It was precisely at the moment of colonial conquest that the indigenous and ethnic *problematiques* emerged in the non-Western world as social phenomena with specific characteristics. These *problematiques* are in origin aspects of the colonial expansion in which racism and the fostering of ethnic differences formed part of the strategy for domination. This in turn resulted in complex structures of social relationships in which racial, ethnic and class differences interacted to maintain patterns of inequality.

The case of the adivasis[2] in Bihar's Jharkhand region is inscribed in India's colonial history, and marked by the process of 'nation-building,' developed after independence. Attention is given in this study of the Jharkhand case to the correlation between ethnic ascription and class situation, the processes of legitimation of ethnic differences, and the historical, political and cultural dimensions of ethnicity.

The different Jharkhand[3] communities share common basic traits (related languages, culture and aspects of social organization) as well as historical experiences and a long history of migration into the area. Jharkhand's adivasis are basically peasants: 89 per cent

---

[2] *Adivasi* (from the Sanskrit *adi-vasi*—original inhabitant), labelled 'tribal' in India. The use of the term *adivasi* is not without problems (see N. Sengupta 1984; 1986). The term *indigenous* is used in this book in the same sense. I add to the semantics of the term the civilizational dimension which refers to the long historical duration of specific socio–cultural styles. The terms *subaltern* or *subordinate sectors/classes* are used to refer to small peasants, subsistence agriculturalists, rural landless labourers, marginal workers, and generally those in the lowest economic echelons of society.

[3] Jharkhand is conceived in its wider expression as a cultural region extending over Chotanagpur and Santal Parganas, in Bihar, parts of West Bengal, Orissa and Madhya Pradesh.

of them live by agriculture; forests supplement the agrarian economy. At the same time, the expansion of industries in Bihar since the fifties and the development of the commercial exploitation of the forests have accelerated a process of land alienation and limited alternative sources of subsistence, undermining the adivasi peasant economy which was already marked by bonded labour and chronic indebtedness. An unequal labour market has developed in Bihar's industrial sector in which poor and landless adivasi peasants are integrated as unskilled workers. To this economic picture one should add the effects on this population of mechanisms to maximize the uses of ethnic differences in the process of domination: discrimination, social degradation, deculturation, and the distortion of cultural traits. Jharkhand has been the setting of a sustained agrarian-based *tradition of protest* with ethnic overtones since the end of the eighteenth century. In present-day Jharkhand, this tradition continues not only in political movements but also in *cultures of protest*, counterparts of a *culture of oppression*, a pervading feature in Bihar.

In approaching ethnic phenomena, I would like to pose a series of theoretical proposals as an alternative to the perspectives current in the field. These proposals will be tested while examining the case under study.[4] The analysis of a situation such as that of contemporary Bihar heavily depends on the social sector that is taken as the main focus and on where we place ourselves thematically and theoretically. The focus of this book is on the subaltern sectors. This gives a specific angle to the perception, understanding and analysis of the phenomenon under study. The researcher's life experience in non-Western societies, and his/her social location will also have direct relevance for his/her perception of a 'Third World' society and to the selection and analysis of data. Therefore, in this book there is an implicit answer to Maquet's (1964) request for the researcher's clear-cut self-definition *vis-à-vis* the subject of study: the researcher only occasionally appears explicitly in the text but is always there because, as E. Said says, 'No production of knowledge in the human sciences can ever ignore or disclaim its author's involvement as a human subject in his own circumstances....' (1979: 11).

[4] The theoretical proposals suggested below attempt to attain, as any theoretical formulation does, a certain level of universal applicability. In the present case, this level is particularly addressed to non-Western societies, given the commonalities in their histories which have conditioned the structuring of ethnic relationships.

Ethnicity: The Faces and the Masks— A Theoretical Proposal

Cultural, ethnic, linguistic and religious factors have often given political movements a source of solidarity and a basis for mobilization *at one moment* of their development. In this context, ethnicity serves as a dependent variable in the social formations of the 'Third World', and not as a product of vaguely defined 'primordial sentiments' (*cf.* with Geertz 1963.). Ethnicity should be seen as a *historical phenomenon*, subordinated to existing class and centre– periphery contradictions, and as an element operating in cultural dialectics.

There has never been a single discourse of ethnicity. Rather, there has been a *plurality of discourses*. By looking at the ways in which ethnicity has been articulated in the ideological discourses of antagonistic classes and of the state, and at the realities of uneven development, two salient faces of the phenomenon are differentiated:

1. Ethnicity can serve as an element of support for the hegemony of the dominant classes and of the state. In this case ethnic strategies confirm the state, its policies and the *status quo* of class domination (as in populist nationalist discourses). The ideological uses of the tribal construct in India fall into this category.
2. Ethnicity can also be a counter-hegemonic force in the instances where ethnic ascription and economic and political subordination correlate (as in the cases of indigenous peasantries in Latin America and India, African workers in South Africa, 'marginalized' workers in the Pacific, etc.). Grass-roots proposals for Jharkhand are a case in point.

In the first case, the recognition and fostering of different identities by the ruling sectors and by an indigenous elite with similar interests, have been used to justify and structure unequal social and economic relationships. In the second case, ethnicity may contribute to develop an awareness of the contradictions existing in the society at large as they are experienced by the social sectors concerned. Thus, the most visible part of the iceberg, ethnicity as a metaphor for opposition, becomes 'subversive' in the eyes of the state and the ruling classes, especially when it is articulated into ideological formulations and a social practice that stimulates the conception of a radically different future. In the light of recent world events, there is a dark side to consider in ethnic assertion posed as an ethnic-only issue. The phenomena of ultra-nationalisms (like in Europe) and of the reinforcement of exclusivistic community-based identities (like in Asia with so-called 'fundamentalism'), may be viewed as extreme forms of identity assertion that back a rigid and exclusive conception of state-nation, negating (often violently) any expression of diversity, turning towards xenophobia, racism and intolerance.

Diversity becomes particularly 'subversive' in the realm of culture, where the resilience of indigenous styles demonstrates the limits of the hegemonic forces. For instance, in a number of multi–ethnic societies, the languages of indigenous inhabitants and ethnic minorities are marginalized or their existence is denied, while the language of those in power is imposed as the official one. In such a situation, indigenous cultures, vernacular languages and diverse modes of knowledge have been debased by the power-holders as 'folklore', 'dialects' and [little or popular] 'tradition'. In the Indian case, the anthropologist G.S. Ghurye (1963) recommended the eradication of adivasi languages. Why this attitude towards language? The answer resides in the great potential language has for practical political purposes and for maintaining a people's identity. Language is a people's particular code, a field where collective identity and the perception of reality are constantly reformulated, hence a terrain difficult to conquer by those external to it.

In the political practice of the subaltern sectors, the revitalization of fundamental elements of a specific sociocultural style gives ethnic-based grass-roots movements a potential beyond mere political tactics and strategy. The efforts at reconquering their own history, at re-inventing it if badly destroyed on the basis of whatever collective memory has kept, should be seen in this light. This reconquered history is opposed to official history, which is never sympathetic to the subaltern sectors.

Looking at the problem in this way, the role played by ethnic identity and consciousness in everyday life in general and in the political field in particular suggests a series of theoretical concerns:

1. At the level of the historical processes, it is important to clarify

under what conditions cultural differences are stressed and become one of the bases for political action.

2. At the political level, the process of formation of an ethnic consciousness needs to be decoded and its role in impairing or favouring the formation of a class consciousness needs to be considered.

3. At the level of the wider social system, patterns of domination translated into 'inter-ethnic' relations and the ways in which ethnic and class differences are structured should be disclosed.[5]

A Mythological Hydra? The Problem Re-stated

The different faces of ethnicity have to be distinguished. On the one hand, there is the *theoretical construct* created by social theorists to catalogue phenomena and social groups, and the elements this construct contributes to the ideological discourses of the ruling classes to justify and implement special policies and practices. On the other, we encounter ethnicity as it is actually *lived*, as a dynamic process with a specific present, entailing a particular mode of social experience. Taking into account these two aspects, ethnicity appears as a dependent variable whose dynamics are subordinated to the diverse ideological and practical needs and interests of the hegemonic as well as of the subordinate sectors.

Not being an ahistorical subject—as it is usually portrayed in liberal sociological writings—ethnicity should be conceived as a process evolving through time. Time provides the necessary ground on which ethnic styles are maintained (recreated) and collective identities formulated. The time dimension (not linear but social time) either gives these styles and identities substance (as in the case of collective identities practised in everyday life) or legitimation (as in the case of 'imagined communities' [B. Anderson 1983] and 'invented traditions' [Hobsbawm and Ranger 1983]. The evolution of the *être historique* of a society—that synthesis expressed in a global

---

[5] The application of analytical categories such as class to a situation like Jharkhand's poses a series of problems given that we are looking at, first, phenomena in evolution and, second, a 'situation of convergence' (peasants, ex-peasants, workers, etc. combined with a diversity of ethnic and regional ascriptions).

ethnic or national style (Abdel–Malek 1981: 151–59)—is not removed from the objective reality of social contradictions, class formation and class conflicts. Although it is a constant point of reference, this *être historique*, this 'style' will be differently lived and expressed by the different classes and class sectors. Being firmly grounded in the concrete history of a particular social reality, an ethnic style cannot be understood as the immutable and intangible 'essence' of a given people, or as a fixed sociological idealized type (seen by Abdel– Malek [1963] as deriving from the West's 'hegemonism of possess- ing minorities'; also Said 1979: Ch. 1). Consequently, processes of renaissance and collective self-assertion are not accidental 'happen- ings' in an ideal 'existential communitas' guided by a spontaneous urge for brotherhood (*cf.* with V. Turner 1969: 119ff.)

Ethnic styles are expressed in quotidian life in codes of com- munication, culture, modes of social reproduction and consumption, the reference to a common past and usually to a territory. At the same time, formulations of what the community is or should be emerge, making use of traditions, modes of thought and acting ascribed to a certain ethnic style. We thus observe the 'invention' and legitimation of communities and their conversion into constructs.

Benedict Anderson, when examining the phenomena of nation and nationalism, defines nation as 'an imagined community... [that], regardless of the actual inequality and exploitation that may prevail [in it]...is always conceived as a deep horizontal comradeship' (1983: 15–16). Anderson's definition broadly cor- responds to Hobsbawm's 'pseudo-community' category (1983: 10). This definition can be applied to state-ist conceptions of the nation, in which the nation-state is portrayed as an all-embracing inter- class collectivity, a supercommunity with no internal contradictions. Often, and particularly in the ex-colonial societies of the 'Third World', it is this key construct that regional and ethno-national movements challenge with their alternative projects. Anderson's proposal, on the other hand, is not adequate to understand those aspects of collective identity that are not imagined but have been built up in the course of time: the constant elements that provide the basis for the formulation of collective identity as it is lived.

While interpreting ethnic styles, care must be taken not to perceive their manifestations as simply a world of symbols, or as expressions of an idealist 'mentality' without reference to socio-economic factors. Neither can all communities be considered to be constructs of the imagination in which all the points of reference for their sustenance are invented. Constructs of communities and the traditions that legitimate them can be defined within temporal and ideological limits. Beyond these constructs there is a concrete world in movement, with reference to which—through a process of re-interpretation—constructs are built. This process is not unidirectional. While constructs have the curious property of elevating themselves to the rank of the real—becoming *the* realities they allege to describe—they are also liable to be questioned, usually in the political domain. This dialectic does not preclude, however, the emergence of new constructs. The question is: when and among whom do constructs arise and what needs and conditions do they respond to?

It is particularly in *times of high density* (the unfolding of deep social transformations, threats of destruction of existing socio-cultural patterns) that the collective imagination is activated and new formulations of communities arise. In the case under discussion, an 'imagined community' overrides the picture: a statelist conception of the Indian nation. Regional and ethnic-based movements do challenge this construct. The colonial creation of administrative units on the basis of the arbitrary delimitation of territories and the spatial reorganization of peoples, was bequeathed to the new ruling sectors after independence. These, in turn, rephrased this creation as the abode of 'the nation'. Thus, the independent state, although the project of a few, has come to act as the true and sole interpreter of the nation(s) it seeks to embrace. Ultimately, in the state-ist conception of the nation, state and nation become one, an 'imagined community' that ignores the various nations/identities/histories it may include. To maintain this conception of the nation–state it is necessary constantly to stress the existence of only *one* possible cultural model, *one* history, *one* language, *one* social project. At the most, diversity can be 'tolerated' by the state but not fully accepted. In this effort to impose a constructed national unity, two apparently contradictory strategies have been followed. On the one hand, cultural plurality is underplayed in the name of 'national integration'. On the other, differences based on 'racial', ethnic or cultural grounds are reinforced to cover the contradictions arising out of domination, class relations and conflicts, the real nature of social struggles, and to maintain specific modes of exploitation. In India this strategy is seen in the coexistence of the ideology of the Indian unity, and the practice of preferential policies (*cf.* with Weiner *et al.* 1981).

In such a context, cultural diversity is preserved as a museum exhibit ('exoticism', 'culture for tourists'), isolated from social reality and thus innocuous. Moreover, the state appropriates for itself the expressions of culture of the subordinate sectors and attempts to integrate these expressions in a modified form into its discourse of national unity. The state has constantly to find ways of incorporating alternative projects and initiatives that may challenge its dominance with the aim of defusing their oppositional potential and subsuming all possible antagonisms under a unitary umbrella. This effort at incorporation is always limited and selective, and does not touch a wide spectrum of social experience, alternative perceptions of social relationships and the material world or the dynamics of political consciousness. It is in these areas that the subordinate indigenous communities build up *zones of resistance* in order to develop a strategy for survival and political action.

By means of populist nationalist ideologies based on imagining the community of the 'nation', the elites attempt to attain monopoly control over the social project. Cultural revivalism provides legitimating support for these ideologies in the shape of 'invented traditions'. Parts of the history and elements of the indigenous cultures are selected and re-structured into a 'tradition' that the elites use in political discourses to call for a broad 'national' ('regional', 'ethnic') solidarity. The culture and history of the different populations composing the nation–state are censored; ethnicity is codified and made immutable in response to the needs of the codifiers acting as self-styled 'true' spokesmen of their societies. These invented traditions are concerned with establishing a legitimating continuity with the past, not with understanding historical discontinuities and the evolution of social contradictions. These new versions of identities and traditions refer to models of ideal and, at the same time, imperfect brotherhoods which may not necessarily coincide with the perceptions, aims and realities at a grass-roots level.

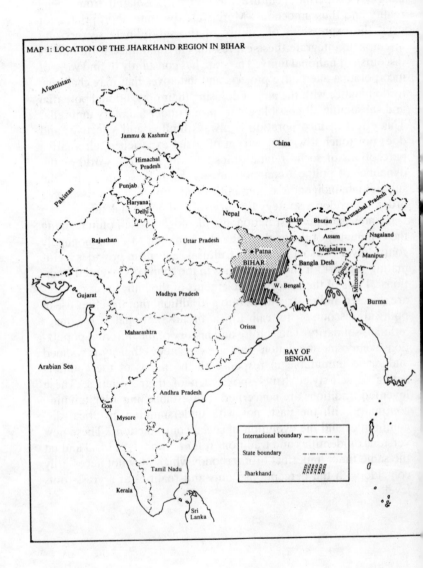

MAP 1: LOCATION OF THE JHARKHAND REGION IN BIHAR

Part One

THE TERRAIN OF IDEAS

1

The Conceptualization of Ethnicity

In the last two decades ethnicity has emerged as a key concept in the writings of numerous social scientists. Societal developments which once may have been explained by economic, political and social factors are increasingly viewed as manifestations of ethnicity. A host of social phenomena around the world is seen to represent the ever growing repertoire of ethnicity (for instance, in Cohen 1974a: ix, xix–xxi) to the extent that today we see an entire 'industry' devoted to the service of this concept: academic journals, university departments, television channels and government departments in some countries. Some 'settler' societies have even adopted it as part of their political culture (like the state ideology of multiculturalism in Australia and Canada. De Lepervanche 1980; Devalle 1990).

Ethnic phenomena[1] in central as well as in peripheral social formations have been approached from theoretical perspectives

[1] The terms 'race relations' and 'ethnic relations' are sometimes mentioned together when discussing theoretical approaches which use them. The position that focuses on the political dimension of these phenomena uses the word 'nationalism' and its derivatives (*cf*. Connor 1972 with Nairn 1975).

within the liberal socio-anthropological tradition. These perspectives have translated into the culturalist-assimilationist approach, the culture of poverty theory, reconstructive ethnography, and the theory of the plural society and other pluralist models. Of late, ethnicity has also been approached from the Marxist perspective. A civilizational approach has also developed. It is in these two related approaches to ethnicity—Marxist and civilizational—that new insights and theoretical discussions on the subject have recently arisen.

European Expansion and the Invention of a Discourse

Myth deprives the object of which it speaks of all history...
Roland Barthes, Mythologies

In modern times ethnic differences were structured in the non-Western world under specific historical circumstances: colonial expansion, the persistence of residual colonial forms of control, the development of neo-colonial structures for the exploitation of people, land, strategic geographical positions and natural resources, and the processes of state formation. In this context, legitimating ideologies phrased in racial or ethnic terms·have been formulated to maintain political domination and unequal socio-economic relations. At the same time, science contributed justifying arguments to this process. The sociological constructs of 'race relations' and 'ethnicity' were applied to specific situations from perspectives that subordinated the nature of the existing socio-economic structures and class relations to the primacy of the racial or ethnic factors. *Inequality* was paraphrased as *difference* ('racial' or/and cultural). Scientific *texts* have not only resulted in a mode of knowing reality, but often ended up acquiring credentials as *the* actual realities they attempted to describe.

The ethnic and the indigenous *problematiques* emerged as specific historical and social phenomena the moment conquest took place. The constructs of 'tribe' and of 'race' as a social category became elements through which Europe reconstructed—intellectually as well as in administrative practice—part of the reality of the·societies that came under its dominance. The categories 'tribe', 'caste' and 'religion' performed this role in colonial India. 'Racial', 'ethnic' and 'tribal' stereotypes were forged, conflating a variety of modes of production, forms of social organization and cultures, ignoring the complexities, dynamism, history and civilizational patterns of the societies thus catalogued. In the end, taxonomies acquired the power of truth.[2] In sum, these societies were rendered ahistorical. The indigenous societies' socio-cultural diversity was given new meanings. Existing differences were enhanced to preclude any unified action of the colonized people. A new opposition expressed in racial and/or cultural terms came into being, i.e. the one between the superordinated European group and the people under their domination.

While the constructed categories were ideal models, the ideology derived from this perception was and is very concrete and functional (Mafeje 1971; Wolpe 1972: 454) in supporting and reproducing patterns of power relationships and in justifying the expansion of cultural hegemony. As with the Orientalists' Orient (Abdel-Malek 1963; Said 1979), I believe we also have comparable discourses on the rest of the 'Third World'. The mode in which the West constructed and reconstructed the non-Western world profoundly marked the way in which ethnic and indigenous issues were posed and addressed. Thus various discourses arose: the Pacific-Paradise, 'tribalist' Africa, passive and 'unprogressive' *Indian America*. Parallel to the evolution of these discourses, anti-colonial movements and efforts at ethno-national assertion developed in the subordinate societies.

In multi-ethnic modern nation-states, the state formulates a project for 'national integration' with the help of intellectuals and administrators and little or no participation by the people to be 'integrated'. In this context, state policies generally run along the lines of paternalism, assimilation or planned aggression (from genocide to acculturation as ethnocide). In the best of cases, these policies aim at an asymmetrical integration. In agrarian-based societies (like India, or more massively, in Latin America), where sectors of the peasantry have clearly defined ethnic contents, integration has come to mean the unequal incorporation of these sectors into the prevailing economic system as peasants or as a reserve labour force. This is the case of the adivasi peasantry in Jharkhand.

---

[2] The categories *Criminal Tribes* and *Criminal Castes* in India up to the fifties are cases in point.

The state is informed by social theories that provide specific objects on which to exert particular social policies. Intellectual constructs of socio-cultural identities function in this way. In India, the official category *Scheduled* or *Backward Tribes* artificially determines a 'special' sector entailing a 'special' problem (phrased as weakness and backwardness). In consequence, the objective situation of the catalogued populations is ignored, and the structure of inequality is validated by attributing its causes to deficiencies assumed to be inherent in these subordinate sectors. Furthermore, in using cataloguing systems and special policies, state paternalism obstructs the forging of alliances across ethnic demarcations. The de-historization and deculturation[3] of subordinate peoples and the imposition of constructed identities have helped in the process of economic and political domination. Subordinate ethnic groups have opposed these processes by means of reaffirming their threatened historical and cultural specificity and by forging alternative social projects. Ethnic consciousness may then serve as a strategic axis for solidarity and for political action at one moment in the development of social movements.

The question of the acknowledgement of the internal contradictions present in the society at large as well as in the ethnic group/community itself, beyond ethnic demarcations, should also be highlighted. In this respect, the discontinuities in the processes of decolonization and 'nation building' call for a consideration of those internal contradictions. For instance, by ignoring these contradictions, the indigenous elites are able to use ethnic identity and alliances to contain the process of decolonization (Fitzpatrick 1980: 198–99) or to monopolize the project of the independent state in ex-colonial societies. The examination of the role of an adivasi elite in Jharkhand provides an opportunity to look into these questions. On the other hand, the existence of a consciousness of historical permanence[4] and

[3] *Deculturation* refers to processes usually concealed under the labels of *modernization*, *Westernization* and *acculturation*, entailing the obliteration or distortion of a society's culture, promoting its replacement by the culture of the dominator (see Ribeiro 1968).

[4] Following A. Abdel–Malek's notion of *depth of the historical field* when discussing the time dimension as a 'component part of the patterns of social maintenance' though historical evolution since: 'Culture and thought...express the sum total of social maintenance, the *global depth reality*, the achievements, the balance sheet as well as the prospective potentials of a given society' (1981: 171. Italics in the original).

the maintenance of social, cultural and semantic fields and endogenous forms of organization provide grounds where counter-hegemonic practices can emerge directed against the conditions created by colonialism, neocolonialism, or by the attempted all-pervading control of the modern state. As shown later in the text, all these elements are present in Jharkhand.

The Construction of the 'Object'

The Orient and Orientals [are considered by Orientalism] as an 'object' of study, stamped with...a constitutive otherness of an essentialist character....
        Anouar Abdel–Malek, L'Orientalisme en Crise

Tribe has been the most salient category used in the study of adivasi societies. The way in which it has been conceptualized in the field of anthropology in general and in India in particular, calls for some comment.[5] Generally, anthropologists defined tribe as a type of society characterized by political autonomy, a subsistence economy and territoriality. This resulted in the construction of a fixed idealized type, and in a perception that divorced 'tribal' societies from the historical processes that affected them, most notably the colonial situation in which 'tribal studies' initially developed.

The vagueness of the category 'tribe', its uses, its derogatory implications and its lack of correspondence with reality, has made anthropologists increasingly dissatisfied with it.[6] A thorough critique of the category and its uses in the intellectual construction of reality developed in the field of African studies. The tribal construct has been traced to the colonial administrations and the social theories

[5] 'Tribe' is used with two meanings: as a type of society, and as a stage in social evolution (Godelier 1974: 198–222). The latter aspect was dropped from the definition until M. Sahlins (1968) and other neo-evolutionists redefined 'tribe' with its former dual meaning. This version of 'tribe' appears to underlie many of the Indian anthropologists' view of adivasi societies.

[6] In the early sixties Aidan Southall stressed the need to take into account 'colonial rule and industrialization or participation in the exchange economy' (1961: 2). Also Gulliver 1969: 7.

that informed them (Southall 1970: 33ff.; Argyle 1969: 51ff.). When the state of the social sciences was evaluated in the seventies, the role social theories played in the colonial context and the ideology of 'tribalism' attracted further criticisms (Mafeje 1971; Essien-Udom 1975: 243; Asad 1975b; Onoge 1977).

Notwithstanding the doubts regarding the category 'tribe', anthropologists continued to use it. Two factors seem to account for its persistence. First, the continuation of microstudies which ignore the societal macrolevel, historical processes and structural transformations. Second, there has been a confusion between idealized types and reality. The category 'tribe' was *constructed* out of ideas about what societies were thought to have been in the pre-colonial past. This construct was in turn projected onto the colonial situation and mechanically applied to societies which were already incorporated in a capitalist economy and in the world market (Mafeje 1971). Hardly any of the so-called tribes can be defined by their political autonomy, isolation and subsistence economy. A reality that included a new articulation of modes of production, new division of labour and system of power inaugurated with colonial rule and, afterwards, the structural changes that took place in the modern states, bring to question the validity of this idealized type.

The roots of the so-called 'tribal problem' have often been sought in the socio-economic characteristics of the 'tribes' themselves, as a 'problem' stemming from their past (as in Mair 1936: 264).[7] This perspective excluded from analysis the contradictions that arise from colonialism and, later, from the operation of political and economic forces in the independent states, and the nature of the process of class formation. Moreover, the construction of a 'tribal problem' on these premises served to create a spurious social sector, 'the tribes', whose arbitrarily defined peculiarities greatly helped, as in India, to set this sector aside from the rest of the society for policy purposes.

Possibly the most serious consequence of this kind of anthropological perception of indigenous peoples has been the construction of a still persisting derogatory image of these societies. It suffices to see the currency in academic parlance of terms like 'primitive', 'simple', 'backward', and the 'underdeveloped' of later vintage. This image

[7] The term *tribalism* alludes to this 'problem' in Africa. In India it is called *particularism*, although the word *tribalism* has also been used (as in Roy Burman 1968; N.K. Bose 1964: 7ff., who equates it with nationalism, and D. P. Sinha 1972).

reflects prejudices that have been put to scientific use. It is an image not only advanced by the central societies (now under the guise of developmentism), but also by sectors of intellectuals and planners in the 'Third World' (Mafeje's 'converts', 1971: 253). Thus we find in multi-ethnic states a variety of assimilative, integrative and indigenist policies, instances of ethnocide and even genocide, all justified in the name of 'progress'.[8]

From Tribe to Ethnicity

In the seventies, a noticeable shift in terminology occurred. A vast range of phenomena formerly subsumed under tribal, racial, cultural, linguistic and religious differences, became increasingly identified with the term *ethnicity* despite some initial reluctance. For instance, Gulliver considered the term 'ethnic group' a euphemism (1969: 2). Recently, de Lepervanche has made a similar point, although on different grounds.[9] The shift in terminology did not necessarily entail a deep transformation in theoretical approach. Sometimes, this shift was justified solely on the basis of the researcher's preference (as in Southall 1970: 47), given the disfavour 'tribe' and 'race' had incurred due to their association with the colonial project and racist ideologies. The less evocative and deceivingly neutral term *ethnicity* provided an appropriate substitute and a basic element to reformulate discourses legitimating social inequality (as in Glazer and Moynihan 1976: 11–12).

While the term *ethnic* is old, *ethnicity* is relatively new.[10] Rather delayed, the shift to the ethnic terminology was practically imposed on the researchers by the changes that had taken place in the international scene after World War II: the end of the colonial order and the emergence of the so-called 'Third World' (anthropology's former 'object societies') in international politics. These events brought with them a realization that the previous context of anthropological research and the position of advantage Western researchers

[8] The case of the Amazon indigenous population in the years of Brazil's 'economic miracle' is a clear example (Davis and Mathews 1976; Ramos and Taylor 1979; Aspelin and Coelho dos Santos 1981).

[9] She considers the change in terminology and perspective part of 'a series of ideological transformations in the recreation of hegemony' (1980: 25).

[10] Possibly first used by David Riessman in 1953 (Glazer and Moynihan 1976: 1).

had enjoyed until then had to be relinquished.[11] Despite the fact that this awareness resulted in a shift from fixed categories to processes in anthropological analysis, the term 'ethnic group' is still regarded with suspicion (see S. Silverman 1976:626).

The Tribal Construct in India

A tribe is a tribe which is included in the list of scheduled tribes....

Tautology creates a dead, a motionless world....
                                                      Roland Barthes, Mythologies

According to the Indian 1981 Census of India, the population officially called *Scheduled Tribes* numbered 51,628,638 persons (7.53 per cent of the total population), distributed in 427 communities, and divided into six major linguistic groups.[12] The British colonial government in India used the category 'tribe' as an element of classification for administrative purposes, and as such it has continued to be used in independent India. In India, 'tribe' is clearly a *colonial category* in origin and in content. It has been reformulated in the context of the Hindu model of caste-ideology, a context observable in the conceptualization of adivasi 'backwardness' and in the alternatives espoused for social mobility. Thus, 'tribes' only exist in relation to the 'mainstream' complex (N. Sengupta 1986).

In India, the category 'tribe' has not developed as a conceptual category, independent from administrative practice, possibly because anthropology there has tended to be applied anthropology. Defining 'the tribes' is the task of government officials (Indian Constitution: Art. 342). The official selection of criteria to define the *Scheduled Tribes* is questionable for its lack of correspondence with reality and its ethnocentric bias.[13] These criteria were so unsatisfactory

[11] Maquet 1964; Copans 1974; Asad 1975b. I discussed this issue in Devalle 1983.

[12] Austro–Asiatic, Mon–Khmer, Munda, Tibeto–Burman, Dravidian and Aryan. Bilingualism was reported in 15.75 per cent of the adivasi population (Schemerhorn 1978: 72–73).

[13] The traits selected included: isolation, racial characteristics, the use of 'tribal dialects', 'animism', 'primitive' economic activities, eating habits (non-vegetarian), dress ('naked or semi-naked'), nomadism, propensity to drink and to dance (1952 Report of the Scheduled Castes and Tribes Commission).

that A.R. Desai (1961) considered they could only apply to 20 per cent of the adivasi population, while K.S. Mathur dismissed the classification as 'a typical case of fiction-creation by Government officers' (1972: 460).[14] Furthermore, the whole exercise has resulted in the legitimation of derogatory stereotypes. Recently, A.K. Danda has questioned the adequacy of the category 'tribe' in its Western sense and its application to the Indian situation (1988: 317ff.; see also Pathy 1988: 20–26).

From the studies of British colonial administrators like E.T. Dalton (1872) and H. Risley (1891), to the pioneer works of S.C. Roy (1912, 1915) and V. Elwin (1943 and many monographs), as well as the bulk of contemporary writings on the adivasis, the term 'tribe' has remained vague, not adequately conceptualized and, consequently, of weak methodological value (see Pathy *et al.* 1976: 401–6; Pathy 1982: 23–48). Indian 'tribalist' anthropologists comfortably accepted as tribes those people registered as such in the official list. Thus, 'precision in defining and identifying a tribe is generally avoided. For every researcher "a tribe is a tribe which is included in the list of scheduled tribes"' Pathy *et al. ibid.*: 402). There also seems to be a lack of awareness about the colonial connotation of the vocabulary used to address adivasi history, as with 'revolt' and 'uprising' to name their anti-colonial movements (Moser 1978: 123–24).

Most Indian 'tribal studies' have remained synchronic and descriptive, ignoring the economic and political transformations that affected the populations studied. 'Tribes' were seen as homogeneous units, forming an undifferentiated bloc (although set in a hierarchy of 'more' and 'less primitive groups'), marked by 'backwardness'. While the anthropological view of 'tribes' in India may have abandoned the stereotype of isolated groups and moved to observe social interaction (K.S. Singh 1982: 1318), the point of reference—to define 'tribe' and social mobility patterns—continues to be the dominant Hindu model. A persistent assumption has been that 'tribes' have a shallow conception of history. Their history then easily becomes 'mythology', a trait that is accompanied by an 'overall tradition-orientation' (Dube 1960: 11–12). 'Tradition-orientation' has often been equated with 'backwardness in the scale of civilization'. On these grounds and from a particular (Western and alien) conception of 'progress',[15] the adivasis' sense

[14] See also Dube 1960: 11; Roy Burman 1960: 17; Bailey 1961: 10.

[15] Following fallacious dichotomies like those of the 'tradition–modernity' and the 'dual society' models (see Gunder Frank 1966; Stavenhagen 1981: 2–6; Leclerc 1972, among others).

of history and their culture are declared to be retrograde, a 'negation of progress', a perpetuation of backwardness.[16] In this way, backwardness becomes a trait inherent to these societies. At the same time, endogenous innovations and change are never mentioned.

Indian anthropological literature seldom introduces the term *ethnicity* with reference to the adivasis, and when it does, it is often in an ambiguous way (Surajit Sinha's 'tribes' as 'certain ethnic groups' [1965: 57–83; 1974]; Dube's 'tribal ethnicity' [1977: 1–5]). Only very recently has the term ethnicity been applied to the so-called 'tribes' in India (for instance, in Pathy 1988). On the whole, however, Indian anthropologists have remained faithful to the old category of tribe. This measured shift in emphasis seems to derive from an acknowledgement of emerging ethno-regional movements, not from an analytical exercise (K.S. Singh 1977). In this context, B.K. Roy Burman preferred the notions of *national identity* and *nation society*, qualifying adivasi political expressions ('processes of identity expansion') as 'infra' and 'protonationalisms' (1983b: 1174). This qualification seems to stem from an identification of 'the nation' with the state.

Lastly, adivasi societies have been defined in terms of a contrast with non-adivasi society (usually understood as Hindu society) and set at one end of several variously defined ahistorical *continua*: the tradition-modernity paradigm (leading to G.S. Ghurye's conception [1963] of adivasis as 'backward Hindus'); the tribe-caste *continuum* (basis for assimilationist models like Srinivas' [1966] Sanskritization model[17], and the developmentalist traditional-modern *continuum* for administrative use (V.K. Mathur 1967: 11–25). M.K. Gautam (1978a: 20) has already called for a perspective independent from the Hindu caste model, and N. Sengupta (1986) provides an excellent discussion of the 'tribe-mainstream' dichotomy.

One last mode of defining the adivasis on the basis of a *continuum* has been to place them in relation to a 'peasant pole', 'tribals' and

---

[16] For B. K. Roy Burman:
'Empirical data from the different parts of the world shows that when an underdeveloped people develop separatist tendencies, they tend to vest symbolical value to some or other aspects of *their backwardness and try to perpetuate the same....* They are overtaken by the social malady of stagnancy and ultimate decay' (1960: 19, italics added).

[17] However, Srinivas was aware that Sanskritization meant only positional and not structural changes (*ibid.*: 7, 30ff.).

peasants conceived as 'two idealized evolutionary levels of socio-cultural integration' (S. Sinha 1982: 3).[18] It is the conception of some adivasis as peasants and not the shortcomings inherent in these *continua* that has aroused opposition. This fact derives from the way the category 'peasant' has been defined (for instance, Roy Burman 1983b: 1173). The neat compartmentalization of 'three types of communities: tribal, caste and peasant' in Mathur and Agrawal (1974), and Vidyarthi's (1967a) 'three dimensions of Indian society: primitive, peasant and industrial', should be noted in this context. On the other hand, K.S. Singh (1982) considers that in many of the 'tribal areas' a peasantization trend started at the end of the eighteenth century, while B.B. Mandal concludes that the agricultural 'tribes' in Bihar can be considered to be peasants (1975: 355–62; Beteille 1974). In the present study, when address-ing specific sectors of the adivasi population as peasants, T. Shanin's definition will be followed.[19] This, however, is not the end of the problem. The fact that adivasis exist in the frame of a class society and that their relationships with it cannot avoid the operation of class forces, are issues that, with few exceptions (Pathy 1982, 1988; N. Sengupta 1980, 1986), have not yet been subjected to analysis.

A Deluge of Scientific 'Texts'

One sees how much, from the eighteenth to the twentieth century, the hegemonism of possessing minorities...[is] accom-panied by eurocentrism in the area of human and social sciences, and more particularly in those in direct relationship with non-European peoples....

Anouar Abdel-Malek, L'Orientalisme en Crise

In the last two decades, the ways in which 'race relations' and ethnicity were studied became a matter of serious concern among

[18] Earlier expressed as 'tribal–caste/peasant continua' (S. Sinha 1965). See also F. G. Bailey's application of the tribe–caste *continuum* (1961: 13ff.).

[19] 'The peasantry consists of small agricultural producers who, with the help of simple equipment and the labour of their families, produce mainly for their own consumption and for the fulfilment of obligations to the holders of political and economic power.' (Shanin 1972: 204).

some social scientists. A critical appraisal of current approaches began, leading to the analysis of case studies beyond the limitations of established anthropological, psychological and historical perspectives. This appraisal was first encapsulated in the critique of an isolated discipline—anthropology—moving by the mid-seventies to the evaluation of positivist theories in general, including economics and the political sciences, inheritors of anthropology's former 'objects': the 'new' states (Mafeje 1976).

Ethnic studies in the liberal Anglo-Saxon tradition do not usually take into account theoretical developments produced outside this tradition, particularly by 'Third World' scholars.[20] Therefore, for many the last word on ethnicity has been pronounced by F. Barth (1970). Considered the last watershed, it has originated the expression 'B.B. and A.B.' (before and after Barth), in which the 'A.B.' seems to be final. However, the self-named New Ethnicists have lately been added (see Hinton's critique, 1981: 14–19).

Two important aspects of ethnicity have been largely absent from the liberal tradition's concern. First, the *historical conditions* under which ethnicity emerges as a major element in social organization, solidarity and conflict. Second, that of ethnicity *as lived by* the people themselves, as an expression of civilizational alternatives, its potential role and strategic value in the process of decolonization and in the development of a social consciousness among subordinate social sectors.

Various and changing realities were reduced to fixed types (ethnic groups, tribes, interest groups), ultimately becoming *autonomous subjects* abstracted from the global social reality, which provided the basis for fundamentally ahistorical studies (Asad 1975b: 29; Saul 1979: 365–66). Furthermore, maintaining the position of advantage of the observer and his/her illusion of objectivity, studies on ethnicity have usually been conducted on the basis of the outsider's perspective. Intellectual conceptions of socio–cultural identities have thus been put forward as the actual identities of the societies studied, mostly on the basis of visible cultural and/or behavioural elements. Some indigenous intellectuals are now

---

[20] A general situation in the social sciences not exclusive to the field of ethnic studies. See S. Bhattacharya's remarks in relation to history (1982: 3) and Denoon (1985: 119). In anthropology, French Africanists have developed a critical reappraisal of the situation (Copans 1974). See also Abdel–Malek's remarks in his critique of Orientalism (1963: 109–42).

denouncing precisely these constructs of identity and their uses (Langton 1981: 16; Documentos: 1979). This is not to say that any further inquiry should stop after noting the ethnic groups' self-perceptions. The determinants of these self-perceptions are factors that should be explained in context (see Wolpe's remarks, 1971), an aspect that is considered in this volume.

A critique of current socio–anthropological approaches to the study of ethnicity and a search for new perspectives started to develop both in the Marxist tradition in the central societies and among 'Third World' intellectuals concerned about the processes of decolonization and 'nation building'. Despite the critique and the limitations of the process of decolonization in the social sciences themselves, some Western academics are finding it hard to stop playing 'the role of unchallenged interpreters and translators...of cultures' (Owusu 1978. Also Onoge 1979: 54).

The study of the relations into which the 'Third World' was drawn by the West, marked from their inception by the colonial experience, was approached by anthropology with the concepts 'racial difference' and 'cultural contact'. Ethnicity, of later use, came generally to be restricted to the perception and uses of cultural differences among either the indigenous peoples themselves or recent newcomers in the central societies, those swelling the waves of the international migratory labour force. Once the social field was thus divided and conceptualized, *race* and *ethnicity* emerged as conceptual tools divorced from the social totalities of which they were integral parts, masking the realities of the colonial past, the current international forces at work, the presence of neocolonialism and dependence, and the nature of the modern state. 'Racial' and ethnic relations were conceived of as developing in situations of hypothetical social balance, favourable to gradual and non-conflictive processes of change called 'modernization' and 'Westernization'.[21] Conflicts inherent in relations established by force, and resistance to domination were rarely considered in their full social dimension. This aspect, however, was treated in the Marxist tradition (starting with Balandier 1955). For the general state of the studies in this field of inquiry, H. Wolpe has already suggested a corrective:

[21] So-called 'Third World' societies have been depicted as passive recipients of externally induced changes. Thus the illusion, in Selbourne's words, that 'the Indians—or the Africans, or the Latin Americans, or the Arabs—are (variously) congenitally inert, lacking in 'political will', 'fatalistic', or passive' (1979: 36).

What is needed is, on the one hand, a description of the ideology and the political practices of the ethnic, racial and national groups and, on the other, an analysis of how they relate to the mode of production and social formation in which they are located.... (1971: 238).

What follows is a discussion of the ways ethnicity has been approached. However, the vast number of studies on the subject has not yet produced a school of thought in the sociological sense. Of late, we find in the influential Anglo–Saxon tradition variants of the same basic approach, mostly under the influence of F. Barth and/or C. Geertz, translated into pluralist models. These influences are generally absent from Indian anthropology which has remained linked to earlier approaches.

The cultural–assimilationist approach centres on cultural aspects and belongs to the old ethnographic tradition developed along with the West's colonial expansion. Considerable effort was devoted to the systematic study of the cultural aspects of subordinate societies in the colonies, the 'ethnics' of the moment. Knowledge of the cultural field provided the foundations for assimilationist policies and what was often called 'cultural transformation' (in fact a process of deculturation). Assimilation and deculturation ultimately aimed at the establishment of an all-embracing hegemony.

Political, economic and cultural confrontations were concealed under the 'cultural contact' disguise. Functionalism described colonialism as 'culture clash, 'culture contact' and 'acculturation'. With the introduction of the concept 'social change', colonialism was further reduced to just one aspect of this general change. Social change was perceived as a natural and uniform process with 'modernization' as its final goal. Neither the colonial system nor the implications of acculturation were critically examined.[22] The assumptions that guided acculturation studies until the fifties were reformulated after the breakdown of the colonial order to fit new

[22] In a review of functionalist anthropological approaches to Africa, O. Onoge remarks:

By far the most disastrous consequence of the functionalist Africanists was their general amnesia over the objective social situation in which Africans were at the time implicated. I refer of course to the colonial situation.... The unit of study always remained the 'tribe' ....The very contradiction of *life in a colony*... [should have received] primacy (1977: 36–37; italics in the original).

socio–political realities and be applied to situations of inequality in which racial, ethnic, minority or national groups were involved.

The inevitability of the assimilation process of all subordinate 'minorities' to conform to the dominant models, values, world-view and economic–political orientations has been the implicit assumption underlying the theories of acculturation and modernization. These theories have failed to see that 'resistance to change' was really based on the people's realization that 'Progress in the abstract meant domination in the concrete' (Nairn 1975: 10). Changes in emphasis in the assimilationist perspective, still dominant in the United States, can be exemplified with the works of Glazer and Moynihan, where they make assumed deficiencies in different ethnic groups responsible for social inequality.[23] The focus on assimilation–acculturation is particularly noticeable among social scientists engaged in 'welfare-relevant research' and among applied anthropologists working as government advisors, a common feature in India.

Indian anthropology has operated within borrowed theoretical frameworks: British functionalism and, after the sixties, under a growing American influence. On the whole, and especially with reference to 'tribal studies', it has, barring very few recent exceptions, not produced an independent line of thought. On the other hand, the tradition of applied anthropology, based on the assimilationist perspective, was taken up in earnest. American influence resulted, in turn, in studies focused on the village as the unit of study, and in a further impetus to 'community development' (for instance, Pande 1968: 33–57). 'Community development' complemented applied anthropology and justified the role of some anthropologists as government planners (Saberwal 1979: 245, 247). These scientists-cum-administrators adopted the basic derogatory attitude toward the societies they studied characteristic of applied anthropology. For instance, V.K. Mathur echoes one of Lucy Mair's consistent lines: 'The program of community development is one of...peaceful *replacement of old undesirable tribal practices* with

---

[23] See the first and second edition of *Beyond the Melting Pot* (1963, 1970), and *Ethnicity: Theory and Experience* (1976). In *Ethnicity...*, it is said:

Men are not equal; neither are ethnic groups.... As to the origins of this inequality...it arises from *differential success in achieving social norms....* Individuals and...ethnic groups have different levels of success in attaining *the desired condition* (1976: 11, 12, 17; italics added).

new scientifically accepted *superior* practices' (1967: 16; italics added). The emphasis on the need for 'desirable modifications' appears often in the writings of Indian anthropologists, some of whom openly express their support for 'directed cultural change' towards the dominant Hindu model (for instance, Sahay 1980: 25–71).

The notion of cultural deprivation derived from Oscar Lewis' works and his 'culture of poverty' theory (1966, 1980), has also been used to equate 'racial' or ethnic differences to negative social, cultural and psychological traits. These traits are seen as the cause of the problems the subordinate sectors suffer. A fallacious notion of 'poverty' is constructed, as a condition inherent in some social sectors, ignoring the historico–economic basis of this condition.[24] Although the culture of poverty theory as such was not applied to the study of the adivasis in India, explanations on similar lines have been offered to characterize their 'backwardness'.

Substantial research has been conducted in the shape of recon- structive ethnography ('salvage anthropology'). From this pers- pective, indigenous cultures are seen as broken residues of past traditions that have to be rescued as if they were museum specimens. A perception of culture as social and historically conditioned is absent. Indigenous cultures are supposed to have succumbed under the impact of 'civilization' and been reduced to the category of 'traditional remains'. These cultures are seen as static, and their living carriers often 'without a culture' (as this is considered to belong to the past), or with a 'lesser' form of culture. 'Salvage anthropology' has been one of the constants of fieldwork in the ethnographic tradition.

A considerable amount of research has developed in India in the line of reconstructive ethnography. With V. Elwin's proposal to establish Bhaiga and Gond reservations, this approach reached the point where whole societies were to be 'living museums' (1943, 1960. See Grigson's comments [1946: 81–96]). Given the belief in the inevitable acculturation of the adivasis, the study of cultural change as 'an urgent necessity' has received attention since the sixties (Sachchidananda 1964). It was the *loss* of culture and not

[24] Even more dangerous than the culture of poverty's negative equations are the racist analyses based on the 'race-civilization' equation, used as the background ideology for special legislation addressed to sectors catalogued according to racial indexes, for instance, Australian Aborigines (comments in Tazt 1982: 15–16).

the adivasis as *creators* of culture that became the research focus. According to the assimilationist perspective, what should be preserved are only 'the rich, colourful and conducive traits of tribal culture' (V.K. Mathur 1967: 21), following a pedestrian conception of 'folklore' (*cf.* Jaulin 1979b: 85–90; Leiris 1976: 303–20). The rescuing spirit is still strong in India judging by the recent drive for the development of anthropological museums where, inevitably, the products of adivasi cultures fall under the headings 'primitive' and 'tribal' art (Koppar 1976).[25]

The theories of the plural society give 'race' and ethnicity the key roles in the dynamics of modern society (Kuper and M.G. Smith 1969; Kuper 1974). Although pluralist theorists acknowledge a possible correlation between economic differences and ethnic ascription, they fall back on models based on the assumption of social equilibrium, such as that followed by the modernization school.[26] The theory of the plural society avoids the problem of the structuring of society into classes. The central idea of a society divided vertically into ethnic or 'racial' blocs, complementary to and interdependent on each other, is one characteristic of F. Barth's still very influential model (1970). Interest converges on interaction in terms of expected or rejected forms of behaviour, and on the interdependence of social sectors defined by their ethnic ascription. The dynamics of the social and historical processes that encompass ethnic phenomena are not explored. This approach stresses adaptation to an established social order and not the possibility of structural changes.[27]

Present ethnic group theory considers ethnicity a 'new social category' (Glazer and Moynihan 1976: 3), the only one that can be observed and even measured. This can be stated because only the visible cultural traits and behavioral aspects of ethnic phenomena are considered. On this basis, ethnic categories were defined as devices forged by ethnic groups to organize social interaction.[28] In

[25] See also other articles in *The Eastern Anthropologist*, 1976.

[26] Pluralist models received a new impetus even after the idea of the 'melting pot', prominent in the United States, did not produce the expected result of a harmonious blending of people of different origins into the dominant culture. The 'melting pot' ideology is echoed in Australia's 'multiculturalism'.

[27] Compare the results of one case-study from two different perspectives: Siverts' study of ethnic relations in Chiapas, following Barth's model (1970: 101–16), and R. Stavenhagen's study of the same (1975: 223–43).

[28] For J. C. Mitchell, 'The cognitive framework of ethnicity…[is] a set of shared meanings attached to socially identifiable ethnic cues that provide the actors with sets of expectations of behaviour' (1974: 14. See also Epstein 1973: 232).

this line J.C. Mitchell (1974: 14, 23) was able to determine patterns of 'social distance' between ethnic groups in which this distance is quantifiable but the reasons why this distance exists are not explained. The picture of a 'cognitive framework of ethnicity' is said to predict behaviour. Only the assumption of social equilibrium and an ahistorical perspective[29] can support this kind of prediction. The ideological proposition for the existence of an ultimate social order allows social relationships to be placed in terms of balance or as transactions among equals, leading to adaptation.[30] In some works within the pluralist perspective, ethnicity is perceived as a political phenomenon. Politics, however, is reduced to the attainment of power. Ethnic groups are seen as 'interest groups' (a vague theoretical category), and the emphasis is put on manipulation (A. Cohen 1969) to obtain short-range aims in a situation of assumed open competition (Despres 1975, among others).

The socio–anthropological literature on ethnicity in the liberal tradition either avoids or explicitly rejects class analysis. It is maintained that interest groups, and not class, operate in concrete reality (A. Cohen 1974b: 17) on the basis of competition (Barth's 'choices', 1970: 33),[31] and that ethnicity, and not class, is 'seen' (Glazer and Moynihan 1976: 15). The confusion arises from a conception of class as 'a thing' or a cataloguing category instead of 'a process' (E.P. Thompson 1968: 9–12; Hobsbawm 1971: 5–21).

One of the latest developments on ethnicity from this perspective has been the New Ethnicity (Despres 1975; J.W. Bennett 1975). The notion of ethnicity as an adaptative mechanism is central in the volumes edited by Despres and Bennett, either as a strategic device (Bennett) or in the context of competition for resources (Despres). The New Ethnicists are also quick to separate ethnicity from class. Only in one article in Bennett's volume is the issue of class discussed (Robbins 1975: 285–304). The New Ethnicists

[29] The historical dimension is often reduced to a mere background. Social phenomena are not seen as historical products. Ethnicity acquires primacy over historical processes.

[30] See, for instance, Glazer and Moynihan's conception of society and of the state (1976). Cf. with Sklar 1967: 4–5, 9.

[31] While Despres differentiates ethnic from class stratification (1975: 195), van der Berghe gives ethnicity the same analytical value as class and, with others, ends up giving it primacy (1976: 242, 251–52). A. Cohen is more explicit: 'Classes are figments of the imagination of sociologists. What actually exist are large numbers of interest groups....' (1974b: 17).

acknowledge Barth's influence and that of social transactionalism and strategy analysis (Despres *ibid.*: 3; Bennett *ibid.*: 4). A further source has been C. Geertz's notion of 'primordial attachments' (1963). Thus, C.F. Keyes (1981) combines the cultural interpretation of ethnicity as a primordial characteristic of identity and its manipulation to attain goals. The New Ethnicity does not represent a fresh contribution to socio–anthropological theory but rather, a readaptation of former views held in the pluralist tradition.[32] Some of the New Ethnicists and pluralists themselves are aware that ethnic studies have reached a theoretical impasse (Keyes 1981: 4; A. Cohen 1981: 307).

A product of the most recent scientific effort made in central societies to understand 'otherness' seems to be the sudden proliferation of 'diaspora studies' ('Asian', 'Sikh' and 'African') in the United States and Canada (see Hamilton 1990; Barrier and Dusenbery 1989). Theoretical contributions to this field of study are uneven. In general, studies on non-European immigrants within this approach suffer from an insufficient definition of the 'diaspora' notion. It is also significant that a whole area of reality has until now escaped the analysis of 'diaspora' specialists: that of the nature of the 'receiving societies'. There is also an attempt to separate 'diaspora studies' from the study of ethnicity and of international migrations, when in fact these should be integral parts of the new field.

In the Marxist analyses of ethnicity, class is placed at centre-stage. Ethnicity is considered a political phenomenon, grounded in the system and relations of production. Generally, the reinforcement of 'racial' and ethnic differences is seen as a mechanism for the recreation of hegemony and the reproduction of socio-economic inequality. Issues such as ethnic struggles in relation to class struggle, the emergence of an 'ethnic problem' as a result of colonialism or related to internal colonialism, have been raised within this perspective. Nevertheless on the whole, the crucial issue, the structuring of ethnic and class differences, is still the subject of discussion and further elaboration.

Class theories on ethnicity can roughly be divided into those centred on the issue of superexploitation and those based on the internal colonialism thesis. Some Marxist studies focus on the nature of national liberation movements, self-determination, and

---

[32] Despres (1975), for instance, rephrases the concept of plural society as 'poly-ethnic system', using for that purpose ecological analogies.

ethnicity's strategic political role. Ethnicity is not seen as a natural outcome of socio–cultural differences. In some cases it tends to be portrayed as an instance of 'false consciousness' and its potential in situations of domination is dismissed (*cf.* Bridges 1973: 335ff.). Marxist reaction to the liberal sociological approaches to ethnic and 'race' relations has produced economistic analyses which leave ethnicity unexplained, or explained as a vague superstructural phenomenon serving ruling class interests (for instance, de Leper-vanche 1980).[33] The approach that centres on the issue of the super-exploitation of the workforce, in its turn, sees the demarcation along ethnic or racial lines at the workplace as a mechanism to keep the workforce divided and to preclude the development of class conscious-ness (Cox 1970; Nikolinakos 1973. See Miles' critique 1980).

The notion of 'internal colonialism'[34] used by some Marxist scholars to study the nature of cultural and political domination and the economic exploitation of subordinate ethnic groups emerged out of the conceptualization of underdevelopment by A. Gunder Frank (1966, 1969) and the writings of P. Gonzälez Casanova (1965) and R. Stavenhagen (1968, 1973, 1975, 1982). While the internal colonialism thesis acknowledges the class nature of the oppression of subordinate ethnic groups, it emphasizes the 'colonial' nature of this oppression (Stavenhagen 1982: 25). H. Wolpe has criticized this approach on the grounds that it treats class relations as residual and that it does not explain the relations between systems of class exploitation and domination on ethnic or cultural grounds (1971; also Sloan 1979). Although cultural assimilationism and re-constructive ethnography still dominate the field of 'tribal studies' in India, a group of scholars, starting with S. Jones (1978), have recently applied the notion of 'internal colonialism' to the Indian situ-ation. The issue of uneven development and internal colonialism has been explored by Nirmal Sengupta (1982a: 3–39) and S. Corbridge (1982: 40–62) while examining the situation in Jharkhand. Lately, J. Pathy (1988) has examined the situation of 'ethnic minorities' in Orissa from the perspective of political economy, considering

[33] On the insufficiency of 'immediate' economic explanations, see Saxton 1979.

[34] A. Gunder Frank (1966) defined underdevelopment on the basis of the existence of unequal metropolitan–satellite relationships, as an essential feature in the devel-opment of the capitalist system on a world scale. For P. Gonzalez Casanova, 'internal colonialism corresponds to a structure of social relations based on domination and exploitation among culturally heterogeneous, distinct groups' (1965: 33). See also Stavenhagen's 'First thesis' (1968).

ethnic expressions a 'product of uneven development' in the process of nation-building, and approaching the class dimension of ethnic phenomena.

Exploring class and ethnic relations that resulted from Western expansion, some recent studies have focused on the indigenous bourgeoisie and the use they make of ethnic or nationalist ideologies to mobilize mass support. For instance, Fitzpatrick (1980) studied the emergence of capitalist relations and the preservation of traditional modes in Papua New Guinea, identifying 'race' as a fundamental ideological category in the colonial context and in the national bourgeoisie's project for decolonization.

The civilizational approach, developed in Latin America and Africa, is specifically addressed to the realities of present 'Third World' societies and, particularly in the Latin American case, to the situation of indigenous populations. It emerged in opposition to both extremes in the perception of ethnicity: to perspectives that maintain the autonomy of ethnicity, and to economistic reductionism. At the base of this approach one finds the ideas of scholars like A. Abdel–Malek (1975) and Darcy Ribeiro (1968, 1969, 1981, 1984), and echoes of Cabral's thought (1973). Ethnicity is seen from this perspective as an expression of civilizational alternatives based on a people's awareness of the historical depth of their collective socio-cultural style. The existence of this awareness phrased in ethnic, national or cultural terms, is considered to indicate the possibility for a veritable process of decolonization to develop (Abdel–Malek 1975: 20–21). This approach views conflicts expressed in ethnic terms as confrontations with economic as well as with socio–cultural domination.

A new concept of *civilization* is central to this perspective. Abdel–Malek locates the driving forces behind present world political transformations in the non-Western social formations where combined processes of renaissance and national liberation movements have taken the shape of 'an explicitly civilizational process'. Importance is given to the 'depth of the historical field', the crucial factor for the maintenance of an ethno–national ('civilizational') style, and the concept of specificity is used as a main conceptual tool.[35] Darcy Ribeiro considers combined ethnic and

[35] 'The study of specificity is...undertaken...within the framework of the concrete evolution of given societies.... To talk of societal maintenance is to address oneself to the long historical duration that moulds events, not to contingency....' (*ibid.* 164–65).

class demands as a possible channel to develop wars of liberation, as happens, for instance, in Guatemala (1984: 28–29). For Ribeiro, ethnic formations are 'operative units of the civilizational process' (1968). He gives the 'Emerging Peoples' (*Pueblos Emergentes*) a central role in the forging of a new society. These peoples correspond to the historico–cultural configurations of oppressed national ethnic groups who are presently 'stressing their ethnic and cultural profiles as national minorities...aiming at self-determination' (1984: 28).[36]

Critiques of the civilizational approach have come from some Marxist anthropologists who underline the weak treatment given to the location of indigenous movements in the class structure of the specific nation–state (Medina 1983), the idealization of the 'ethnic essence' and a 'return to the sources' (Ortega Hegg *et al.* 1983), and the emphasis on the confrontation of ethno–national groups with the West as a basic contradiction.[37] This controversy within Marxism regarding ethnicity opposes an economistic to a political perspective. The civilizational approach has, in fact, considered issues on the class articulation of indigenous populations and the role of the state (see Varese 1979), and the crucial issue of class and ethnic consciousness.

Production in the field of ethnic studies is plentiful. However, this production reveals a series of problems: the inadequacy of some of the social categories in use; a lack of agreement in the definition of the subject of study and, for the most part, limited theoretical advances. Of late, there has been a significant shift in the approach to the problem. First, there have been new insights from a Marxist perspective and second, a turn from reductionism (be it cultural or economic) to a social and political perspective. Consequently, there has been a change in the conception of the 'object'. Are we then witnessing 'the end of ethnicity'? To obtain an answer to this question, culture and the development of collective identities will be explored in the following chapters.

[36] In this respect, Stavenhagen points out that, in Latin America, there is rather 'an emerging social movement and an incipient ideology based on ethnic criteria' (1984a: 201). The aims of indigenous movements in Latin America are summarized in Bonfil Batalla 1981. See the *Declaration of Barbados* (1971) and the *Second Declaration* (1977) (Documentos...1979).

[37] Earlier, Jean Copans had expressed his doubts on the 'chevaliers of ethnocide' (a direct reference to R. Jaulin [1973]), viewing with suspicion what he considered a new praise of 'primitiveness' (1974: 144).

Part Two

REALITIES

2

The Myth of
the Tribe

Father of the Earth ours is the land...
In Nagpur, our ancestors left their footprints.
In the country reclaimed by us, you made others sit in our
property.
Our ancient order was wiped out....

Birsaite song

British colonial and Indian administrative ethnography, combined with applied anthropology, have generated an epistemology which views Bihar as a living museum of tribes. In constructing these representations, facts in the history of Jharkhand's ethnic communities have been largely ignored or altered to uphold the 'myth of the tribe'. The existence of different systems of production, the incorporation of these communities into a cash economy and later into a colonial economy, and their subsumption under the capitalist mode of production, processes of class formation, changes in the social division of labour and in the relations of production, and the evolving nature of power relationships are not discussed in existing ethnographies of Jharkhand. The concrete realities of Jharkhand's populations, the transformations they had experienced over time, and their economic–political location in the wider social context, were ignored. Instead, partial socio–economic indices were arbitrarily attributed to them, in order to make them fit the construct of 'tribe'.

It is my contention that the tribal construct in India is a *colonial category*, and that it formed part of the colonial legitimizing ideology. As such, this category operated as a device to catalogue conquered populations, to formulate imperial policies and to facilitate the incorporation of these populations into the colonial system. The ideology of tribe did not dissolve with the end of colonialism. It is still functional in independent India's underdeveloped capitalism, as will be shown in the next chapter.

Jharkhand's ethnohistory reveals not the existence of 'tribes', but rather a variegated development of its indigenous societies and processes of transition from lineage and communally-based societies to a class-based society. A review of Jharkhand's ethnohistory makes visible the historical depth of its adivasi communities' socio–cultural styles, and how social maintenance and the attachment to land and territory have acted as an axis for the reproduction of collective identities. These dynamics were present in the past, and they survive today.

Jharkhand's reality challenges the myth of the tribe with the evidence provided by history. To evaluate this evidence, this chapter focuses not on isolated communities but on key processes that affected adivasi societies.[1] For that purpose, illustrative instances are presented to show the processes of transformation which Jharkhand's adivasi societies underwent in the course of time. Internal discontinuities occurring in these societies, like the development of social differentiation, are also observed in these cases. An analysis of the modes of incorporation of Jharkhand's adivasi societies into the colonial system follows. The tribal paradigm is questioned by examining both different specific 'histories' and general processes like colonialism.

In sum, I will argue that there were no 'tribes' in Jharkhand until the European perception of Indian reality constructed them and

---

[1] To isolate particular communities would have meant to reproduce the perspective that has ensured the existence of the tribal paradigm. The intention is precisely to demonstrate that the elements used to characterize Jharkhand's adivasis as 'tribes' (isolation, inherent egalitarism, autonomy, economic independence, slow change) are invalid.

MAP 2: JHARKHAND REGION (BIHAR)

Nepal

Uttar
Pradesh

Champaran

Darbhanga

Saran   Muzaffarpur

Saharsa   Purnea

Ganges R.

Patna

Shahabad   Monghyr

Gaya   Bhagalpur

BIHAR

Santal Parganas

Palamau   Hazaribagh

JHARKHAND

Dhanbad

Madhya
Pradesh   West Bengal

Ranchi

Singhbhum

Orissa   JHARKHAND
                            (Districts before
                            reorganization)

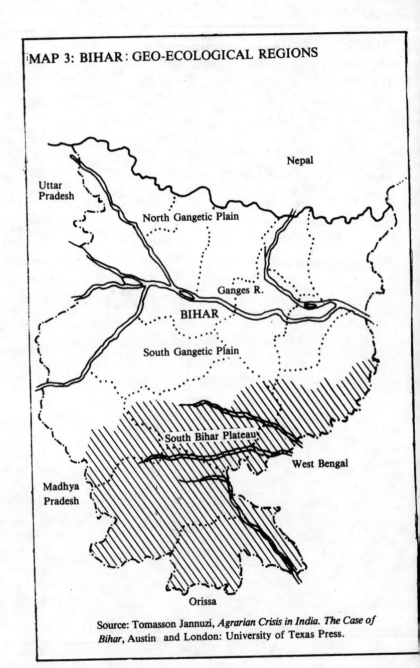

MAP 3: BIHAR: GEO-ECOLOGICAL REGIONS

Nepal

Uttar
Pradesh

North Gangetic Plain

Ganges R.

BIHAR

South Gangetic Plain

South Bihar Plateau

West Bengal

Madhya
Pradesh

Orissa

Source: Tomasson Jannuzi, *Agrarian Crisis in India. The Case of Bihar*, Austin and London: University of Texas Press.

colonial authorities gave them their administrative sanction. The tribal paradigm is ill-suited to categorize past and present adivasi societies. In Jharkhand, these societies are now basically peasant societies inserted in a class society, portraying *at the same time* specific ethno–cultural styles.

The Region

With 5,810,867 persons registered as Scheduled Tribes out of an all-India total of 51,628,638, the state of Bihar[2] has one of the largest proportions of indigenous ethnic communities (8.31 per cent of the population). Of the total Scheduled Tribes population in Bihar, 5,329,283 persons (91.7 per cent) are located in its Jharkhand region (CI 1981: series 1, part II–B, iii).

More important than Bihar's existing internal administrative divisions is the geo–ecological regional differentiation of the state, resulting in three well-demarcated regions: North Bihar to the north of the Ganges River, the South Ganges Plain or South Bihar, and the South Bihar Plateau comprising Chotanagpur and Santal Parganas (*Map 3*). The distinctive geo–ecological characteristics of these areas have partially conditioned the development of systems of production and the emergence of socio–cultural patterns. The Ganges River divides Bihar into two physically different regions: the fertile plain of the north, and the south which, being fertile along the Ganges, becomes hillier as one proceeds south into the Chotanagpur plateau. In the past, the Ganges divide already marked the development of two different regions.[3]

Until the middle of the sixteenth century, when Akbar acceded to the throne of Delhi, Chotanagpur seemed to have been little

[2] The modern state of Bihar borders on the north with the Nepalese Terai, on the east with the state of West Bengal, on the south with the state of Orissa, and with the state of Uttar Pradesh and Madhya Pradesh on the west.

[3] The state of Videha on the north was already on the decline in the sixth century BC, and the state of Magadha in the south rose to prominence around that time. The hilly and forest region of Jharkhand (Jharakhanda: 'forest territory') may have formed part of the Magadha state during Ashoka's reign (273–32BC) (Thapar 1966: 50–69; Spear 1958). The name Jharkhand for Chotanagpur appears in the late Sanskrit literature and continued to be used by Muslim historians, changing to Kokrah (possibly from the Oraon *Kurukh*) in the sixteenth century (S.C. Roy 1912: 151, 176, 359; Bradley–Birt 1903: 10, 12; Pandey 1963: 111).

affected by external influences. Under the Mughals, the Raja of Chotanagpur was made a tributary. Whatever independence and isolation Chotanagpur had enjoyed in Mughal times was relative. Chotanagpur was surrounded by a cash economy and, if this economy did not penetrate the entire area it was because the lower productivity of its land was not particularly vital for the reproduction of Mughal 'feudal' economy (Habib 1963). In 1765, the East India Company acquired the Diwani of Bengal, Bihar and Orissa, which included Jharkhand.

Today the Jharkhand area of Bihar comprises practically half the state's territory, extending over the districts of Palamau, Hazaribagh, Santal Parganas, Dhanbad, Ranchi and Singhbhum (*Map 2*). Jharkhand, however, denotes more than a geographical region. Together with the adjacent districts of the states of West Bengal, Orissa and Madhya Pradesh it forms part of a distinct socio–cultural region: Greater Jharkhand.

Demands for a separate state for this region were presented in 1928 to the Simon Commission and later, in 1954, to the States Reorganization Commission.[4] In 1973, the Jharkhand Party demanded a state comprising over 72,619 sq. miles of territory with a population of 30,598,991, covering three districts of West Bengal (Bankura, Midnapur, Purulia), six from Bihar (Ranchi, Singhbhum, Dhanbad, Hazaribagh, Palamau, Santal Parganas), four from Orissa (Sundargarh, Keonjhor, Majurbhanj, Sambalpur), and two from Madhya Pradesh (Raigarh and Sarguja). Greater Jharkhand can be claimed to extend even further if the hilly and jungle areas of Rajasthan, Maharashtra and Andhra Pradesh are included on the basis of their pattern of uneven development and ethno–cultural composition (A.K. Roy 1982a: 5).

Paths Leading to Jharkhand

F.B. Bradley–Birt noted at the beginning of the century: 'Nothing

---

[4] Jharkhand was to embrace 63, 859 sq. miles of territory with a population of 16,367,175. This proposal differed from later claims in that it excluded some parts of West Bengal but included larger areas of Bihar and Madhya Pradesh, and the hill and jungle areas of southern Uttar Pradesh.

but a special volume...could attempt to give a detailed account of all the tribes and castes that people Chota Nagpore.... All the races of Northern India seem to have collected in this corner of the empire' (1903: 22). From ancient times Jharkhand received people who migrated into the area. Major adivasi groups like the Mundas, Santals, Oraons and Hos and other early settlers reached Jharkhand after a series of migrations.[5]

The ancestors of the adivasis have been identified as the native opponents the Indo–Aryans encountered when they entered the subcontinent. They were the *dasas* and *dasyus* of the *Rig Veda*. The differentiation between Aryans and adivasis persisted across the centuries, later formulated on a racial basis as the one between 'superior' and 'inferior' communities. The racial basis (the construct of 'racial purity') which has sustained this dichotomy is untenable on historical grounds, not to mention its ethnocentric–racist bias. As pointed out by N. Sengupta (1982b), attention should shift to the evolution of a different mode of production in the fertile river basins after the discovery of iron and the development of agricultural technology and irrigation, leading to an intensive use of land and to economic specialization, social differentiation and regional integration. This process did not take place in the hilly areas because the terrain did not allow such intense land utilization. The developments that were possible in the plains were understood as expressions of a 'higher civilization', while the people of the hills and the jungles were seen as not so technologically advanced and, following a fallacious correlation, as belonging to an 'inferior race'. These regional–economic identifications did not become fixed until the advent of colonialism, when different pre-capitalist societies were integrated in the capitalist system in various ways. Existing differences were used by British colonial administrators, and isolationist policies towards the adivasis were shaped with a rhetorical protectionist intent. In the background of these policies stood a history of military repression and economic exploitation of adivasi land and labour. The process of unequal integration based on the construction of fixed categories (Scheduled Tribes) continued after independence.

[5] Pioneer ethnographers like S.C. Roy (1912, 1915), E.T. Dalton (1872) and W.W. Hunter (1868, 1877) attempted to reconstruct the early history of these groups on the basis of archaeological and linguistic data, the analysis of Hindu scriptures and adivasi oral history.

From a Variety of Indigenous Formations to the Forging of 'Tribes'

The Stigma of the 'Tribe of Predatory Freebooters': the Paharias

In the nineteenth century, the Paharias[6] were described as 'thieves and murderers' (Heber 1861: 120). The appellation dates back to 1770 when the British administration became interested in the Paharias, a 'tribe of predatory freebooters, raiding and terrorizing the plain country from the foot of the hills to the Ganges' (Russell 1916: 155). That was precisely the year when the great Bengal famine of 1770 started to be felt with severity in the region between the Rajmahal hills and the Ganges. In the years that followed, the Paharias systematically plundered the plains to such an extent that these were abandoned by the cultivators (Hunter 1877: 303; O'Malley 1910: 34–35).

In such years of scarcity and starvation, plunder was an activity not restricted to the peoples of the hills, but one to which many peasants resorted to after having been forced by famine and drought to abandon their lands and to take refuge in the hills. Wandering *sannyasis* were active in Rungpur, Rajshahi and Malda in groups of 50,000 strong (Monckton Jones 1918: 180, 212, 213; Hunter 1868: 70ff.). They were joined by crowds of starving peasants. Bands of up to 500 men moved, unresisted, across abandoned villages and lands from Kharakpur to Rajmahal. In the winter of 1772, these starving masses fell upon the Lower Bengal fields, burning and plundering. Dacoity became 'a standing trouble present in all parts of the provinces and at all seasons of the year' (Hunter *ibid.*: 178), the result of the general economic conditions at the time, of the insensibility of an administration mostly worried about the collection of revenue, and of the hoarding of grain.[7] Despite the famine, revenue was rigorously collected.[8]

[6] The Paharias are the Maler or Savaria Paharias in the present subdivisions of Rajmahal, Pakur and Godala in Santal Parganas District (Vidyarthi 1960: 26). They maintained that 'the human race was first produced on the hills', and their traditions do not speak of migrations. Oraon oral history, however, mentions the Paharias' migration from Rohtas when driven out by the Indo–Aryans. Some then went towards Chotanagpur and others to the Rajmahal hills (Dalton 1872: 236, 255–56).

[7] Monckton Jones *op. cit.* letters and documents: 207, 211–212; Patwardhan 1971, Fort William–India House, letters dated 4 February, 31 August, 11 September 1770, 28 August 1771, 9 March 1772: 117–31. 361–68; B. Prasad (ed.) 1960: 191–94, 224–29.

[8] The East India Company was informed in 1772:

Deep transformations in the land tenure system occurred in the 1770s. According to Hunter:

> Before the commencement of 1771, one-third of a generation of peasants had been swept from the face of the earth and a whole generation of once rich families had been reduced to indigence.... In 1776 the scarcity of cultivators had completely transposed the relations of landlords and tenants in Bengal....(1868: 56, 59–60).

The process of depopulation continued for 15 years after the famine; cultivators fled to the cities; the impossibility of paying the revenue resulted in many going to prison.

The situation of disorder and scarcity brought about by the famine affected the Paharias to a lesser degree since they could retreat to the forests for survival. It added, nevertheless, to the changes that had been taking place in the agreements between them and the zamindars of the plains. At that time, the economic life of the Paharias could be characterized as based on a communal system of production, dependent on a territory of forests and hill slopes (Pathy 1982: 37–39). The Paharias used land mainly as a 'subject of labour'.[9] They depended on forest products and hunting but practiced some agriculture, which puts them marginally into the agricultural self-sustaining category. Labour was family-based and followed the principle of reciprocity. Today they still live off the forests and practice slash-and-burn cultivation on the flat hill-tops. On the low hilly areas they have taken to plough cultivation where the forests have disappeared, and to a combination of both forms of cultivation at intermediate altitudes (Vidyarthi 1960: 26–27). Their original mode of production in which shifting cultivation and the right to its usufruct were collectively vested in the community

---

The influence [of the 1770 famine] on the revenue has been yet unnoticed, and even *unfelt, but by those from whom it is collected*; for notwithstanding the loss of at least one-third of the inhabitants of the province, and the consequent decrease of the cultivation, *the net collections of the year 1771 exceeded even those of 1768.* (Letter from the Revenue Department, Fort William, 3 November 1772. Prasad *op. cit.* 417–30; italics added).

Revenue collection was made under pressure (Forrest 1910: 265–66).

[9] Conducive to 'a type of "instantaneous" production whose output is immediately available, allowing a process of *sharing* which takes place at the end of each enterprise' (Meillassoux 1972: 99) as in the case of hunting and gathering.

became endangered by the immigration of non-adivasi cultivators and a consequent reduction of forest lands when these were opened to intensive agriculture.[10]

The Paharias had until the end of the eighteenth century a history of independence. The Mughal government only exerted nominal control over them and seemed to have accepted the idea that no revenue was obtainable from the hilly areas. In my view, by the eighteenth century, a modified version of the arrangements based on reciprocity had already been extended beyond the community in the form of the annual agreements with the zamindars of the plains, whereby divisional and village headmen (*sardars* and *manjhis*) took charge of detecting crime, and Paharia contingents guarded the hill passes and prevented raids upon the plains. The Paharias thus exchanged protection for the zamindars' respect for their economic independence. The *sardars* were given service tenures (*jagirs*) in the plains. However, the zamindars' growing desire for control over people and land became a real threat to Paharia economic self-sufficiency. Raids that took place following the 1770 famine often reflected the need of the Paharias to check the advance of the cultivators from the plains. More than survival guided the Paharias in their raids at the end of the eighteenth century: by then they were engaged in an open guerrilla warfare to safeguard their independence.

British military penetration into these areas began two years after acquiring the Diwani of Bengal, Bihar and Orissa in 1765. From 1767 to 1778 the British extended their control over these areas with the aim of subjecting them to the payment of revenue. Captain Brooke, Military Governor of the Jungleterry,[11] established armed control over the area and set up a scheme 'of pacification' based on the transformation of the Paharias into instruments of the colonial administration, and on their incorporation into the colonial economy by settling them and establishing markets at the outskirts of the plains (O'Malley 1910: 36). The plan, sanctioned

[10] The Paharia is the only 'Scheduled Tribe' whose population has been constantly declining since 1931 (set at 93,282 in the 1971 Census). The formerly self-sufficient Paharias are now plagued by illness, malnutrition, debts, harassment by forest officials, and by the illegal use of their lands (as for mining) (H. Narayan 1984: 26–27).

[11] The British called Santal Parganas, parts of Hazaribagh, Monghyr and Bhagalpur, the *Jungleterry* or *Jungle tarai*.

by the Government in 1778, was carried out by August Cleveland, Collector of Bhagalpur.

Cleveland's subjugation of the Jungleterry has been referred to as 'the most permanent,...the most rational mode of domination'.[12] But his mode of domination proved not to be permanent and was abandoned after Cleveland died. Cleveland's measures were neither conciliatory nor benevolent, as usually portrayed. They were an example of colonial control tactics.[13] Among other things, he formed a corps of Paharia archers (the Bhagalpur Hill Rangers, disbanded in 1857), who were to be used against their own people. He also set up a tribunal of *sardars*, presided over by himself, to try their brethren and execute the sentences. In this, Cleveland took advantage of the animosity between Paharias and Santals. Santals were sentenced on false charges of dacoity and murder, sometimes to death, by the Paharia Councils he set up. Adivasi protest in the area could thus be repressed by the new bodies of native collaborators created by Cleveland.

Cleveland made explicit his colonial policy in a letter dated 21 November 1780:

The *circulation of money in the hills* by Government appears to me the most likely *bait* to ensure the attachment of the chiefs.... *The enemies of Government are to be considered as enemies by the hill people*.... It shall be...the duty of the Corps to bring all refractory hill chiefs and Gautwalls to terms....(O' Malley 1910: 38–39. Italics added).

Sardars and *manjhis* began receiving regular cash payments for their collaboration. The administration considered the operative 'a financial success' which contributed to breaking the control of the local zamindars and facilitated the Government's direct management of the area.[14]

[12] As stated in the inscription on the monument dedicated to him in Bhagalpur (O'Malley 1910: 41).

[13] See D.C. Ganguly 1958: 19; Forrest 1910: 79; O'Malley 1910: 37; Hunter 1877: 305–7; A. Srivastava 1981b.

[14] Out of the East India Company's experiences in the control of the Rajmahal hills originated the Non-regulation system (*Regulation I, 1796*, on justice). In 1823 the Government promised not to take revenue from the Paharias. By the beginning of the nineteenth century the Paharias were Government tenants with occupancy rights on their lands but unable to dispose of them (*ibid.*: 214–17).

How the Santals Became 'the Day Labourers of Lowland Bengal'

The Santals, although not considered to be as 'fierce...nor as hostile' as the Paharias were nevertheless an obstacle for the regional completion of colonial control:

> Until 1790, the Santals were the pest of the adjacent lowlands....Every winter, as soon as they had gathered in the rice crop..., the whole nation moved down upon the plains, hunting in the forests and plundering the open country on the line of march....(Hunter 1868: 219).

Hunting and gathering—complementary activities for these settled agriculturalists—were considered to be plundering by the British. Paradoxically, Hunter also remarks that amongst the Santals 'crime and criminal officers... [were] almost unknown' (*ibid*.: 217).

The Santals considered land to be a village patrimony. According to customary law, the individual had the right to the usufruct of land but not to its possession nor inheritance. All economic activities were based on cooperation.[15]

At the end of the eighteenth century, important migrations took place among the Santals of Bengal, Bihar and Orissa due to problems they had with the local zamindars and the situation created by the 1770 famine. In 1812, Sutherland, Magistrate of Bhagalpur, recommended that the colonial Government declare the hill tract and the adjacent plains in Paharia and Santal country to be Government property. Subsequently, the colonial Government took possession of the Damin-i-koh as direct proprietor and from 1832 on promoted the migration of Santals, reputed to be excellent clearers of lands and cultivators, to the region.[16] By 1851 there were already 82,785 adivasi and non-adivasi migrants in the Damin, living in 1,473 villages, as well as 10,000 people established beyond the demarcation fence.[17] Only the 1,164 Santal villages

[15] See Dalton 1872; Hunter 1868; Risley 1908; Mukherjea 1943; Man n.d.; Datta–Majumder 1956; Orans 1965; Culshaw 1949.

[16] Migrants came from Orissa, Dhalbhum, Manbhum, Barabhum, Chotanagpur, Palamau, Hazaribagh, Midnapur, Bankura and Birbhum.

[17] The ring fence of pillars marking the Damin-i-koh was 295 miles in circumference and embraced 866 sq. miles of highland and 500 of lowland territory (Hunter 1868: 223 fn. 61a). For details, see Gait *et al.* 1909: 237 ff.; Hunter 1877: 309–10; CR 1856: 238; Roy Chaudhuri 1965a: 74–75; Raghavaiah 1971: 148).

paid rent. The Paharias, meanwhile, remained in the high part of the hills.

What did the creation of the Damin imply? The colonial Government *expropriated* the lands of the inhabitants of the area and created a 'tribal reserve' for its own profit. It exacted labour from the Santals who worked as day labourers to open the area to cultivation. Subsequently, the Santals were transformed into tenants paying rent in cash on lands onto which the then Deputy Collector Pontet brought new migrants. The area under cultivation was thus enlarged and 'a handsome revenue' obtained.[18] A money economy expanded through the new weekly markets and new commodities were introduced (Hunter 1868: 228). The control of the Rajmahal hills was also considered by the British to be a strategic imperative that provided them with a guard post over the Ganges River route. The Santals, transformed into 'the day–labourers of Lowland Bengal', began to be described as industrious, as an agricultural reserve army. However, the moment they challenged the pattern of colonial domination in 1855, they were again depicted as 'blood-thirsty savages' (Hunter *ibid.*: 220–25; CR 1856: 259). It was precisely in the Damin-i-koh where the 1855 Santal Movement started.

From lineage-based Societies to State Formation: Mundas, Oraons, Bhumijs

Chotanagpur's settled agricultural communities shared a similar language and social institutions and, up to the advent of the first Chotanagpur Nagbansi raja (*c.* fifth century AD), followed parallel patterns of social, economic and cultural development. According to S.C. Roy, the Mundas settled in Chotanagpur around the sixth century BC.[19] The lands they occupied were considered to be the

[18] The aims of the administration are clearly stated in the letter Deputy Collector Pontet sent to H.J. James, Acting Collector of Bhagalpur, in 1837 (*cit.* in Roy Chaudhuri 1959: 3 ff.).

[19] At first there were groups of independent villages led by a secular (*munda*) and a religious chief (*pahan*), and a *panchayat*. Later, villages came together in confederacies (*parha* or *patti*), led by a *manki* and a *parhapanchayat*. Mundas were divided in exogamous groups (*kili*), each of whom founded a village. The descendants were known as *khuntkattidars*. *Mundas* and *pahans* came usually from the founding clan.

village's patrimony. The descendants of the founding clan of the village (*khuntkattidars*) controlled the land, protecting their rights under customary inheritance laws. Individuals integrated into the community through adoption[20] could have the usufruct of lands allotted to them for maintenance, but did not have other rights over them (S.C. Roy 1912: 166ff., 433, 435; Hoffmann 1961).

The *khuntkatti* system and the egalitarian character of Munda society began to change with the development of social stratification based on a differential attainment of power over land and with the transformation of the offices of the chiefs of villages and confederacies into hereditary positions. This marked the beginning of a tendency towards the establishment of chiefdoms. The election of a raja among the Mundas and the Oraons, initially with no prerogatives over land, initiated a change in their economic and political patterns which led to state formation. In time, the Raj Nagbansi family of Chotanagpur drew up genealogies to support its claims to a Rajput origin.[21]

Settled agriculture, the continuous occupation of a territory and a territorial administrative organization provided the basis for state formation among the Mundas and Oraons. The emergence of an aristocracy with economic privileges (control over land, labour, services and rent), accelerated the already existing process of social differentiation. The ensuing mode of production has been characterized as 'feudal'.[22] At first, the village community had to make collective payments of a permanently-fixed rent to the overlord, and the peasants had to provide free labour (*begari*). Later, these demands evolved into a system of *awabs* (tributes) levied by the raja and the *jagirdars* (K.S. Singh 1966: 3–4; 1977: 175). Munda society ceased to be egalitarian and based on the communal holding of resources with a collective organization of labour and production. Dalton has noted the emergence of two classes in each village:

[20] They were called *eta haturenko* or *parha horoko* ('men from other villages').

[21] There is no historical account of the emergence of kingship among the Mundas nor on the origins of the Nagbansis. S.C. Roy (*ibid.*: 141; 1915: 136ff.) and Dalton (1872: 164–68) recorded a myth of origin according to which the first raja may have been a Naga adopted by a *manki*. See also P.C. Roy Chaudhuri 1965b: 143–44 and K.S. Singh 1971b: 170.

[22] Pathy 1982; K.S. Singh 1971b; S.C. Roy 1912. There is an ongoing debate on the categorization of pre-colonial non-European social formations and the applicability of the category 'feudalism' to India (see *The Journal of Peasant Studies*, 1985. *Cf.* H. Mukhia 1981 with R.S. Sharma 1965, 1985).

the privileged *bhuinhars* ('the militia of the state'), and the mass of the peasantry working on rent-paying lands (*rajhas*) (1872: 167). The situation was more complicated.

I visualize the system of social stratification based on the control of land and labour that developed in Chotanagpur together with state formation as follows: There was a rent-receiving ruling class at the top composed of the raja, his family and the new landlord sector.[23] There followed a dominant peasant group (*khuntkattidars*, later *bhuinhars*), descendants of the original settlers and principal office-holders. This sector had a privileged position, paying quit rent to the raja and holding some lands rent free. However, they were also found cultivating *rajha* lands ('the share of the raja') and rendering free services. This dominant peasant sector could preserve a relative control over the means of production at the level of production (Mukhia 1981: 290; Stein 1985: 21). To a certain extent this may have also been the case with the next group in the hierarchy: peasants working the lands of the former group and on *rajha* lands who paid rent, produce or both to the upper groups. A fourth layer was that of the landless agricultural labourers working on the landlords' privileged private lands (*manjihas*), paying the landlord in services mostly translated into unpaid cultivation, with no right of occupancy. In general terms, it was the existence of a group's superior rights over the rest of the peasants' lands that allowed the extraction of surplus in various forms: the lord's share of rent, labour, gifts and free services. Given that only the surplus was extracted, the self-sufficiency of the peasantry probably did not break down in the case of cultivators working land under rent or giving part of the produce.[24] It seems doubtful that this applied in the case of the fourth group, who had an insecure position on the land they tilled and were made to contribute forced labour.

The rajas, who became increasingly Hinduized, began to give land grants to brahmins from Upper and Central India, who were brought to spread Hinduism among the population. Hindu and Muslim moneylenders, merchants and potential courtiers followed in their wake, also obtaining land grants from the raja. They eventually appropriated these lands for themselves by dispossessing the

[23] The new landlord sector comprised *jagirdars* (holders of a *jagir*: conditional or unconditional assignment of land for its revenue), the *korposhdars* (maintenance grantees) and the *thikadars* (holders of temporary or permanent land leases).
[24] See Habib (1985: 48) for medieval India.

cultivators who had opened them to cultivation and tilled them.[25] The process of immigration intensified during the seventeenth and eighteenth centuries. Peasants were encouraged to migrate to the area to extend agriculture and thus generate a larger surplus. The raja also brought military mercenaries, who were remunerated with *jagirs*, for purposes of defence and to control the peasantry. Land grants were given to all these alien elements. This led to the emergence of the *jagirdars* who, at first, collected part of the agricultural produce, and later established a cash rent system.

By the beginning of the nineteenth century the raja, his family and the *jagirdars* were already indebted to Muslim, Hindu and Sikh moneylenders and merchants who were paid with permanent or temporary leases (*thikas*), with perpetual leases at fixed rentals and with usufructuary leases. By the nineteenth century many of the original settlers had been transformed through this process of making land grants into tenants. Ultimately, only the wastelands and the forests were left to them. It has been sometimes argued that the raja gave land grants as a way of relinquishing his claims over the surplus generated in those lands in favour of the *jagirdars* (S.C. Roy 1912: 165) but that he did not intend to give them full control over them, which was what eventually happened. In contrast to what happened in the European feudal system (peasants received land grants to cultivate these lands for the lord), Indian rajas gave land grants in order to get the surplus collected. Peasants paid rent to the *jagirdars*, but did not necessarily enjoy security on the land they tilled since they could be replaced by other peasants who provided forced labour in the form of agricultural work (Sharma 1985: fn. 31). The new landlords also intervened in the internal affairs of the villages, restricting the activities of the *panchayat* and exerting pressure on the chiefs in order to preclude independent decisions. Non-economic coercion served to reinforce the economic control over the means and processes of production, and formed an integral part of the pre-capitalist mode of exploitation. A complex land tenure system thus evolved in Chotanagpur together with the rising power of the rajas. All this was later compounded with the changes brought about by British colonial administration.[26]

[25] The concept of service land grants seems to have been alien to the area. The practice may have started quite late since the oldest registered lease dates back only to 1676 (S.C. Roy 1912: 164–65).

[26] See S.C. Roy 1912: app. III, and 1961: 278–323.

A process of 'feudalization' also took place among the Bhumijs. Surajit Sinha (1962: 42) as well as K.S. Singh (1971: 171) suggest that the emergence of the state among the Bhumijs was an endogenous development, a fact that would make them the exception among other Kolarian groups. Dalton earlier noted that the Raja of Dhalbhum, for instance, was unmistakably of Bhumij origin, despite the Dhalbhum rajas' claim of being kshatriyas or Rajputs. Dalton further stated that the zamindars were also of 'the same race as their people' (*op. cit.*: 174).

By the sixteenth century the Bhumijs were already organized in kingdoms and claimed to be Rajputs. At the end of the eighteenth century the British, after encountering the strong resistance of the local chiefs, forced their way into the Jungle Mahals where they found well-established kingdoms in Barabhum and Patkum. S. Sinha (1953) views this development as being one of 'a feudalistic structure [evolving] from a tribal democratic base', in the course of which former administrative units did not change their democratic character. But was this democratic base maintained once the social stratification accompanying a 'feudalistic structure' emerged? This seems not to have been the case. A landholding sector, with the raja or zamindar at the top, included the chiefs (*sardar ghatwals*) of a number of administrative units of twelve villages, the chiefs of each of these units (*sadiyals*), village headmen with service tenures (*ghatwals*), soldiers (*tanbedars* or *paiks*) also with tenures of cultivable land, and the *kuntkattidars*. Poor peasants, artisans and landless labourers came last. The raja obtained his income mainly from agricultural land in the villages over which he had attained proprietorship. The tenants provided free labour and a certain amount of 'tribute' in kind on the occasion of the Durga Puja festival. Artisans gave a share of their products to the raja in exchange for land free of rent. The *sardar ghatwals* only paid a symbolic revenue to the raja, and in fact preserved a great deal of autonomy.

Different communities—brahmins as priests, literate people as officers for the administration, service castes, craftmen and trading groups—were encouraged to immigrate to the territories of the Barabhum, Patkum and Bhagmundi 'feudal' chiefs. These elements did not endanger the supremacy of the Bhumijs, particularly over land. The brahmins, however, acquired economic and political power after receiving generous land and village grants (*brahmottars*).

Many of them settled as tenants or started operating as money-lenders and *diwans* (J.C. Jha 1967: 109–10). In addition, the *ghatwals* (village headmen), entrusted with defence and the maintenance of order, became 'proprietors of states comprising each from one to twenty manors... the most substantial tenants under them... [being] also hereditary Ghatwals rendering services and paying... a very low fixed rent...' (Dalton 1872: 175). The differential access to land and politico–administrative offices, and thus to power, gave rise to a fairly rigid social stratification, ritually expressed in caste-ranking combined with widespread Hinduization.

By the beginning of the nineteenth century, the immigrants' encroachment on Bhumij economic life was considerable, a situation aggravated by the effects of the Permanent Settlement. British law tended to favour the usurious activities of the moneylenders and this adversely affected the indebted rajas and chiefs as well as other sectors of the population. Zamindars and *sardars* had also begun to exact an increasing number of illegal cesses that soon became permanent taxes which added to the toll levied by the petty officials of the East India Company. As we will see later, the common grievance of indebtedness finally induced some rajas and zamindars to join forces with the discontented people in a series of armed insurgencies that swept the Jungle Mahals and Dhalbhum, culminating in the 1832 uprising.

Chotanagpur and Singhbum under Colonial Rule

In 1765, Chotanagpur came under the rule of the East India Company, and the first agreement on rents was reached with the Raja of Chotanagpur in 1771. In 1789 it was suggested that the Permanent Settlement should not apply to Chotanagpur since the revenue received from this area was more a fixed tribute than a tax determined by land production. Nevertheless, the Permanent Settlement was introduced in the last years of the eighteenth century. This caused an adverse reaction in the rural areas among the zamindars when lands on which they had been declared full proprietors came to be auctioned off to cover revenue arrears (Gopal 1949; J.C. Jha 1963; R. Guha 1981). The zamindars' indebtedness and the operation of usurious capital became one of the pivots around which the land market revolved, with the result that land started passing into the hands of moneylenders. With regard to the adivasi peasantry, there was no room in the new provisions for the customary land rights of the original settlers and the village office-holders. These omissions in the new system gave the zamindars increased power to evict peasants from their lands. Customary law was abruptly replaced by contract law.[27] Increasing rent demands began to affect the zamindars. The Raja of Chotanagpur had constant difficulties in paying the revenue, zamindars were ruined, landlors with unlimited power increased the rents of the cultivators, and the oppression and pauperization of the peasantry grew.

In 1817, Munda and Oraon lands were put under the direct administration of the East India Company as part of the District of Ramgarh and the Raja of Chotanagpur ceased to be a tributary. In 1823, the Government took over from the Raja and his *jagirdars* the right to tax the production of liquor, to collect road-tolls, and to tax the products sold in the market. The situation of instability and the incidence of recurrent rural insurgency[28] led in 1833 to an administrative change: the creation of the South West Frontier Agency. With the establishment of courts of justice and military cantonments, the *jagirdars* and *thikadars* continued the despoliation of the adivasi peasantry, but now under a semblance of legality. Around 1856, the *jagirdars*, some 600 in number, had come to control approximately 150 villages each. Munda land inheritance laws were disregarded by the landlords. Backed by British law, the landlord 'regained' possession of lands when there were no male heirs. As Hoffmann noted in relation to laws forbidding adivasis to sell their lands:

> The lawgiver intended the lands to be *inalienable*, i.e., to remain in the possession of the raiyats. The lawyer says: they are *unsaleable*, i.e., the raiyat cannot give his valuable right in the land *for money*, but he can give it *for nothing*.... (Hoffmann 1961: fn. 337. Italics in the original).

[27] The Permanent Settlement vested individual land proprietorship on a host of landholders taken in bloc to be zamindars, who then could freely inherit, sell, mortgage or give away these lands. While the Permanent Settlement reinforced the new zamindars' position, it seriously weakened that of the common peasantry, and created sharp conflicts in the countryside.

[28] For instance: the protests of the Mundas of Tamar in 1789 and 1797, the one led by Dukan Shahi Manki in 1807, those in Rahe and Silli in 1796–98, in Rahe in 1812, the major movements of 1819–20 led by Rudu and Konta Munda, and of the Mundas of Sonepur in 1831–32.

Complete villages could be bought at the Ranchi Court, as for instance, when the village headman went into debt and gave his village as a guarantee. As soon as the creditor won the case, he started acting as a zamindar, demanding rent from the *khuntkattidar* peasants.

The process of peasant exploitation and land alienation commenced in Chotanagpur well before the establishment of colonial control, but it acquired major proportions under British administration with the introduction of an alien legal and tax system and administrative measures that aimed at attaining an effective system of economic exploitation. For instance, the system of rent payment in services (*kamioti* or *beth begari*), which had evolved into a veritable bonded labour system, was regulated but not abolished by different laws that culminated in the 1920 Bihar and Orissa Kamiauti Agreements Act (A.G. Roy *et al*. 1964: 2120 ff; R. Mukherjee 1933: 232).

Alienation of the peasants' land was not contained by the Chota Nagpur Tenancy Act (Act II BC, 1869), neither was the incidence of illegal rent increases controlled by the Chota Nagpur Landlord and Tenants Procedure Act, 1879 (Rent Law). Landlords imposed rents even on trees, especially those that produced lac, as well as making other exactions (Gait *et al*. 1909; S.C. Roy 1912: 292).[29] The Chota Nagpur Tenancy Act, 1908 (Bengal Act VI of 1908) protecting *khuntkatti* rights on land, was enacted when it was already too late. By then few *khuntkatti* villages still existed.[30] The restrictions on land transfers from 'tribals to non-tribals' under Section 46 of the Act also fostered the emergence of a class of adivasis who were moneylenders on a part-time basis (lending as a complementary activity to agriculture) when laws made money-lending to and the appropriation of lands from debtors difficult for non-adivasis (K.S. Singh 1972a: 370–80).

[29] The situation of Chotanagpur's adivasi peasants in mid-nineteenth century was graphically described by the *Calcutta Review* in 1869:

When the oppressor wants a horse, the Kol must pay; when he desires a palki, the Kols have to pay, and afterwards to bear him therein.... Does somebody die in his house? he taxes them; is a child born? again a tax.... And this plundering, punishing, robbing system goes on till the Kols run away. These unjust people... even force the Kols to borrow... (*cit*. in S.C. Roy 1912: 221)

[30] See Govt. of Bihar and Orissa 1931: 8–9, 109ff.; Chapter XVIII, Sec. 242 to 256; S.C. Roy 1961; K.S. Singh 1971a: 102–07.

Further south, the Hos had settled in Singhbhum, a region well suited for defence, after migrating from Chotanagpur. The central plateau was well protected by ranges of hills and thick jungle. To the south, where the hill ranges are higher, lay the Kolhan. The Hos owed nominal allegiance to the Raja of Singhbhum and remained independent, resisting the attempts of the Raja to subjugate them militarily. Only 40 years after the East India Company gained control over Bengal, Bihar and Orissa, did British troops enter the Kolhan. Later, after major military operations in 1836, the Hos surrendered. In 1837, Kolhan was made a Government Estate. Singhbhum was constituted as a new district, and a British officer was posted at Chaibasa with authority over 620 villages and around 90,000 people (Risley 1908). A rent of eight annas for every plough was fixed after the British 1819–20 military campaign. This system was confirmed in 1837. Thirty years later, a settlement based on a fixed assessment on the lands was introduced. This mode of assessment marked the end of the semi-independent life of the Hos whose previous system of government through heads of *pirs* (divisions) and of villages was absorbed into the colonial administration. The *munda* (village chief), for instance, came to act as the village police officer and helped to collect the tax revenue.

The first regular settlement took place in 1897, following the introduction of forest reservation policies and the opening of the Bengal Nagpur Railway.[31] At that time, non-adivasis had already acquired land in the area, and moneylenders were giving loans at high interest and taking land from indebted Ho cultivators. According to Dalton (1872), the Hos were thus 'tamed, softened, and civilized'. In other words, they were conquered and forcibly integrated into the colonial system. The process of despoliation of their lands and resources that then started was to be further accelerated when Singhbhum was acknowledged as a source of industrial wealth.

Jharkhand's Incorporation into the Colonial System

The main factors that marked the incorporation of Jharkhand's

---

[31] The last settlement took place in 1913–18 under the provisions of The Chota Nagpur Tenancy Act, 1908.

adivasi societies into the colonial system may be summed up as follows:

1. Pre-capitalist systems of production were articulated with the colonial economic formation under the dominance of capitalism.

   The changes imposed upon the existing pre-capitalist societies by colonialism were totally different in nature and scale to the ones these societies had formerly experienced. The introduction of individual land-ownership by means of the Permanent Settlement, resulted in the alienation of adivasi lands. in the pauperization of the peasantry, and in the migration of contract labourers—in fact a form of bonded labour—to the tea plantations in Assam and to the coal-mines of Bihar and Bengal. A new legal system came to regulate both land alienation in the form of transfers or sales—since land became a commodity—and the *kamioti* system of exploitation of peasant labour. The pervasive effect of a money economy, the creation of a market in land, the emergence of a moneylending landed sector and the development of chronic peasant indebtedness, were instrumental in producing fundamental transformations in agrarian economic relationships.

   The main conflict that emerged in Chotanagpur as a result of progressive subinfeudation was the one between different kinds of landlords and the peasantry. The adivasi states were small and lacked the necessary resources to give rise to a separate landlord class with autonomous power, able to drastically undermine the resilient communal base. It was the inflow of elements alien to these societies, like merchants and moneylenders, who found in the system of land grants the channel through which to obtain and augment their control over land and peasants. This emerging landlord class was precisely the one that gained from British conquest. The members of this alien class presented themselves to the British rulers *as if* they were zamindars (Hoffmann 1961: fn. 325). The new laws accepted them as such and at the same time ignored the existing *khuntkatti* system. It was colonialism that created the conditions for the emergence of a rich peasant class from among the claimants to the old zamindar status. The first step in this direction, the Permanent Settlement of 1793, was 'as much a permanent settlement of rights as of revenue' (Gopal 1949: 7). The imposition of the capitalist mode of production in its colonial form brought with it the restructuration of the existing pre-capitalist systems which were simultaneously undermined and preserved but distorted to fulfil the needs of capital and colonialism. The transformation of the original communal systems was completed in the 1770s, as in the case of the Paharias when they were 'settled' and incorporated into the market economy. In the case of the Santals, the creation of the Damini-i-koh initiated their transformation into an agricultural reserve army and a pool of captive labour for the capitalist plantations in Assam.

Adivasi societies were shaped by colonialism into units—'the tribes'—and given a subordinate role in the new economic system. They were 'preserved' in this constructed way to permit the reproduction of the labour force and to ensure their survival at the level of subsistence. Capitalist plantations in Assam, indigo plantations in Bengal, and mines in Jharkhand, developed on the basis of the exploitation of the labour of temporary adivasi workers. Their rural communities of origin were also exploited since, besides reproducing the labour force, they took care of the sick, the aged and the jobless.[32] In the context of the colonial economy, the rural community became 'an organic component of capitalist production' (Meillassoux 1972: 103). Wages were kept low, barely permitting the physical survival of the worker himself. In consequence, by the mid-nineteenth century, Hazaribagh and Ranchi were considered 'the best recruiting districts to get labourers for the tea plantations'[33] In the three years between 1864 and 1867, one per cent of the total population of Chotanagpur District had been recruited (many emigrants were not recorded).[34] The drain of migrant labour came from areas that were certainly

[32] Temporary workers in the mines were not entitled to any sick leave or privilege. The very way in which mining companies acquired rights over land under the Land Acquisition Act (1894) was based on the assumption that the rural communities had to perform this supportive role. In Singhbum, a constant supply of cheap labour was ensured when former rights and tenures were trespassed (Corbridge 1982).

[33] See *The Bengalee* 1886 No. 40, 41 43; 1887. Antrobus 1957. Laws passed in 1901 forbade recruitment except by licensed contractors. The 1932 Tea Districts Emigrant Labour Act (Act XXII of 1932) allowed the free movement of labourers and gave them a certain degree of security. The Payment of Wages Act (1936), the Industrial Employment Standing Order Act (1946), and the Industrial Dispute Act (1947), benefited the labourers only marginally (M.R. Chaudhuri 1978: 22).

[34] In the 1901 Census, more than 91,000 persons born in Chotanagpur were registered as working in Assam (Antrobus 1957: 384–85; B.B. Shina 1979: 180).

not overpopulated. At the end of the nineteenth century the effects of this drain were compared to those of the Black Death in Europe (Thapar and Siddiqi 1979: 55). *The Bengalee* stated in 1886 that Santal Parganas constituted 'the mainstay of the labour force' in the Assam tea gardens, supplying 44.7 per cent of the workers (1886: 39). Since the beginning of the nineteenth century the Santals had also been considered to be 'the means of rendering British [indigo] enterprise possible through the whole of Bengal'. They formed a labour force that capital exploited, making use of ethnic stereotypes which marked them for specific forms of wage slavery. These peoples were seen as: 'Patient of labour...able to live on a penny a day, contented with roots when better food is not to be had' (Hunter 1868: 224, 226–27).

The fact that there was an assured pool of labour in Jharkhand also made the rising death-toll of workers due to illness and harsh working conditions a matter of small concern and precluded improvements in the situation. Contemporary reports on the tea plantations clearly indicate a declining birth-rate, abortions and suicides among the labourers, showing that adivasi workers had reached the limits of endurance and were unwilling to perpetuate the group ('ethnic suicide'). From the point of view of the capitalist enterprise, the unwanted workers, disabled by illness or starvation, could not be sent back to their original communities, neither was the enterprise going to incur any social welfare expense. In the light of this, the high death-tolls and the declining birth-rates point to a situation that I call *gradual genocide*.

2. The process of colonial conquest and consolidation was not a peaceful affair. Subjugation, often glossed over as the 'pacification' of territories, was attained by force.

Military operations consistently preceded the establishment of administrative control in all areas of Jharkhand, and were launched every time there were signs of protest. Control was not only attained by the actual exercise of force but by a permanent threat of violence. This total 'culture of repression' (Huizer 1974: 21 ff.) used physical violence as well as other means of coercion which crystallized in a legal and revenue system that fostered the operation of pressure mechanisms like the reproduction of indebtedness and extensive forced labour. It also used native institutions and forms of social organization, putting them at the service of the colonial system.

3. Fixed ethnic stereotypes—'the tribes'—were constructed to denote a variety of systems of production and cultures, ignoring the complexities in the socio–economic organization, law systems, history and civilizational patterns of the adivasi societies. These societies were perceived as an undifferentiated mass from which to extract labour and revenue, a process that was thought to lead automatically to their 'civilization': to the creation of the colonized man in body and soul.

The existing *diku-adivasi* (alien–indigenous) opposition—implying regional/ethnic *cum* economic difference—was indirectly sanctioned by early legal provisions like the Permanent Settlement, and fixed in the new correlations established in the transformed system of agrarian relationships: *diku* landlord—'tribal' tenant/agricultural labourer. The 'alien exploiters' gained added strength when they became zamindars under the protection of a British legal and administrative system which conferred on them the status of private land proprietors.[35] In the new division of labour, 'the tribals' functioned as agricultural labourers and as a reserve of labour force.

Under colonialism, communities that evaded the other dominant cataloguing device—caste—were defined according to the tribal paradigm. It was then that 'the tribes' made their appearance in the Indian scenario. A creation of European origin, 'tribe' was one of the elements through which Europe constructed part of the Indian reality.

4. A final factor must be considered for nineteenth century colonial Chotanagpur: the arrival of German Evangelican Lutheran, Anglican and Roman Catholic missions. In this way, the pillars that have classically sustained colonial penetration and ensured colonial hegemony—the military, a legal and administrative system, a capitalist economy, and the Church with its 'civilizing'/educational mission—were all present in Jharkhand.[36] Education

---

[35] Private property of land was known in India prior to 1793 under Hindu and Muslim rule. In medieval India, the *raiyats* preserved their rights on the land they cleared and tilled, while those who were granted service tenures (*jagirs*) only had a conditional grant and depended on the state. The fundamental change introduced with the Permanent Settlement was to give the zamindars the status of private proprietors.

[36] The core of the Munda area was contained in the Quadrilateral, flanked by the Catholic churches at Bandgaon, Sarwada, Dolda and Burudih. Later on, other Catholic stations were established in Karra (1891), Khunti (1892–96), Darma (1899–1900)

given by the different missions, based on European values, con-. tributed to the adivasis' deculturation, and its effects are clearly observable today.

Some expected consequences resulted from the relations of the adivasi peasantry with the missions: an initial perception of British rule as just, and the use of legal means to channel protest (which would partly account for the long years of legal struggle during the Sardar Movement). In this way, the questioning of the colonial system was controlled, and violent conflict avoided until it surged up with great force at the close of the century in the Birsaite Movement. Other results were not so predictable. Adivasis who came into contact with the missions became more aware of the way in which the colonial system worked, and organized themselves to resist it. Converts refused to work for the zamindars without pay. While the mass of the cultivators held uneconomic holdings and had to resort to migration to survive, some converts had secured their lands through registration, including some *mundas* and *mankis* who retained land for their private use. Moreover, since rents did not increase as much as the prices of agricultural products, a more affluent peasant sector emerged among Chotanagpur's adivasi converts. It was possible for them to transform a certain amount of surplus into savings, as the payment of the cost of many legal procedures during the Sardar Movement seems to indicate. However, their economic power was insufficient to enable them to evolve into a rich peasant sector. Capital, good lands and market control (subordinated to the colonial economy) was in the hands of *diku* zamindars (Thapar and Siddiqi 1979: 40–51).[37]

It is against this background that the history of Jharkhand's adivasis from the end of the eighteenth century should be understood. This

---

and Torpa (1886–89). The Roman Catholic mission attained the fastest rate of conversions (15,000 converts in 1887; 71,270 by 1900). The German Evangelical Lutheran mission was the first to settle in Chotanagpur when it established stations in Munda territory in 1845. It had 40,000 converts by 1895. The Anglicans established their first mission at Murhu by the late 1860s, followed in succeeding years by a series of outposts (K.S. Singh 1966: 13ff.). Santals and Hos rarely converted; the bulk of adivasi Christians were Mundas and Oraons.

[37] Furthermore, it was the landlord class that British legislation protected, especially from the consequences of indebtedness, with laws like the Relief of Encumbered Estates in Chutia Nagpur Bill (1875), and the Chota Nagpur Act (1876).

history later led to an anti-colonial and ethno–national struggle, an aspect discussed later in the text. After independence the situation did not substantially improve with the legal abolition of the zamindari system (the 1950 Bihar Land Reform Bills and the land ceiling legislation).[38] In fact, peasants were evicted by the landlords in great numbers in the sixties, transfers of lands increased, and the landlord class maintained its position, now relieved of the formal responsibility they had towards their tenants (Tomasson Jannuzi 1974; Das 1983; N. Sengupta 1982c). As a result, the process of peasant differentiation accelerated. Many cultivators became agricultural labourers. In the sixties and seventies, class oppositions were translated into an intense class struggle in Bihar's countryside, reflected in the mounting incidents of violence against dalit and adivasi peasants (A. Sinha 1982b). Special laws like the Chota Nagpur and the Santal Parganas Tenancy Act account for the fact that the proportion of adivasi agricultural labourers is lower than among other sectors, and that the amount of land sales in adivasi areas is low (S. R. Bose 1971: 17, 21). However, the proportion of adivasis who are cultivators has decreased[39] since this legislation could not contain moneylending and land alienation through a manipulation of the law.[40]

The Myth of the Tribe

Jharkhand's socio–economic evolution in the course of history, described above, gives evidence that supports my contention that it is erroneous to place Jharkhand's adivasi societies within the

---

[38] Bihar Agricultural Lands—Ceilings and Management—Bill (1955); Bihar Land Reforms—Fixation of Ceiling Area and Acquisition of Surplus Land—Act (1961); Bihar Act (1962). See Tomasson Jannuzi *op. cit.*

[39] Among the Santals, for instance, it decreased from 73.51 per cent in 1961 to 54.9 per cent in 1971, while the proportion of landless labourers increased from 12.19 per cent to 34.26 per cent in the same years (Hrach 1978: 100).

[40] This occurred despite the amendments to existing laws like the Chotanagpur Tenancy Amendment Act (1969), and the Moneylenders' Act (1974). Although rural indebtedness is endemic in Bihar, the Bihar Scheduled Castes, Scheduled Tribes and Denotified Tribes Debt Relief Act, and the Bihar Moneylenders' Act were only passed in 1974. Bonded labour, regulated by the 1920 Act, is still a feature of rural Bihar.

artificially-created framework of 'tribe'. The assumed egalitarianism, the 'primitive' subsistence economy with little or no external trade, the autonomy and isolation of such an ideal unit, are not to be found among Jharkhand's adivasis either now or in the past.

Well before the incorporation of adivasi pre-capitalist societies into the capitalist system through colonialism, internal social differentiation had already emerged. The collective holding of lands, characteristic of a communal mode of production, gave way to privileged hereditary holdings in the hands of some members of the community (*mundas, pahans* and *mankis*). There is evidence of the development of an 'aristocracy' in some of Jharkhand's adivasi societies when a family acquired special prerogatives and power over land and people. This happened among the Mundas and the Bhumijs where some lineages became ruling ones. The development of a social division of labour, which partially replaced former collective labour forms, and a differential distribution of the products of work, wealth and access to land gave rise to class divisions and to state formation in these societies. Social differentiation also started appearing in societies like that of the Paharias, based on a communal system of production, when the zamindars began to reward the headmen with service tenures in the plains. No longer was the emergence of a social hierarchy precluded. *Jagir* lands were employed as an instrument for production and the Paharia *jagirdars* became involved in new relations of production (zamindar–intermediate *jagirdars*–cultivators).

In sum, given the qualitative aspects of the social and economic organization of the adivasi pre-capitalist societies of Jharkhand in pre-colonial India as well as after their subsumption under colonial capitalism, their categorization as 'tribal' is, at best, out of place and, at worst, ahistorical and sociologically groundless. There were in fact no tribes in Jharkhand but ethno–cultural configurations developing in specific socio–economic contexts. In essence the 'tribes' were a parthenogenetic creation of the British colonial administration. Therefore, only a curious trick of historical reversion could give support to the idea that tribes exist nowadays in Jharkhand.

3

The Poverty of
Development

*Underprivileged people always take the trash of civilization
and later on realize what they have lost....*

An adivasi intellectual

*On the periphery... people... learned quickly enough that
Progress in the abstract meant domination in the concrete, by
powers they could not help apprehending as foreign and alien ....*

T. Nairn, The Modern Janus

Indian social anthropology, with very few exceptions, has focused
on the microlevel. The result has been a plethora of monographs
on Indian villages, castes and tribes. The epistemological basis on
which Indian society has been studied has only recently begun to
be examined. The results have been shattering. The much talked-
about self-sufficiency of the Indian village has been questioned,
caste ranking seems to have had more to do with British administrative concerns rather than the realities of India, and tribes to
have been one of the metropolitan–imperial taxonomies that
helped in the process of colonization.

In order to question this pattern, the focus has been set on the
situation of the majority of the adivasis in Jharkhand's social formation, and not on ethnic groups in isolation. Only some researchers

(contributions in N. Sengupta 1982a; G. Heuze 1989) have attempted a sociological analysis at a regional level. The efforts at producing a theoretical–methodological rupture with the still prevalent tradition of 'tribal studies' are recent.

The situation in Jharkhand is one of the clearest examples of a process of 'development of underdevelopment' taking place in underdeveloped capitalist formations (like India).[1] One can observe in the small universe of Jharkhand how different factors have acted to produce an apparently paradoxical situation in which a much praised industrial development is accompanied by agrarian impoverishment.[2] The economic side of the phenomenon is combined with social and ideological instances that make underdevelopment a unitary and complex phenomenon. That the paradox is apparent and the ensuing 'dualistic model' false, can be proven precisely by showing the simultaneity of both processes—development and underdevelopment—and the role the latter plays at a certain stage in capitalist development.[3]

The dualistic model opposes a stagnant 'traditional society' to an economically progressive 'modern society', the first conceived as an obstacle to the economic development the second is supposed to entail (Frank 1966; Stavenhagen 1968: 14–31, see his 'First Thesis') Adivasis have been qualified as 'backward'. They are usually blamed for this condition, the blame being placed on what is perceived as their attachment to 'tradition' and their not readily adopting changes that are allegedly introduced for their or the nation's interest. This view was expressed in the course of interviews with people engaged

---

[1] *Underdeveloped capitalism* refers to societies 'which have been incorporated into the international capitalist economy by the imperialist expansion' and in which pre-capitalist and capitalist modes of production are found in articulation (see Post 1979: 281–82).

[2] I will not deal with the relationships between Jharkhand's economic formation in the Indian context and the international system, a logical follow-up to the present discussion. These limitations are essential to maintain the focus on the main issue under study: ethnicity.

[3] In Meillassoux's words:

The 'dual' theory is intended to conceal the exploitation of the rural community, integrated...as an organic component of capitalist production....The agricultural communities, maintained as reserves of cheap labour, are being both undermined and perpetuated at the same time, undergoing a prolonged crisis and not a smooth transition to capitalism (1972: 103).

See also Magubane 1976.

in rural development projects in Chotanagpur.[4] These interviews talk about the adivasis' 'traditional background', their 'lack of understanding of how market economy works' and of 'competition and profit'. All these factors were indicated as major obstacles to their development. In reality, the adivasis have been maintained in their backwardness, which is *neither inherent nor old* but has specific origins and causes. This 'backwardness', that is, underdevelopment, must be understood as a historical product, born out of capitalist expansion in non-industrialized areas, inaugurated with colonialism and later evolving as an integral part of underdeveloped capitalism in India. In Bihar's Jharkhand region, the structuration of ethnic and class differences is an integral part of the historically determined totality of economic, political and ideological instances which together make up Jharkhand's social formation. Underdevelopment is reproduced through the use of non-economic forms of coercion, the creation of a 'coolie–proletariat' and of 'labour reserves', and the uses of ethnic differences for economic ends.

Jharkhand's Socio—Economic Profile

In our fields,
In our lands,
There is a world of riches....

Santal song

An Economically Depressed Population

The majority of the Scheduled Tribes' population of Bihar (97.7 per cent), together with two of the ten million persons registered as Scheduled Castes in the state, live in the Jharkhand region.[5] This fact is of prime importance for the socio–economic configuration of the area as well as for regional political formulations.

---

[4] Refer to testimonial data in Chapter 5.

[5] Over 98 per cent of the Scheduled Castes of Pan or Sawasi, Ghasi and Bauri, of the state of Bihar reside in Jharkhand. Not only are they viewed as part of the original inhabitants of the area but also as of 'tribal' origin (Mehta 1982: 93ff.).

Scheduled Tribes and Castes together amount to 42 per cent of Jharkhand's population.[6] The massive presence of Scheduled Tribes and Castes, a high proportion of lower Backward Castes, and a considerable number of poor migrants, point to one of the fundamental characteristics of Jharkhand: a significant economically depressed population in an underdeveloped region. Of the state's total Scheduled Tribes population, 75 per cent reside in the districts of Ranchi, Singhbhum and Santal Parganas (*CI* 1981). The regional distribution of the major adivasi groups can be clearly appreciated, with the Santals in the north, and the Mundas, Hos, Bhumijs and Oraons in the south of Jharkhand (Map 4).

The equation indigenous (non-caste) people = tribes, which emerged under colonial rule, was legitimized the first time 'tribes' were recorded in the Census. It was reformulated in independent India in the equation adivasis=tribes, distorting the broad concept of indigenous ethnic group (N. Sengupta 1986) which is based on regional and historical self-identification.[7] One should note that the adivasis are not the only people presently to consider themselves Jharkhandis. Furthermore, in the recent redrawing of states' boundaries, major ethnic groups like the Santal have ended up divided among different states. Their territorial integration into viable separate units has thus been precluded, and their numerical strength in the political arena weakened. By an administrative artifice, major ethnic groups appear as minorities in 'non-tribal' states, a situation further aggravated by the steady inflow of migrants into these areas.

According to Census data, 89 per cent of the Scheduled Tribes' and 74 per cent of the Scheduled Castes' working population in Jharkhand were engaged in agriculture. Meanwhile, they showed

[6] The percentages given in the Census understate the number of depressed communities. Communities that are as economically depressed as other Scheduled Castes are not included in the list. Census data are taken as general indicators. There are many inconsistencies which make comparisons between Census data not very reliable. Since to have a picture of the economic situation in Jharkhand we have to follow Census data, we are constrained to use the official categories Scheduled Tribes and Scheduled Castes.

[7] For instance, the Kurmis or Bauris of Jharkhand were at first (1913) included in the Scheduled Tribes' list and later excluded from it. They had been living in the area as long as the Mundas and the Santals had or even longer, and could rightly be considered natives of the place. In the seventies they demanded to be included again in the Scheduled Tribes' list (Mehta 1982: 94 ff.).

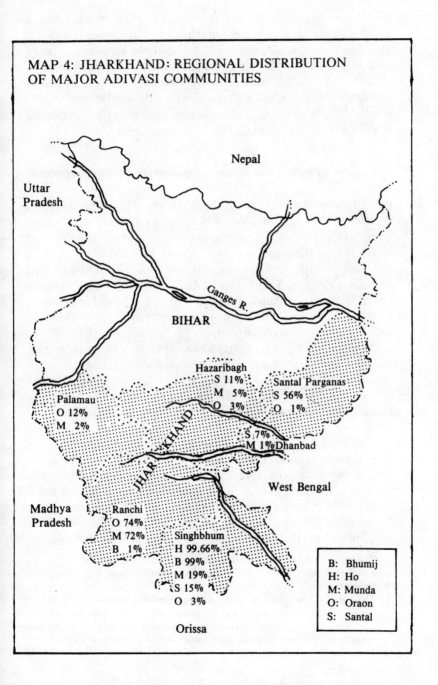

MAP 4: JHARKHAND: REGIONAL DISTRIBUTION
OF MAJOR ADIVASI COMMUNITIES

Nepal

Uttar
Pradesh

Ganges R.

BIHAR

Hazaribagh
S 11%
M 5%   Santal Parganas
O 3%   S 56%
              O 1%

Palamau
O 12%
M 2%

JHARKHAND

S 7%
M 1% Dhanbad

West Bengal

Madhya
Pradesh

Ranchi
O 74%
M 72%
B 1%   Singhbhum
            H 99.66%
            B 99%
            M 19%
            S 15%
            O 3%

Orissa

B: Bhumij
H: Ho
M: Munda
O: Oraon
S: Santal

low percentages in the industrial categories. They amounted to 32 per cent of the total workforce in mining and quarrying (*CI* 1971). This percentage was further reduced after the nationalization of coal-mines in 1971 (Kumar 1981a and b) followed by the massive retrenchment of Jharkhandi miners,[8] who were replaced by Bihari immigrants who received higher wages than the local miners. Afterwards, the labour market suffered some changes with the opening of the competition for jobs to the local population.

The 'Ruhr' of India: the Foundations of Underdevelopment

Bihar has been called 'the Ruhr of India'. The largest mineral deposits in the state are located in the heart of Jharkhand, where more than a fourth of the mining in India takes place. In 1980, coal production in Bihar reached 44.35 million tons out of an all-India production of 109.10 million tons. Important coalfields are located in Jharia, Bokaro, Ramgarh and Giridih. Inferior grade coal is mined in Santal Parganas. Iron ore is mined in Singhbhum where Gua and Noamundi are the main mining centres. This district is also the only producer of copper. Manganese ore deposits are found together with iron ore. Ranchi and Palamau Districts produce bauxite, mostly used for making aluminium. Mica is found in north Hazaribagh; chromite in Singhbhum; clay in Singhbhum, Ranchi and Santal Parganas; fire-clay in the Jharia coalfields and in Hazaribagh; apatite (useful as a fertilizer) in Singhbhum (*GI* 1982).

Jharkhand receives a fifth of the total public sector investments in industrial pursuits.[9] The Tata Iron and Steel Co. Ltd. (TISCO), one of the most profitable concerns in the private sector, runs some of the mines, including Noamundi. Other important landmarks in Jharkhand are the steel plant at Jamshedpur, the Heavy Engineering factory at Ranchi, the copper plant at Ghatshila, the mica industry at Giridih, the aluminium factory at Muri, and uranium

[8] The number of retrenched workers in the first week after nationalization was estimated at 50,000. Further retrenchments occurred during the Emergency (N. Sengupta 1980: 667).

[9] The majority of the iron ore mines in Singhbhum are worked under the Indian Iron and Steel Co. Ltd. (ILSCO) and the Bokaro Steel Plant, subsidiaries of the Steel Authority of India (SAIL). ILSCO is responsible for the Gua, Chiria and Manoharpur mines, and Bokaro for the Kiriburu and Megahataburu mines.

mining at Jaduguda.[10] The production of cement, brick and tiles, glass and glassware in Bihar is overwhelmingly carried out in Jharkhand where six out of the ten cement factories, and five out of the total six glass and glassware factories in all of Bihar are found (*GI* 1968: 207). Half of the state's factories making heavy machinery and tools, and nearly half of the manufacturing and assembly of non-electrical machinery and general engineering goods are located in Jharkhand (*Ibid.*: 209).

The rapid pace of industrialization in Jharkhand was accompanied by fast urban growth and by a steady increase in the rate of immigration. These three factors, operating in the midst of an already depressed agrarian economy, have to be taken into account in trying to understand the reproduction of underdevelopment in the region. Despite spectacular urban growth in the Jharkhand area of Bihar, a very small percentage of the population classified as Scheduled Tribes and Castes lives in urban areas and enjoys their facilities. The lack of investment in agriculture, land alienation for industrial development, restrictions on the use of forest resources, the super-exploitation of adivasi labour to sustain industrial development, and the fact that the beneficiaries of this development are not the majority of the Jharkhandis, must be considered.

For the adivasis, industrial development has resulted in increasing land alienation and displacement since all large public industrial projects in Bihar are situated in its Jharkhand area. Displacement has been inadequately met by slow rehabilitation programs.[11] Many of the displaced persons were not rehabilitated, received less land than what they had prior to displacement, or received compensation in cash below the market rate and not on the basis of land value appreciation after industrial development. The cash received in compensation was not adequately invested and quickly spent (*GI* 1967: 71). The displaced persons could not find suitable land in these areas. Displaced adivasis remained in the vicinity of the new industries, hoping to get employment, clustered in the poor quarters around the new complexes where living conditions

[10] In 1981 it was announced that the uranium mine at Jaduguda was to be expanded, three uranium mines were to open and another two established. The existing mines were then producing 67,000 tons of uranium (*TI* 1981c).

[11] For the period between 1951 and 1961, 17 per cent (7,961) of the displaced families in Bihar were adivasis, a high proportion considering that the percentage of Scheduled Tribes in relation to the total population of the state was 9 per cent (M.L. Patel, 1974). The process has accelerated with further industrialization.

were precarious. With inadequate or no compensation, adivasis who owned land before displacement became landless labourers and, only during the industries' initial building stages, unskilled workers. The lack of compensation, the vagueness about the compensation rates, the methods of land acquisition, the nature of resettlement schemes and the uncertainty of future employment for displaced persons, became a focus of tension in the industrial areas. Later on the value of land acquired for industrial purposes was reassessed and some of the displaced persons were given jobs. In this way, some of the economic demands were partially met.

Natural resources (minerals, timber) are extracted from adivasi areas in Jharkhand and absorbed by the more developed urban and rural areas of the plains. Few adivasis benefit from urban-industrial development and in fact most have been adversely affected by it. In the process, in addition to being displaced from their lands to make room for industrial schemes, they have been largely excluded from employment in the modern sector or maintained as a pool of cheap labour. As part of the pattern of resource extraction, the electricity generated in the area is not predominantly for rural Jharkhand, but for the industrial and urban centres, despite the fact that Jharkhand produces 90 per cent of the electricity in the state of Bihar and that it is the biggest producer of power in India.[12]

Regarding irrigation needs, rainfall variability is low in most of Jharkhand.[13] Theoretically, there is a fair degree of rainfall reliability. Accordingly, the administration has considered these areas' irrigational needs to be low. However, the characteristics of the soil and the terrain in the area are unfavourable, tending not to retain water. Indigenous methods of irrigation—the collection of water in embankments (*bundhs*)—a feature noticeable in Santal Parganas and Singhbhum, have been left to deteriorate (N. Sengupta 1985: 44). Jharkhand's irrigated area has been substantially reduced since the fifties, adversely affecting the agrarian economy (A. N. Das 1983; N. Sengupta 1982b, 1982c, 1985). The danger of crop

[12] Hazaribagh has the greatest generating capacity and is the largest generator of electricity in Bihar, followed by Dhanbad and Singhbhum. In these and other districts of Jharkhand, almost all the power generated is consumed for industrial purposes and a very low percentage is used for irrigation and other public purposes.

[13] Rainfall has moderate coefficients in the north of Hazaribagh and Palamau, north-western Santal Parganas and south-western Singhbhum.

failure due to the lack of rains has proved to be more than a mere possibility. There is no major irrigation project in Santal Parganas. Paddy, maize and rabi crops depend totally on rainfall. The district has been affected regularly by drought. Paddy crops failed totally in 1955–56 in the Damin area. In 1967, drought and famine affected 73 per cent of the population in Central and South Bihar on account of deficient rainfall from 1965 to 1967 (S.R. Bose 1971: 127–35). From 1979 to 1982 Santal Parganas experienced drought in various degrees, culminating in 1982 in the loss of 72 per cent of paddy crops and the near-starvation of the peasants. No prompt relief measures were put into practice. The official response to relief appeals was repression.[14]

The neglect of irrigation has created increasing tension in the rural areas since it accentuates already existing problems. The result has been a growing number of peasants who are jobless for most of the year, since only one crop is possible without irrigation. This in its turn has led to a seasonal exodus in search of work and to trafficking with young Jharkhandi labourers to take them to work under miserable conditions in far-removed areas (like the Punjab). Maharaj and Iyer (1982) point to a general problem in rural Jharkhand: the flow of funds and loans available for the construction or maintenance of irrigation works is appropriated by rich non-adivasi peasants who then do not invest them in productive activities in the countryside. In consequence, Government-sponsored schemes rarely improve the economic conditions of the common peasantry.

Regarding natural resources, four-fifths of Bihar's forest areas are found in the Chotanagpur plateau.[15] All the forests in Bihar are considered marketable and the aim of the Government is to develop the forests commercially. This has meant that increasing restrictions have been put on their use by the local people. In any case, a relatively small amount of the forests is presently commercially exploited (Jones 1978: 58). Forests are an essential complementary

[14] In this particular instance, it ended in the firing on starving adivasis asking for relief at Palajori Block headquarters on 7 October 1982. Four days later, a demonstration of 15,000 adivasis led by Sibu Soren (JMM), protesting against the firing and demanding relief, met police violence after Section 144 Cr. PC, restricting the gathering of people, had been invoked (*Link* 1982a, b, c).

[15] 9,770.38 sq. miles out of a total of 12,105.4 sq. miles. Forests cover more than 45 per cent of Palamau and Hazaribagh, 33.92 per cent of Singhbhum and 23.83 per cent of Ranchi districts (*GI* 1983: 65).

source of livelihood for the adivasis. They used to reclaim land from the forest for agricultural purposes, and had traditional rights over the collection of forest products. The restriction of the adivasis' forest rights goes back to the British Forest Policy Resolution (1894), according to which the adivasis could no longer claim the forests as their own. Independent India's forest policy was formulated in 1952, clearly stating that village communities would not be permitted to use forests 'at the cost of national interests' (Kannan 1982: 936). One of the national needs was to generate 'the maximum annual revenue in perpetuity' (Kulkarni 1983: 192). The effects of this policy have been considered disastrous (N. Sengupta 1982a: 17). The rights of the adivasis to cultivate foodcrops and to collect forest products were transformed into 'concessions'. At the same time, from the fifties onwards, more forest areas have been declared reserved forests.[16]

Future plans for the commercial exploitation of the forests and not the assumed ecological damage caused by the way they have been traditionally used (as stated by the National Commission on Agriculture), are the main reasons for the growing exclusion of the adivasis from the use of forest areas. Land reclamation from the forest has been substantially curtailed by increasing reservation, thereby eliminating one balancing factor which helped in coping with the growing population pressure on land. The collection and sale of forest products (lac, honey and *mahua*) as a second means of livelihood is also becoming difficult for the adivasis. Moreover, the introduction by the Forest Development Corporation of teak plantations in Jharkhand with purely commercial goals, has resulted in continuous and violent tensions in the area. Peasants have been displaced from lands in the forests which were suitable for cultivation (a cultivation that did not endanger the traditional forest) when the Government decided to introduce commercial trees.

Not only is teak useless for the adivasis (unlike sal, which is being replaced) but it also tends to adversely affect the soil, since

[16] For 1977–78, 17.2 per cent of the total forest area of Bihar was declared reserved, 82.5 per cent protected, and 0.17 per cent unclassed. Practically all the area is under the control of the Forest Department; a small margin of 0.15 per cent is controlled by civil authorities. The Indian state earned a gross revenue of Rs. 2.6 billion in 1978–79 at an all-India level. For Bihar, the amount was Rs. 181 million, to which Jharkhand contributed a significant part given the extension of its forests. Only 5.5 per cent of the total area in the state was afforested (*GI* 1982: 66–71).

other crops cannot grow at its side. In the South Bengal region of Jharkhand, eucalyptus (its wood is used to make paper) has developed as a monoculture after the clearing of sal, *mahua* and *kendu* forests. Massive deforestation has brought the total area under forests from 33 per cent in 1947 to 10 per cent in 1980. Droughts and soil erosion, both with disastrous consequences for agriculture, have increased with deforestation. Forests, legally owned by the Government of India, started to be auctioned by the state governments, and the rights over them handed over, for instance, to paper mills (*EPW* 1982b: 1901–02). New restrictions, as under the Indian Forest Bill (1980), and commercial monoculture in the forests have been opposed by organized popular protest and questioned by experts in the field (Kulkarni 1983).

Locals and Migrants

One important issue to address is that of the changing composition of Jharkhand's population after independence. These changes accompanied urban-industrial growth and resulted from a heavy inflow of immigrants. Twenty years ago, approximately 10 per cent of Jharkhand's total population were immigrants (*CI* 1971). Despite their low percentage, they tended to occupy more than 50 per cent of the industrial jobs (N. Sengupta 1982a: 15, 18), were better paid as skilled workers and hired mostly on a permanent basis. Professionals, big traders and administrative officials are usually also migrants. The situation is one in which some of the immigrants tend to get the benefits of development in Jharkhand, while the adivasis together with other Jharkhandis have largely remained unskilled workers and peasants. Areas of Jharkhand like Ranchi and Singhbhum that had almost an entirely adivasi population at the end of the nineteenth century, experienced a radical change in their composition over a period of three quarters of a century (*CI* 1961; 1971). In all districts of Jharkhand, immigration continued to increase after 1971.

This picture should not be taken as a reflection of the easy equation outsiders–exploiters *vs* Jharhandis–oppressed workers. This equation has been one of the constant themes in Jharkhand by which social contradictions have been explained, and it also fits well into the internal colonialism thesis. In this way, problems of class differentiation and the nature of the economic system as it variously affects the different social sectors tend to be submerged under the ethno-regional question. There is not and there never was in Jharkhand a strict correspondence between class and ethnic ascription. As was shown in the previous chapter, internal social stratification has long been present in the indigenous groups. The 'sons of the soil' do not constitute a single bloc in class terms (*cf.* with Weiner *et al.* 1981).[17] However, there is a trend in the labour market that makes it appear as if the growing number of outsiders were monopolizing the existing jobs. Following N. Sengupta's suggestion (1980: 668), various sectors among the immigrants should be differentiated: (*a*) the rural poor who migrate in search of work in the industries and are as ill-paid and ill-treated as Jharkhandi workers; (*b*) the skilled workers in the organized industry, small traders and employees who rarely identify with the plight of the first group, and (*c*) the *dikus* (in the 'outsider-exploiter' sense): moneylenders, corrupt officials, muscle-men and profiteers in general.

The emphasis on the presence of outsiders and their characterization as exploiters is not new and has persisted, although with changes, in the definition of who these aliens are. The term *diku* ('they' in Kurukh, according to a Munda informant) has been specifically used in Jharkhand to name the 'outsider-exploiter', more precisely those from outside the community or the region, who came to control land by illegal or dubious means and the moneylenders. It does not apply, however, to exploitative elements in the local communities, nor to groups that have lived in the region for a long time. Moneylenders, traders and individuals eager for land on a big scale, zamindars and *jagirdars* who started pouring into the area in the first decades of the nineteenth century, all fell into the *diku* category. In the fifties, the term came to be applied to upper-class non-adivasis. Later on, it was used to identify people of North Bihar, 'those who earn their living here and send their earnings out to their homes in Bihar' (Sen 1972: 434; K. S. Singh 1972a: 377–78).

---

[17] Jharkhand shows the emergence of a fragmented working class within the frame of a subsistence economy. This is partially related to the development of 'industrial enclaves'. The expansion of industrial capitalism and the growing strength of a rural bourgeoisie have affected the rural class structure resulting in a growing number of agricultural labourers, a pauperized peasant sector working as bonded labourers, and a semi-proletarized mass of reserve labour

The old pejorative and xenophobic connotation in the term *diku* still persists to address, in the words of a Munda elder, 'the dirty, filthy, bad outsider-exploiter'. Moreover, 'when politics come into it, worse things are said of them'. For the most part, the use of the term persists because the social sectors at whom it was aimed are still active in Jharkhand. It took a long time to reformulate the 'we-they' opposition into one that combines regional and class elements. In the seventies, one of the terms of the dyad was defined anew: a Jharkhandi ('we') was described as a producer working in Jharkhand.

Mechanisms for the Reproduction of Adivasi Underdevelopment

Non-economic Coercion

The apparently humanitarian ideals of the protection of 'traditional' culture and forms of social organization, the rhetorical avoidance of changes that might disturb 'traditional society', were and are deeply rooted in the capitalist economic logic of how best to use existing conditions to make them serve an economic system of profit maximization at the lowest possible cost. In the crudest sense, Jharkhand's adivasi peasants have maintained their subsistence form of agriculture not just from an assumed love for tradition, but because it is the *locus* of their struggle for survival, in the last instance, to avoid simple starvation. This circumstance favours the logic of development at a minimum cost. The peasant and the rural migrant cost nothing. It is their social environment—'traditional society'—which bears the burden of the reproduction of the labour force and ensures its survival.

At the same time, there is, at the level of collective identity, another side to this defence mechanism: cultural and social patterns are preserved to avoid de-historization. Adivasi peasants strive to survive not just in mere physical terms but also as historical subjects (and not as 'objects'). The tendency towards preservation, while not fostered by the 'modern' economic rationale (although 'used' in economic practice) and constantly undermined by politico-ideological means, is nevertheless used by the sectors in power to

support domination in Jharkhand by placing the legitimating ideological focus on 'racial', 'tribal' or ethnic issues. The tribal construct
becomes functional in this context, facilitating the operation of
non-economic methods of coercion. A lethal combination of condescending and derogative attitudes merge to mould a perception
of the adivasis that directly bears on the way they are treated. Both
attitudes presuppose the inferiority of the adivasis and are instrumental in the operation of a *culture of oppression* in Jharkhand.
This condescending–derogatory attitude has given rise to the idea
of the adivasi as an 'object' for development, a role some adivasi
intellectuals have internalized. In this line, I heard one of them say
at a public meeting: 'We, the tribals, are so grateful for your (the
anthropologists' and administrators') concern for our development. You are developing us.'

Social degradation, racial discrimination, deculturation and
cultural distortion have acted as effective mechanisms in the process
of economic control and exploitation of the adivasis, pervading all
aspects of their lives. In this way, for instance, in the eyes of non-
adivasi interlocutors, the prejudiced image of adivasi women as
'free' and 'naive' justified their social degradation into prostitution
and their exploitation around the industrial towns, and even their
becoming the 'natural objects' of rape. There was no moral judge-
ment against the responsible agents of prostitution and rape when
these belonged to the dominant social sectors. When this topic
arose in interviews with non-adivasi women (particularly with
development officers' wives), the portrait they painted of adivasi
women mixed references to their 'free' behaviour with the fact that
they 'work and earn': 'They are the ones who work. The men pay
a brideprice depending on how much the women can work and
earn. Adivasi women are too free, go out of the house, work, and
are cheated'; 'Anything can happen to them since they go around
so freely.' Remarks on the 'freedom' of adivasi women relate to
the more general 'danger' that free behaviour among subaltern
sectors may entail the 'freedom to act'. Peasant adivasi women not
only 'work' and 'earn' but also have become politically active. In
this context, the sharp reaction of adivasi men to the rape of adivasi
women by the powerful is, among other things, a response to a
manifestation of class violence.[18] In Bihar's countryside, rape is a

[18] Maria Mies precisely points at rape as an instrument of class oppression 'of
one class of men to punish or humiliate another class of men' (1982: 13).

form of non-economic coercion to reinforce subordination, grounded in the landlord's arrogated rights over the people that work his land.

The issue of alcoholism among the adivasis provides another instance of social degradation as a form of non-economic coercion. Alcoholism among the adivasis is not a 'traditional vice' but an acquired and patronized one. In the mines, the contractors have been at the same time the owners of liquor shops, thus exercising a combined control over the miners. Adivasis have fought degradation by alcoholism with the early Jharkhand Mukti Morcha (JMM) anti-liquor campaign. Non-economic coercion, essentially a pre-capitalist method, is used in Jharkhand for capitalist ends. In this respect, A. K. Bagchi remarks: 'A continual inter-change between capitalist and pre-capitalist relations has not ceased [after Independence].... Capitalist profit-making itself uses pre-capitalist methods....' (*cit.*, in Thorner 1982: 1998). The use of non-economic means of coercion is not a 'feudal' remain, but a mechanism used by the upper classes, the police and the administration to control the peasantry. In Jharkhand, social degradation is directly translated into economic exploitation, the outcome of development for the adivasis. As concisely put by a concerned government officer: 'Industrialization has made them landless and destitute. Now they are relegated to be rickshaw-pullers, porters, prostitutes'.

The economic super-exploitation of the adivasis in the rural and industrial areas, justified and reinforced by social and racial discrimination, is supported by violence. As discussed in detail later in the text, this violence permeates Bihar society, is directed against its economically depressed sectors, and is fuelled by the prevailing racist preconceptions. The entrenched nature of this upper-class violence is shown in the frequency of atrocities perpetrated against dalits and adivasis in Bihar. Usually portrayed as 'caste wars' or outbreaks of communalism, these incidents, particularly in the rural areas—place of origin of adivasi peasants and workers alike—are in fact expressions of fierce class confrontations. The triggering elements have been the peasants' economic demands and their will to organize themselves independently.

Segmentation of the Labour Force Along Ethnic and Regional Lines

Prejudiced stereotypes work against adivasi workers. They are considered unreliable and lazy, as people unfit for the regular work needed by modern economy. In the eyes of industry, they make a very undisciplined labour force. They are the unskilled workers, seen as unable to become skilled. For instance, two engineers based in Dhanbad commented: 'It is practically impossible to plan industrial production on the basis of tribal workers. They come one day and then disappear for two or three. They get drunk and do not come to work. It is impossible to make them work'; 'Tribals are not suited for our modern economy. They are not skilled and are ill-fitted for the industrial environment.' It is not so much the level of skill that counts but the 'traits' ascribed to the adivasis which define their 'suitability' for certain jobs and not others, and influence recruitment practices (see N. Sengupta 1983). In interviews with an industrial consultant and an engineer working for the collieries it was considered that, 'tribals are strong-built and do work that does not ask for precision but for energy, like loading and unloading', 'tribals are honest but with no sense of money or deadlines', and that 'one cannot give them jobs that require responsibility'.

It appears that adivasis are reluctant to abide by the time–work–discipline that capitalism demands to reach its targets of productivity and profit. It is no surprise to find a message displayed on huge placards at the Hatia industrial complex: 'Your time is gold, don't fritter it away'. Time is monetarized; it can be saved, wasted, sold. The adivasi vision of time–work control is quite different from that of industrial managers. In the words of an adivasi with experience in wage labour, 'After working all day at the mercy of somebody else, we find our stomachs empty.' The attitude of the adivasis is not only related to different conceptions of time and work in the pre-industrial context—where life and work cycles are closely interrelated—and in the industrial setting—where time is marketed. It also refers to their resistance as workers to being totally subordinated to the tyranny of time control linked to labour exploitation (see Thompson 1967).

All the factors mentioned regarding the current stereotype of the adivasi worker contribute to maintain the adivasis in the position of a reserve of unskilled and temporary labour force, and justify the low wages they are paid. As an example of how the adivasis are perceived in relation to work (in this case with reference to the rural areas), the words of a non-adivasi social worker may be illustrative: 'Bonded labour is more common among the lower castes than among the tribals because the adivasi is not so much of a *slave* and leaves. *Ordinary men*, the small landowner and moneylender, will not *employ* the adivasis as such.' A distorted conception of bonded labour as 'employment', of who are 'ordinary men', and that adivasis are not considered good working people *compared to slaves*, are elements worth noting in this quote. Furthermore, an adivasi 'psychological nature' has been constructed which is seen as an obstacle to development and, at the same time, to control the adivasi workers. For instance, a development planner said: 'They do not have an outlet to release tension and, when they cannot bear it any more, they turn to violence.' Once again, adivasis are not reliable and, moreover, are potentially dangerous. They are not wanted for the permanent working force in the organized sector, but are nevertheless considered 'suitable' to work as *coolies* to support industrial development at a low cost and in unfavourable working conditions. The labour market is thus segmented along ethnic or regional lines, and a secondary labour market of insecure, lowly-paid jobs evolves.

Through racism and by unfavourably stressing cultural and pseudo-psychological traits, adivasi workers are artificially separated from the rest of the working class. This separation has been reinforced when workers from outside the region were hired under better working conditions and then compared to the local displaced or badly-paid working force. The rationale behind the preference given to a migrant labour force is clear. First, there is the idea that only in the very long run ('two or three generations') would local workers become properly skilled. Second, a migrant labour force does not have social links in the host society that could provide a basis for solidarity, especially in labour politics. Third, the employment of migrants in a region where ethnic differences are important and where unemployment and semi-employment are the norm, contributes to divide the working class. The result of this segmentation has been the emergence of a 'labour aristocracy' in Jharkhand's working force.

The implications of these labour tactics are clear for those politically involved. In the words of a political worker, 'the contradictions between skilled and non-skilled workers are used by the employer to divide the mass of the workers'. Others also said: 'It is the ideal situation for the industry. It pays the local workers little. They can be fired and just left to fend for themselves. There is always the village to dump them in'; 'Migrants are paid well but must behave as the industry says. They do not understand our problems. They do not want to mix (with us). They are not like us. They do not think like us.' Despite this segmentation, local as well as migrant workers are exploited by the same moneylenders and contractors, a common grievance that in some cases has helped the workers to attain a temporary unity, as in Dhanbad under the leadership of A. K. Roy. In this context, it is also more profitable for capital not to modernize certain jobs, like sectors of the building and mining industries, as long as a cheap and abundant reserve of labour is available.[19] Starting in 1977, however, heavy mechanization was introduced in the mines, further contributing to the workers' segmentation.

The Creation of a 'Coolie–Proletariat' and 'Labour Reserves'

The clue to the simultaneously developed and underdeveloped nature of Jharkhand's economic formation lies in the articulation of non-capitalist modes of production with the capitalist mode, to which the first are subordinated.[20] Jharkhand's economic formation appearing both as capitalist and non-capitalist is an illusion. In Jharkhand there is no such a thing as a 'traditional system of production' any more. Modes of production may have remained pre-capitalist *in form* but, while not fully transformed, they have been restructured and subordinated to the needs of capital.[21] The opinions expressed to me by informants engaged in developmentalism, saying that 'Chotanagpur is not yet involved in the market economy', amounts to a dismissal of practically two centuries of history. In Jharkhand, the tendency towards the complete dissolution of the

[19] The role of the Jharkhandi workers, particularly the adivasis, can be considered to be similar to that of the immigrant workers in Western Europe who, in Castell's words: '*Do not exist because there are "arduous and badly paid" jobs*...but, rather... [these] *jobs exist because immigrant workers are present or can be sent for to do them*' (1979: 365. Italics in the original).

[20] For a discussion on the articulation of modes of production, see Wolpe 1980. For a characterization of pre-capitalist and capitalist relations of production by Indian economists, see Rudra 1978: 919.

[21] For similar comments see Bettelheim 1972: 297–98; Mc Eachern 1976; Dhoquois 1976.

non-capitalist economic modes has been restrained in order to allow for the continuation of a level of subsistence high enough to maintain the reproduction of labour, and at the same time, low enough to insure a reserve of semi-proletarianized labour force which will be compelled to migrate or to accept marginal lowly-paid jobs. Rural 'backwardness' is reproduced.

The production of commodities by means of non-capitalist forms of production in the rural sector once the capitalist mode becomes dominant, includes labour as a commodity. This last aspect shows a specific form of surplus extraction from the peasant economy—the one that covers the reproduction of the reserve of labour—by the capitalist mode of production. The task of reproducing the labour force rests on the village communities. This accounts for the payment of low wages to Jharkhandi workers. That is, the costs of reproducing labour, as well as of the means of production on which this process is based, remain unpaid by the workers' wages. In this way, elements of the non-capitalist modes like village and kinship-based reciprocal obligations of mutual support (the peasants' 'social security system'), are also made to function for the benefit of capital while the payment of indirect wages is avoided (see Meillassoux 1972: 102). In the words of an adivasi peasant/temporary worker: 'When I got sick in the chest, I came back [to my village]. My family did not have enough for medicine. The mine does not care if I die. It takes us (our lives) and does not give anything [in return].'

In this context, the Jharkhand Party has failed to understand the economic dynamics in which Jharkhand's village communities have long been involved. Ethnic loyalties are thought to be able to defy the dominant economic tendencies. The President of the Jharkhand Party considered that: 'Those who migrate to town areas do not like to return to the villages. I tell them: "You are a Munda. You are a tribal, so you *must* [return]". Munda economy has been broken. We need to recover the self-sufficient economy *as it was*.' Adivasis, as a relative surplus population, whether or not they like to stay in the towns to work, stay as long as needed. They are easily expelled and *have to* return to their villages. The problem is not that they 'must' stay in the villages, but that they *must sell their labour power*, cheaply at that, in order to survive. Their economy cannot become self-sufficient 'as it was', neither can it change while no alternative socio–economic project to the existing one is proposed. This alternative seems to be absent from the Jharkhand Party's program.

Some areas of Jharkhand have become suppliers of specific kinds of labour. I perceive them in terms similar to Samir Amin's African 'labour reserves' (1974: 172), but without institutionalized segregation. Chotanagpur and Santal Parganas were made into areas from where labour was extracted for the tea plantations in Assam. As long as mining remained technologically unsophisticated, Jharkhand was used as a ground to recruit miners. Industry particularly benefited from the gang-system, the gang composed of families, including women and children, paid by piece-rates. The inclusion of women and children in the workforce, with wages lower than those of an adult male, directly contributed to lower the general wage level still further. It was this system—which transformed the agriculturalist adivasis' tradition of collective work into a device for their super-exploitation as semi-proletarianized labour—that Bradley–Birt glorified at the beginning of the century.[22]

The continuing *sardari* system of recruitment of adivasi labour, particularly of women, is based on the same principle of wage-depression by creating a bonded labour force with long working hours (12 to 14 hours per day), no medical arrangements and, in the women's case, sexual exploitation. Bihar's 'tribal belt' functions as a huge 'labour reserve' for contract (bonded) labour which is sent, for instance, to the brick kilns in and outside the state, despite the provisions of the Bonded Labour System (Abolition) Act (1976) (Devi 1981a; S. Kumar 1978). 'Forest villages', significantly called 'labour camps' by the Forest Department, function as small reserve units with a practically captive labour force. Not having tenancy rights, the people in these villages are under constant threat of eviction. They have to work for the Forest Department whenever it demands. They receive poor wages and cannot take up other paid jobs without permission (interviews; Jones 1978: 57; *Link* 1978: 21–23). Profits resulting from the exploitation of adivasi labour in the forest areas are immense, thanks largely to the low level of wages.[23]

[22] 'The opening out of the [Jherria] coalfield has altered the whole face of the land as if by magic....The coolies always work in gangs....The labourer who lives close-by scores most of all....The lucky ryot cultivates his well-watered fields and earns besides a good day's wage in the colliery close at hand....' (1903: 282–86).

[23] Contractors controlling sal seed collection pay Rs. 50 per quintal to the labourer, and resell it for Rs. 250. Sal seeds reach finally a multinational soap manufacturer which realizes a profit of up to Rs. 15 per kg of seed processed (Ramachandra Guha 1983: 1890).

Not truly proletarianized, Jharkhandi workers now function, as Simeon puts it, as a 'reserve army of coolie–proletariat for capital' (1982: 227). They are that part of the relative surplus population of disposable labour power and pauperized sectors of society Marx called 'the victims of industry'. The aftermath of the nationalization of the coal-mines in the early seventies brought about the retrenchment of Jharkhandi workers and their replacement by immigrants once the working conditions improved. This is a clear example of how this reserve of labour is used. After nationalization, adivasis continued to be employed as cheap labour in illegal private mining operations run by outsiders (*F* 1980b: 2–7) and in mines controlled by the public sector SAIL (Ahmed 1983: 50–53). Two hundred mines were closed during nationalization as being uneconomic. Five years later, however, there was a shortage of coal and illegal mining started. Most of the illegal miners were adivasis who had been retrenched in the past.[24] In general, the minimum wages of Rs. 6.65 *per* day for unskilled workers are not paid in the mines, and wages are also sometimes withheld for two or three months.[25] Legal procedures to acquire land for mining purposes have been largely ignored. As a result, peasants are driven out of their lands to make place for illegal mining operations, lands for which, nevertheless, they continue to pay tax (*EPW* 1981: 1525). At the Giridih mines, where daily wages are Rs. 3 to Rs. 4, the risks for the workers are immense. Some 20 miners, including women and children, die each month in working accidents.[26] Hazaribagh's mining area has been called a 'graveyard of coal-miners' (*EPW* 1982a: 1641). Accidents have resulted from the Government policy to step up coal production at the lowest cost, disregarding safety regulations. According to this logic, the workers killed were cheap and easily replaceable. Similarly, preventive measures against coal-miners' occupational diseases are inadequate.[27] Furthermore, in fear that

[24] Although the mines still belong to the Central Coalfields Ltd. (CCL) and are a Government property, their illegal mining is now controlled by private gangs.

[25] In the approximately 250 mines in the Kolhan area (Singhbhum), mostly privately operated, daily wages were Rs. 3 to Rs. 3.50. In the iron–ore mines they amounted to Rs. 15 weekly (*EPW* 1981: 1525).

[26] On Badua hill, for instance, some 20 mines collapsed on 13 February 1981, killing between 300 and 500 miners, 200 of them adivasis. No rescue operations or investigation seem to have ensued (Ranjan 1981: 19–21; J. Singh 1981: 19).

[27] Pneumoconiosis, produced by exposure to fine dust, bronchial asthma, filariasis, and abdominal diseases are common.

he may lose his job, the sick miner continues working and does not get treatment (A. Sinha 1982a: 118, fn. 6).

S. Jones maintains that the adivasis do not face either ethnocide or genocide (1978: 64), but on the basis of current evidence one is inclined to disagree. Ethnocidal attempts (leading to the elimination of a people's identity) have been part of an uninterrupted process affecting the adivasis, whose origins can be traced to about the mid-nineteenth century, and its effects are noticeable today. Regarding genocide (the decimation of specific populations), one finds in Jharkhand what I call gradual *genocide*. This is not the result of any official policy but of the working out of social and economic forces and of administrative negligence. Gradual *genocide* for the adivasis takes place by means of the starvation and illnesses arising from growing pauperization caused by the decline in land production due to the effects of industrial waste, the neglect of irrigation, and the curtailing of alternative sources of subsistence like forests. To this one must add the prevailing physical violence perpetuated against Jharkhand's subaltern sectors. This violence is political in nature, a way of maintaining the labourers 'in their place' and of precluding any effort at labourers' organization on independent grounds.

One may ask: why such treatment for a population that has obviously been a profitable reserve of labour? The demand of capitalism for this kind of labour is limited (Bradby 1980: 116–18; Mafeje 1981: 134). Control over land and natural resources seems to be gaining primacy over the need for an expanded reserve of labour. The demand for a reserve of labour decreases with growing industrial employment requiring skilled labour. Since adivasi workers are not given skills to satisfy this demand, they tend to become redundant in certain sectors, an unwanted labour force which is expelled back to the countryside where its chances for survival are minimal. Thus, the village communities may pass from being the cradle of a reserve of labour to become the graveyard of the unwanted adivasi worker. This reverse tide to the rural areas may not be favourably received by the rural elites, since it tends to sharpen existing contradictions and to introduce new elements (experiences, ideas, principles of organization, that the returned worker may have acquired at the industrial setting) that could eventually have political uses.

The operation of all these forces combined has tended to acquire the character of an attack on the very survival of the adivasis. This situation was at the base of the recent rural movements in Jharkhand which took up the questions of access to land and resources, endogenous patterns of organization, and human rights issues. In the coal-mines of Dhanbad, political and human rights, and not just economic demands, became in the seventies the focus of the workers' political struggle, lately to revert to a economistic position (see Heuze 1989: 294–301).

The Question of Natural Resources and Internal Colonialism

In Jharkhand, the arguments of 'primitiveness' *vs* 'development', and 'traditional society' *vs* 'progress', have served to justify the exploitation of natural resources on adivasi territories in instances where labour extraction has become secondary and the reproduction of surplus labour begins to appear as a liability. In the last case, the tendency towards the dissolution of non-capitalist forms may gain primacy over the conservation tendency. What are seen as errors in planning, like the massive displacement of rural communities under inadequate rehabilitation programs, could instead be understood as part of the drive towards dissolution, congruent with purely extractive aims.

The extractive nature of capitalism in Jharkhand accounts for the situation being perceived as 'colonial'. However, what we observe now in such dependent formations is not just a reflection of former colonial processes in the form of 'internal colonialism'. In order to extract labour, raw materials and resources, capitalism employs in Jharkhand mechanisms of a 'colonial' type, including the manipulation of ethnic differences. The direct producers in Jharkhand are working for capital in various ways in the context of India's underdeveloped capitalism incorporated to the international capitalist economy.

The links between the exploitation of labour and resources in remote Jharkhand and the international market managed by multinational corporations from the central capitalist countries can be traced. For instance, sal seed collection at the lowest cost is transformed into profits for the international cosmetics industry. For this reason, it has been considered advantageous to preserve some sal forests. In other cases, the existing forest has been replaced with 'desirable' commercial species like eucalyptus, pine and teak. The US Agency for International Development made a recommendation to the Indian Government in 1970 stating that, by exploiting forest resources and 'one of the lowest wages in the world', foreign exchange could be generated from the export of furniture and paper (Ramachandra Guha 1983: 1889–90). The planting of teak in Jharkhand has followed the same aim of profit maximization. These projects have been opposed by the local adivasi population. Among some adivasis there is an awareness of the links of these projects with the international market. A Munda village headman in Chotanagpur's 'deep country' told me, 'There is a lot of lac in Chotanagpur, but it goes to Japan and the United States, and the people of Chotanagpur get nothing.'

'Racial'/ethnic justifications that back the exploitation of labour and resources in Jharkhand do not stop at the regional or country level. In the neocolonial era, international capitalism has consistently looked at those areas of the world that formed part of the colonial realm, and specifically to regions rich in natural resources with a population labelled as 'primitive', to scientifically plunder them. Their populations are considered expendable in the name of progress. This situation raises the question of indigenous rights over natural resources in the territories these populations occupy.

Jharkhand's Combined Ethnic/Class Domination

What we find in Jharkhand is a system of class exploitation and domination reinforced by the ideological uses of ethnic differences. Ideological justifications are phrased in 'racial' or/and ethnic terms, not in class terms. We are not, however, in the presence of two different phenomena (class domination and ethnic domination) but of *one*.[28] The way in which the capitalist mode constructed its relations with the non-capitalist modes in Jharkhand from the moment colonial capitalism began its expansion in India, resulted in the structuration of ethnic and class relations and marked their

[28] Ethnic relations do not exist independently of the concrete structure of specific social formations, but depend on the nature of class relations present in them, and the relationships established among different modes of production in the given economic formation.

later evolution. In Jharkhand, subordination is simultaneously regional (and ethnic, in the adivasis' case) and economic, is conditioned by specific patterns of economic development and by class factors (see Simeon 1982). For analytical purposes, however, it is convenient to keep in mind the difference between the content and the form of this subordination. The content refers to the essential class character of exploitation in Jharkhand. The form points at the ideological instances used to exert domination, as with ethnic and regional differences.

From the point of view of the Jharkhandis themselves, oppression is perceived and experienced in its *combined* ethno/regional–class form. An awareness of this global form of domination has given the ground for the adivasi grass-roots protests that reject reformism. The adivasis are 'decided to struggle to the end, making no compromise', because for them, 'to preserve the integrity of the community is vital' (from an interview with a political activist). There is then no demarcation in their perception of the situation between economic and socio-cultural issues, but a globally experienced reality. Grass-roots struggles precisely show the present class contradictions in the configuration of ethnic differentiation in Jharkhand.

Subaltern Discourses: People Confronting Development

In the course of interviews, adivasis from across the political spectrum criticized the present pattern of development in Jharkhand. Development was variously called 'civilization' and 'progress', and was not necessarily considered to be positive. In many instances, it was perceived as an autonomous force with as much of an 'evil' content as a plague that has befallen upon the adivasis. This view, however, was balanced with realistic remarks. For instance: 'We are the victims of progress. Without self-determination there is no development'; 'Civilization has not been good for the tribes. Fifty lakhs of families have been uprooted in 33 years. Jharkhand is very important in minerals and forests. Everybody's food is cooked here. For this reason, they will not agree easily to have a Jharkhand state. The big industrial projects are colonial-oriented, exploitative, not for the benefit of the common man'; 'Underprivileged people always take the trash of civilization and later on realize what they have lost'; 'Civilization, development, have little to offer. They are corrupting.'

S. Jones has already remarked on the illusory nature of development in Jharkhand where 'industries have remained small modern non-tribal enclaves in the middle of large areas of rural, tribal underdevelopment' (1978: 55). The fact that development has not been translated into concrete benefits for the Jharkhandis but rather into further pauperization and extraction of resources, has been understood by the people of the area. This is evidenced in their open rejection of several development schemes.

The continuing opposition to the Koel Karo project provides an instance of this awareness. The project's capacity to produce 732 MW will be at the cost of 45,000 acres of agricultural and sacred land (sacred groves and burial grounds), and the means of livelihood of peasants from 200 villages. Peasants whom the project was to displace practically stopped work on it since 1981. According to the President of the Jharkhand Party, the cash compensations were not enough, although they surpassed the amount the Government has given in similar cases. After many past broken promises, adivasis refused to take this offer as a serious one. An adivasi stated: 'Part of the money is taken by the Government officers and the moneylenders. After displacement we become labourers, unskilled workers, migrants.' The question of employment for members of the estimated 15,000 families to be displaced by this project is uncertain. At Koel Karo, protest turned to boycott since, 'nobody lifted anything of the building material', and 'at Torpa road blockades were set up, tents burnt and engineers harassed'. In 1984 the Government sent armed police to supervise the operations (*TT* 1984: 7). The Subarnarekha river multipurpose project in Singhbhum produced a similar response from the local population after survey operations started in 1970. The project involved the displacement of around 75,000 people. After appeals made in 1978 to the Government proved ineffective, the peasants refused to collect their compensations, paid at rates much below the amount demanded. Protest took the form of a fasting program which ended in police firing (A. Sinha 1978c: 750–51; *TI* 1978a; *NR* 1980e and f). In 1982, severe repression was launched in the area which resulted in police firing and killing, the beating of villagers and the assassination of

Gangaram, the anti-dam protest leader, by the police (R., personal communication).

Protests against industrial projects continued cropping up in all areas of Jharkhand. Around 15,000 peasants stopped work at Hazaribagh and Kujju coalfields of CCL and Tata's West Bokaro Colliery in July 1980 by digging trenches and blocking roads, succeeding in paralysing the works for several days. They demanded employment for the local people and due compensation for the lands appropriated by the management of CCL and Tata. Peasants regained possession of some 500 acres of land by force and started ploughing. Two platoons of the Central Reserve Police were sent to contain the protest (interviews; *NR* 1980b: 3). In March 1982, a group of Mundas blew up the foundations of the future microwave tower at the Sukunburu hilltop in Chotanagpur (the abode of Buru Bonga and a pilgrimage place). In this case, they responded not only to an aggression on their *khuntkatti* land rights but also on their culture. Protest ended with the imprisonment of several people (Amit Roy 1982: 2–3).

Protest in the forest areas against the growing encroachment on land and natural resources have occurred since the fifties. In the eighties, protest became widespred and militant. The opposition to the replacement of the sal forest with teak has been met with police repression, launched as a 'preventive measure' before any confrontation takes place (like in Ichahatu and Serengda in the late seventies (*PUCL* 1979: 9–16). As an adivasi put it: 'Teak is killing us.' This was not just a metaphor. Thus, the so-called 'felling craze' started. As a political activist explained in the course of an interview:

> The Government wanted to remove *sal* and *mahua* to plant commercial teak. We cannot use teak, so we cut it. We feel the traditional forest is being destroyed and that we do not get anything out of it. Therefore, it is better to make the land cultivable. In the Himalayan track there is a movement against jungle cutting and the land becoming an income for the Government. In Jharkhand, we could not prevent the cutting of the forest...but we do not want the teak.

Around 1978, the Jharkhand Party initiated a one–month protest on the issue of teak, with the purpose of negotiating with the Government. In its President's words: 'We oppose teak. We want to protect the traditional forest on which our economy is based and to reclaim our land.' Repression and not dialogue ensued.[29] When the negotiations of the Jharkhand Party failed, the Jharkhand Mukti Morcha backed the continuation of the protest to the Party's annoyance since, 'the Mukti Morcha continued with the protest and stopped our discussions with the Government; they began to cut trees and if we cut trees, we will suffer'. Jharkhand Mukti Morcha (JMM) leader Sibu Soren, meanwhile, curtly stated: 'Adivasis will stop felling trees when their needs are met.'

Why was the Government reaction to the forest protests so out of proportion? On the one hand, the authorities feared that the protesters could implement their threats to stop dispatches of coal, iron-ore, bamboo, timber and minerals. On the other, what was called a 'felling craze' was directly related to the demands for land restoration and for a Jharkhand state. The JMM was then (1980) backing the *jungle kato* movement in Singhbhum with the aim of reclaiming land for cultivation in the forest tracts. The control of forest lands and resources had become a highly political issue. The confrontations with Government agencies culminated in September 1980 in the Gua killings in Singhbhum.

The underdevelopment of the adivasis is part of the reality of Jharkhand's social formation. It cannot be understood as a result of a reluctance to change 'traditional tribal society' but has to be related to the pattern of development espoused in the region. Non-economic coercion and ideological instances that make use of ethnic differences have served to reproduce the underdevelopment of Jharkhand's subaltern sectors. The fact that the adivasis are at the vortex of this process challenges the conception of them as 'tribes', as units isolated from the operation of general economic forces and with peculiar problems. The situation in Jharkhand also raises questions about the need to attain a proper balance between national and regional interests in development planning.

Development has been taking place in Jharkhand under the threat of guns. Behind the repression that accompanies development lies a perception of the adivasi peasantry as physical obstacles in the

[29] Like the first of the 1978 incidents in Goelkera (Singhbhum) where three were killed by the police and the President of the Jharkhand Party arrested while delivering a speech.

drive to gain full access to land, raw materials and natural resources. They stand in the way, persistently despite repression, while the expansion of extractive capitalism demands their removal. It is against this economic background and that of the region's history that the present socio–economic conditions of the adivasis in Jharkhand and their political expressions should be evaluated.

Part Three

THE POLITICAL TERRAIN

THE POLITICAL TERRAIN

4

The Tradition of Protest: The Experience of Unity

The true word is in the land...
the word of the land is with us....

Birsaite song

The initial development of an ethnic consciousness among the adivasis of Jharkhand can be traced to the colonial period (from the end of the eighteenth century through the nineteenth century), a period in which the adivasis unmistakably appear as actors on the stage of history. This process of emergence of an ethnic consciousness and its development in the course of political actions became expressed in Jharkhand's *tradition of protest*.[1] The previous discussion of Jharkhand's ethnohistory helps to set the adivasi tradition of protest in context.

Agrarian insurgency shook Jharkhand from the time the British first attempted to integrate the region into the colonial system. It is my contention that in the colonial situation, when socio–cultural

---

[1] I first used the concept *tradition of protest* in Devalle 1977a.

identities were distorted to facilitate a new division of labour, the adivasis in Jharkhand responded by forging wide ethnic solidarity links. Ethnic and class solidarity usually combined giving impetus to many of the nineteenth century adivasi movements. The existence of this tradition is clearly revealed in moments of 'high density', that is, when the tension between socio–economic and political transformation and historico–cultural identity maintenance becomes acute.

Starting at the end of the eighteenth century, social contradictions encouraged economic oppositions that were simultaneously perceived as ethnic or regional. In this situation, the 'they' in the *we–they* opposition came to refer to the *dikus as well as* to the colonizer, the other 'alien–exploiter'. The confrontation with the colonial power was, however, the key factor that shaped the mode in which social, economic and cultural differences were structured starting from the end of the eighteenth century. The *other* was no longer the *diku* in isolation, but a complex and plural *other* incarnated in a combination of powerholders: landlords and moneylenders, and the colonial government, its representatives and allies. It was against this composite *they* that the Jharkhand peasantry launched its protests grounded in its ethnic and class solidarity. In the changed context of independent India, the *we–they* opposition in Jharkhand began to be expressed in regional/community and class terms, in accordance with a reality in which socio–cultural differences had become constitutive elements in the maintenance of capitalist development.

In the present century, the centre of political activity among Jharkhand's adivasis shifted towards urban pressure groups and regionalism, and a mostly Western-educated urban leadership. This shift culminated in the formation of the Jharkhand Party in 1950. However, the agrarian factor surfaced again by the end of the 1960s as the main *locus* of adivasi political action. The conditions in the rural areas and at the industrial centres of Jharkhand led in 1972 to the emergence of a regionally-based movement, oriented towards class struggle.

The rise of a political consciousness among the urban adivasi elite is evident to the observer since it is expressed in formal political terms. The same does not apply to the development of a political consciousness among the adivasi peasantry, which usually becomes evident in exceptional moments when peasant protest takes the shape of mass movements, not infrequently bursting into armed struggle. This is what happened with Jharkhand's adivasi peasantry in the nineteenth century.

Modes and Contents of Peasant Protest in Jharkhand

In 1974, K. Gough (1974) stressed the fact that, despite their absence in historiography, peasant expressions of protest had been common in India under British rule.[2] Peasants repeatedly rose against the oppression of landlords, moneylenders, tax collectors, the military and the police, sometimes in widespread and numerically strong movements. Only a few of the many instances of peasant protest in colonial India have been studied since the mid-seventies. Nevertheless, these few cases challenge the view of a passively subjugated Indian peasantry.

Some of these protests, like the Ulgulan of 1895, were expressed partially in religious terms, and consequently have been studied as primarily religious, usually with reference to the main Indian religion or to Christianity. The political character and the agrarian base of these movements were largely ignored (e.g. Fuchs 1965, E. Jay 1961). The 'partial isomorphism' of agrarian classes with major ethnic, religious or linguistic categories, already noted by Gough (1974: 1403), often obscures the actual occurrence of class struggles and may partly account for the way in which peasant movements in India have been perceived by some scholars.

Since a mere description of the formal aspects of peasant oppositional actions seems insufficient to understand them, I prefer to look at two dimensions in this social phenomenon:

1. The first is what I call a *tradition of protest*. Such a tradition presupposes that peasant protest is not confined to the isolated events when peasants openly rebel. A tradition of protest refers to a continuous, not just occasional, stance of opposition to the established power when this is experienced as oppressive.

[2] Peasant protest, sometimes violent in form, was present in pre-colonial times as well. The seventeenth and eighteenth centuries were marked by revolts against the Moghuls accompanying the extension of commercial relations and increases in taxes.

The concept of a *tradition of protest* serves to disclose the temporal distribution of different kinds of peasant protests and their condensed occurrence in times of crisis. More importantly, it reveals the long historical duration of peasant struggles, a duration which enables the formation of a pool of cumulative experiences from which new political actions may develop (Devalle 1977a; Agüero, Devalle, Tanaka 1981).

2. The second dimension is that of the development of *cultures of protest* among the peasants, a theme that will be discussed later in this book. This dimension refers to the existence of a consciousness of opposition and resistance among the peasantry. The ideas that back political actions, their emergence and development, the means to channel protest in daily life and at the special times of overt rebellion, can be found in this culture. This culture does not remain static but is transformed in the course of history (Devalle 1985a).

By considering these two dimensions in peasant protest we can avoid judgements about its rare successes and usual failure to attain power. Its 'failure' is relative. Peasants fight an unequal war against powerful opponents. In the cases under study, rural insurgency challenged the colonial apparatus of control, the state and the many ways in which the dominant groups sought to impose their hegemony over society. In this light, peasant movements should be evaluated not in terms of their 'success' or 'failure', but in terms of their role in the history of the subaltern social sectors.

Peasant protest in Jharkhand presented a double-faced, coordinated resistance to the established order: first, as an agrarian struggle, a struggle common at all times of history to peasants who strive for economic redress as epitomized in the struggle for land; secondly, as a defence of the historical identity of the community. This coordinated resistance is reflected in the meaning given to land as territory and to its defence. That is, land is not only conceived as a means of production but also as an anchor for self-definition.

Colonialism was perceived as a situation in which aggregated levels of domination reinforced each other. To previous injustices, new socio–economic inequalities were added. This resulted in a general dislocation of the social order and in a reorganization of the local economies which became subordinated to the colonial system. At another level, the indigenous cultures came to be threatened by the culture introduced by the colonizers through the Christian missions, a new system of education and new moral and legal codes. Colonialism also implied the enhancement of socio–cultural differences with a racist perspective, creating new inequalities that proved functional for the colonial system. These differences not only separated the colonizer from the colonized, but also strengthened existing social divisions such as the opposition between 'hill' and 'plains' people. In nineteenth century Jharkhand, the contradictions arising from the unequal relationships between colonizer and colonized people were reflected in inter-ethnic relations.

The peasantry normally relies on non-violent means to exert pressure, for instance, by withdrawing from or slowing down the process of production. Even when the limits of endurance have been reached, peasants remain legalistic, requesting justice from the authorities. They take to violence only when all possible ways to obtain redress fail. However, when they resort to violence through organized actions, this violence is always selective, measured according to the strength of the opponents and with a clear perception about who these opponents are. Peasant wrath has rarely been blind or irrational.

The causes of the protests that occurred in the nineteenth century among the adivasis of Jharkhand under British rule included the following: the establishment of outsiders on adivasi lands and land dispossession, tax and rent increases, violation of forest rights, the generalization of forced labour in payment of debts, and socio–cultural dislocation. Originally, protest arose as an immediate response to the need to solve conflicts of an agrarian character. The early uprisings and the actions of 'social banditry' and non-cooperation stemmed from these problems. Sometimes non-violent actions were resorted to, for instance, when peasants and even entire communities abandoned their lands in order to avoid direct confrontation. The effects of these actions were very limited at first, but later they became a real threat to the colonial economy, as happened in the aftermath of the Santal Movement. The pressure on the colonial economy was stronger when peasants decided to abandon cultivation and to stop production, organizing themselves for non-cooperation. This happened during the first stages of the Birsaite Movement.

There were also actions of 'social banditry'. Long traditions of protest of this kind can be detected, for instance, among the Bhumijs, as a way of questioning inefficient authorities. 'Social banditry', however, does not aim at producing structural changes but only at modifying a situation to make it less oppressive (Hobsbowm 1963; 1976). When persisting and endemic, 'social banditry' can be a symptom of generalized peasant unrest. Economic crises in pre-capitalist peasant societies have been often accompanied by a rise in the incidence of 'social banditry'. From the end of the eighteenth century until the first quarter of the nineteenth century, banditry and widespread protest formed the background of a tradition of opposition to colonial rule among the Bhumijs of the then Districts of Jungle Mahals and Dhalbhum, that was to culminate in 1832 in Ganga Narain's movement (Map 5).[3]

To what extent can the Bhumij *chuars* be strictly called 'social bandits'? They were not always opposed to the landlords and the state, nor engaged in the defence of the interests of the rural poor. They certainly resisted a colonial conquest that threatened to destroy 'the traditional order of things'. Their anti-colonial struggle was mostly linked to the defence of established landlords and rajas, and to the maintenance of the positions of power of the upper rural strata. They often rose in response to British intervention in favour of local authorities loyal to the colonizer (see Chart 1). Their protests also involved the peasantry, especially the *bhumihars*.[4] The imposition of colonial rule over Bhumij territories brought about great hardship for the peasants and trouble for the overlords. This situation led different sectors of Bhumij society to join forces to fight the intruder but did not result in a questioning of their society's internal contradictions. On those occasions,

[3] There were numerous *chuar* revolts in the area from the end of the eighteenth century. Particularly since the 1820s, the Bhumij peasantry and especially the descendants of the original settlers, took to arms when rajas and zamindars did not defend them from outsiders (*dikus* and British alike), and when some of them allied with the British (J.C. Jha 1967: 106 ff.). The 1832 movement rose against British intervention in the succession of Ganga Narain as Raja of Barabhum. (Coupland 1911; E. Jay 1961; Fuchs 1965; Bradley-Birt 1903; S. Sinha 1953; Devalle 1977a).

[4] Another source of conflict was the situation in which the *ghatwals* found themselves after losing their rights over the service tenures received for taking care of defence and order. The colonial administration took over these duties. In 1793, Cornwallis introduced the *daroga* system and a police alien to the region. As a result, violent uprisings occurred (J.C. Jha 1963: 266). The colonial authorities had to restore the *ghatwals* their lands in 1800. By that time also, the District of Jungle Mahals was created (Regulation XVIII, 1805).

MAP 5: GANGA NARAIN'S MOVEMENT OF 1832-1833

Concentration of
Bhumij population

Area covered
by the movement of 1832-1833

Source for the data on population: S.C. Sinha, "Some Aspects of Change in Bhumij Religion in South Manbhum, Bihar", *Man in India*, vol. 33, no. 2, 1953.

Bhumij collective identity prevailed over existing socio–economic cleavages.

During the nineteenth century in Jharkhand, the adivasis made their grievances known to the colonial authorities through legal channels: memoranda, petitions and documents asking for justice. These petitions remained unattended. For instance, the government ignored those sent by the Santals before and during the Santal Movement of 1855. The Mulkui Larai or Sardar Movement, antecedent of the Birsaite Movement, is an example of a long and unsuccessful attempt at legal protest by the Mundas.

'Passive' resistance, non-cooperation and legal actions are common among peasants. These forms of protest are not spectacular and frequently pass unnoticed or are explained away as products of a vaguely defined 'peasant mentality'. Eric Wolf (1975) has described some of the difficulties the peasantry faces in developing a sustained rebellion. These difficulties explain the peasantry's apparent slowness in openly rebelling against the oppression of local rural dominant elements or the state. Peasants appear in this light as legalist, respectful of an order that has been imposed on them, eager to negotiate with the rulers and to show them a reality of which they are apparently unaware. Peasants give opportunities to the powerful to correct the situation and to be just. For instance, Santal peasants sent a petition in 1854 to Commissioner Brown, saying: 'We have no protection but Government and pray that inquiry be made and the *mahajans* removed from the Damin and that we be saved from their claws....' (Roy Chaudhuri 1959: 26–27).

Legalist actions were pursued before the start of the two major movements of 1855 and 1895. This legalist approach persisted even at the moment of selecting targets and announcing attacks. Opponents were warned by being sent branches of sal or messages, so that they would not be treacherously surprised. When it became clear that neither protection nor answers to the petitions or justice could be expected from the government, the ideal of an alternative government and a new social order began to emerge. This new social order was to be established by destroying the existing one. In the Santal case, only when all legal channels were exhausted did armed struggle begin. The Santals then proclaimed that the land was theirs and that British rule had come to an end. One of the participants in the 1855 movement, imprisoned at Birbhum after its suppression, explained the reasons why armed action became inevitable: 'You [the government] forced us to fight against you. We asked only what was fair, and you gave us no answer. When we tried to get redress by arms, you shot us like leopards in the jungle....' (Hunter 1868: 254).

Forty years later the Birsaite Movement was to enunciate the same final goal: independence. The targets of attack became all the *dikus*, all the aliens, including the Christians and the *hakims* (the British). The Birsaites foresaw that only with their elimination could the establishment of the New Kingdom of justice be possible.

By means of their experiences in legal and armed protest and their contact with officials of the colonial administration and with people who carried the ideology of the colonizers, the adivasi peasants became aware of the nature of the colonial system and the new unequal relationships in which they had become involved. On the basis of this awareness, the adivasi peasantry began to assert its historical identity (ethnicity) as a part of its political discourse, and began to launch its struggle against the colonizer, his local allies and the social products of colonialism such as the new zamindars. British administration was acknowledged to be the apex of the system of domination in the colony. Direct references were made during the Birsaite Movement to the metropolis, on which the colonial administrative apparatus was seen to depend.

Anti-colonial feelings with clear political content inspired the prayers and songs of the Birsaites as well as the speeches of their leader. Similar feelings were present among the participants in the Santal Movement (K.S. Singh 1966: 98–144; Culshaw and Archer 1945: 220). Both movements were crushed after long repressive campaigns. The suppression of the Santal Movement left the Santals with their villages burnt down and their people decimated and facing famine. The Birsaite Movement also ended brutally with the massacre at Dombari Hill.

The agrarian base, a constant element in the long history of protest of the adivasis of the area, was included in another type of action of resistance. The political strategy came to be based on the establishment of ethnic solidarity links, leading to actions in defence of adivasi cultural and social integrity. In this struggle a colonized people sought to preserve their historical identity, a driving force in all movements for decolonization. Among the adivasis, ethnicity became the vehicle to express their demands for political and economic independence, and an instrument to organize action and form alliances against the colonizer and his representatives.[5]

Practically all the major agrarian movements in Jharkhand during the nineteenth century brought adivasi peasants together across what were tenuous ethnic demarcations. This potentiality of ethnic solidarity for sustaining protest was well understood by the colonial authorities.[6] Ethnic solidarity appeared to be grounded more on a broad historically and territorially defined identity as original settlers than on particular ethnic ascriptions. At the same time, the existence of a correlated class solidarity across the low rural sections of the population—agriculturalists and artisans—in the major peasant movements of nineteenth century Jharkhand, added an important qualitative dimension. This class dimension has been underplayed by contemporary observers, colonial administrators and later scholars whose perceptions of the phenomenon was shaped by the colonial category of tribe. Consequently, these movements have been perceived as 'tribal', with no participation of the general peasantry which supposedly remained passive spectators. Contrary to this perception, there is evidence of the support and participation of the general peasantry in these movements, as in the case of the Santal Movement of 1855 when all sectors of the peasantry—'tribal' *and* 'non-tribal'—were mobilized.[7] By the end of 1855, this formidable rural contingent had joined the movement (Hunter 1868: 250; *CR* 1856: 246), united in a 'brotherhood of class'. It is perhaps in the selection of the targets of attack that the class character of adivasi peasant insurgency is most evident. The rich and the powerful were invariably subjected to violence, while peasants and artisans were carefully spared.

[5] For instance, the alliance of Mundas, Oraons and Hos in the Kol Movement of 1831–32; of Santals and Mundas in the Kherwar Movement of 1871; of Santals and Oraons in the Kherwar Movement of 1891, and of Mundas and Oraons in the Birsaite Movement. The Larka Kols of Singhbhum, although 'they had none of the real grievances of their neighbours' as yet, came forward to aid the Kol Movement as 'the most formidable division of the rebel army'. Insurgency spread to Palamau, where it was taken up by the Kherwar Movement to which most of the adivasi peasantry of Chotanagpur and Palamau provided armed collaboration (Dalton 1872: 169–71; Bradley-Birt 1903: 92–93).

[6] For instance, when disturbances started after Birsa's arrest in 1895 and crowds began to gather at Chalkad, landlords were instructed to forbid the adivasis in the villages under their control to join the meeting (K.S. Singh 1966: 54–55; 63–64).

[7] Blacksmiths, for instance, who usually made agricultural tools in times of peace, provided weapons for the insurgents (Hunter 1868: 250).

The adivasis of Jharkhand sought legitimization and support for their struggle for their rights and independence in their own traditions and in their real or ideal past. This is what Birsa, the Ulgulan's leader, meant when he urged his followers to pay 'homage to the first people of our race'.

The Tradition of Protest Among the Santals

Sidhu, why are you bathed in blood?
Kanhu, why do you cry 'hul, hul!'?
—For our people we have bathed in blood,
since the trader thieves have robbed us of our land....

Santal song

The 1855 Movement started among the Santal peasantry of the Damin-i-koh and later embraced the rural population across an extensive area (Maps 6 and 7). The Damin offered good prospects to traders and moneylenders who started pouring into the area from nearby regions. Colonial administration was satisfied with the Damin as a source of revenue.[8] The conditions prevailing in the Damin were not, however, satisfactory for the Santal peasants who became dependent on merchants for loans in kind or cash at high interest rates. Almost their entire harvest went to pay debts. Santals became trapped in the circle of debts and the *kamioti* system. British Courts declared in favour of the creditor and 'contracts' in dubious terms were signed (Man n.d.: 111–13; R. Mukherjee 1933: 229, fn. 2).[9] The Santal peasant worked the creditor's land without pay and did not have time to cultivate his own. The system

[8] The annual rents on land the Damin peasants had to pay progressively rose from Rs. 6,682 in 1837 to Rs. 58,033 in 1855 (Roy Chaudhuri 1959: 4–11); *CR* 1856: 238). Based on the report by A.C. Bidwell's (special Commissioner in charge of the suppression of the Santal Movement), the Judicial Department stated that the payment exacted was 'moderate in the extreme' (Roy Chaudhuri *ibid*.: 21–30. See also *CR ibid*.: 240).

[9] See transcriptions of some of these contracts in Man *ibid*. and R. Mukherjee *ibid*.

MAP 6: THE SANTAL MOVEMENT OF 1855 (1)

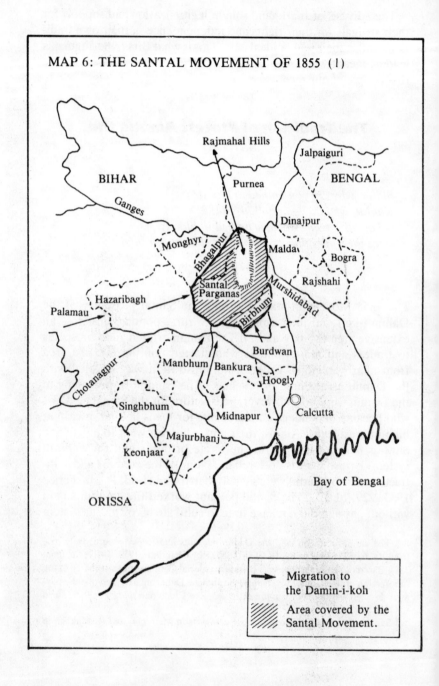

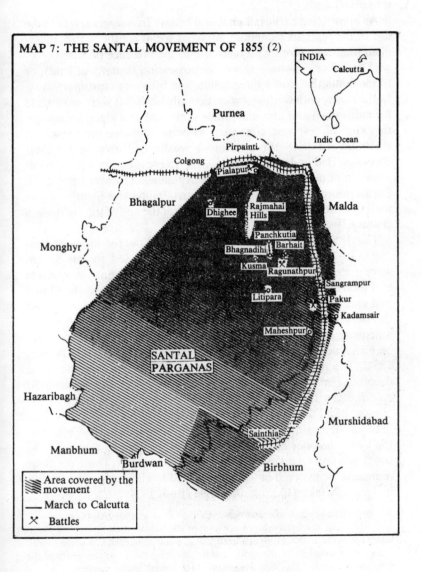

MAP 7: THE SANTAL MOVEMENT OF 1855 (2)

INDIA

Calcutta

Indic Ocean

Purnea

Pirpainti

Colgong

Pialapur

Bhagalpur

Dhighee

Rajmahal
Hills

Malda

Monghyr

Panchkutia

Bhagnadihi

Barhait

Kusma

Ragunathpur

Sangrampur

Litipara

Pakur

Kadamsair

Maheshpur

SANTAL
PARGANAS

Hazaribagh

Murshidabad

Manbhum

Sainthia

Burdwan

Birbhum

Area covered by the
movement

March to Calcutta

✕ Battles

of loans finally forced the Santals to pay their debts with the very lands they had opened to cultivation. These lands gradually passed into *diku* hands.[10]

As mentioned earlier, Santal oral history frequently refers to the use of the 'exodus technique' to avoid social conflicts. Santals explain their migrations with reference to the presence of 'foreigners', who are always associated with dispossession (usually of land), or to incidents that could have resulted in breaking customary laws. In the nineteenth century, when the only lands left were unsuitable for cultivation and only the jungle remained as a place for refuge, this kind of response continued to occur. Among the Santals of Birbhum 'in 1848 three whole townships...throwing up their clearings, fled in despair to the jungle' to escape from a permanent situation of indebtedness to the moneylenders (Hunter 1868: 232). Furthermore, Santals in the area surrounding the Damin had in their tradition rebellions that took place at the end of the eighteenth century.[11]

The 1855 Movement was preceded by different kinds of protests. In 1854, actions of 'social banditry', led by Bir Singh, were reported; these were directed mostly against merchants and moneylenders.[12] By that time, meetings of village headmen and chiefs of *parganas* had already been taking place to discuss the situation and to determine the course of action to follow. As a first steps to eliminate oppression it was decided to exert pressure on *mahajans* and traders. Magistrate Heywood reported in August 1854: 'The number of persons ready and willing to commit these dacoities... may I fear be reckoned by thousands....' (Roy Chaudhuri *op. cit.*: 25). It was acknowledged that these actions received the consent of all the Santal population (*Ibid.*).

From the beginning of 1855 petitions were sent to the Collector, the Commissioner and the Government demanding that usury be contained and all *dikus* expelled from Santal lands. These petitions remained unanswered or were considered too late, when the Santals had already taken to armed struggle (Basu 1934: 192).

[10] See a description of the situation in *Calcutta Review* 1856: 240–41.

[11] According to nineteenth century sources, the Santals tried to organize themselves under the leadership of headman Morgo Rajah, aiming at 'the union into an independent kingdom of the south country, meaning the original country of the Sonthal tribe' (*CR* 1856: 242). Discontent in Hazaribagh is also mentioned.

[12] In my view, these actions of protest did not amount to a 'messianic movement' as Fuchs (1965) considers them.

The Santal Movement followed a clear pattern of development. At first, religious elements served to legitimize the protest and the selection of the leaders. Premonitions and divine revelations marked the beginning of a special, sacralized time, the right moment to gain independence and to create a new and just society. The second stage was legalist. Documents asking for justice were submitted to the authorities. In June 1855 the march to Calcutta was organized. The failure of the shortlived march led on 7 July 1855 to an overt armed struggle, conceived as the last resort to obtain redress. Four Santal brothers from Bhagnadihi village were selected as leaders, symbolically by divine intervention and in practice by the people who decided to follow them. Two of the brothers, Sidhu and Kanhu, emerged as the actual leaders of the movement. They had become landless peasants after their father had lost his lands to the *dikus* (Datta 1940: 14ff.).

Before launching their protest, the Santals sought strength and assurance for the success of their struggle in a series of symbolic actions. They started by differentiating themselves from the rest of men as 'the chosen people'. For the Santals, to belong to 'the chosen ones' meant to be conscious of their collective identity. The main goal of the movement became the elimination of merchants, moneylenders, colonial officials and alien landlords. Later on, final objectives were enunciated: Santal independence, land restoration and the establishment of a Santal government. New letters were sent to the Government, the authorities at Bhagalpur and Birbhum, and some *darogas* and zamindars (Culshaw and Archer 1945: 219–20; Roy Chaudhuri 1965a: 80). Only W.W. Hunter and S. Fuchs mention the march to Calcutta. Others talk of a gathering of between 10,000 to 30,000 people. The aborted march was the last of the legal actions before armed struggle began.[13] Once the avenues for legal protest and dialogue with the colonial authorities were severed, the Santals proclaimed that the land was theirs and that British rule had come to an end.

The consistent pattern in the choice of targets for insurgent

---

[13] The circumstances that ended this march are rather confusing. Datta mentions the killing of five *mahajans* in Panchkutia which provoked police intervention on 7 July. The police party was led by the *daroga* Mahesh Lal Datta, known to the Santals for his past outrages. The marchers captured the *daroga*, tried and executed him. It seems he had been bribed by Hindu usurers and asked to arrest the Santal leaders under false accusations of robbery (K.K. Datta 1940).

violence indicates the existence both of consensus among the participants regarding who their enemy was and a precise organization. The most frequent targets were the moneylenders and the merchants. Starting in 1854 with Bir Singh's actions, the insurgents pillaged the houses of the rich. When the struggle became openly anti-colonial, Government representatives, the police, the railways' high employees and the army, were added to the list. Several Europeans were killed, Bengalis were threatened, houses in some villages were looted and burnt, markets pillaged, and zamindars, local rajas and the centres of trade in indigo attacked.[14] In July 1855 the Santals made their goal of self-rule explicit. The yearning for an independent kingdom was reinforced by the belief, which antedated the movement, that a powerful independent Santal kingdom had existed in the past.

The suppression of the movement was particularly severe. Santal property was destroyed and villages burnt down under the excuse that they were 'full of booty'. The movement, nevertheless, continued to spread, reaching Colong–Rajmahal in the east and Raniganj and Sainthia in the south, and spilling over into Birbhum, Bankura and Hazaribagh (Raghavaiah 1971: 153; Roy Chaudhuri 1965a: 19; O'Malley 1938: 59–60). The escalation of repression finally forced up to 30,000 Santals to take refuge in the jungles. Local zamindars, *ghatwals* and the police aided the counter-insurgency forces, which were also helped by funds provided by the indigo planters.[15] The collaboration of planters and zamindars in the repression was, ironically, in the last instance funded by the income from the peasants' own work (*WBDR* 1855: 1786–97; *Indian Records* 1870: 196 ff.). More than 10,000 Santals died in this unequal war.

Conflicts internal to the movement contributed to its disintegration. The environment of violence and fear and an increasingly authoritarian leadership discouraged and alienated many participants. Many left the movement and fled, only to encounter the troops or their burnt villages. Santals who were arrested were treated

[14] Messages were sent by the insurgents prior to their attacks, promising not to harm the cultivators. Gregor Grant's establishment was captured and destroyed only after two proclamations were sent advising him to leave with all his belongings (*Santal Communiques* and letters, *BJP* 1956).

[15] The planters were alarmed because the indigo cultivators were willing to back the insurgents. The persisting demands of the planters to the Government for compensation contributed to the escalation of the final repression of the movement.

as common criminals. Even the possibility of Santal political dissidence was not considered (*WBDR* 1855: 119–20, 129–30). The colonial administration was worried about the number of cultivators not willing to return to the Damin and who were instead fleeing the area. The editorial of *Friends of India* demanded exemplary punishments for the insurgents—described as 'blood-thirsty savages'—to 'avenge the outrages committed...[and] to restore the prestige of British authority'. *Calcutta Review* saw the problem in more practical terms, and advised:

> [The Santals] should be compelled, by force, if need be, to return to the Damin-i-koh and to the waste country in Bhaugulpore and Beerbhoom, to rebuild the ruined villages, restore the desolate fields to cultivation, open roads, and advance general public works; and do this under watch and guard, for otherwise they will run away....(1856: 262–63).

In short, from the colonialist perspective, the Santals had to be forced again into the mould of the obedient coolie.

After the suppression of the movement, revenue collection was resumed in the Damin with good results for the Government. It was only 30 years later that legislation was enacted to stop land alienation in Santal territories. Since the underlying socio–economic structure was not modified by the new laws, the exploitation of the Santals by landlords and moneylenders continued. Rents were increased further, and village authorities were displaced under external pressure.

But the tradition of protest among the Santals was not broken. By mid–1861 sal branches again carried messages of dissidence among the Santal villages. The time coincided both with a prophecy made by Kanhu in which he promised to return to his people and with a rent increase by the zamindars. In the end, the protest did not materialize in action. Demands for independence surfaced again in the Kherwar Movement of 1871, led by Bhagrit of Taldiha, a movement which was messianic in form and Hinduist in the reforms it sought to introduce. The beginnings of this movement also coincided with an increase in rents. This circumstance shows once again that the formal aspects of a movement (religious elements) concealed causes that had more to do with the economic situation. Incidents continued to take place, especially in 1874 during a serious famine in Santal Parganas. By 1880–81, demands for independence were again expressed, this time under the leadership of Dubia Gosain, a Hindu ascetic. The Kherwar Movement revived in 1891. Its participants announced the end of colonial rule, the advent of self-government, the elimination of rents and the restoration of lands to the adivasis, repeating demands that had been uttered for half a century.[16]

The Tradition of Protest Among the Adivasis of Chotanagpur

White men, go away, hurry up,
Your land is in the West, you must leave.
Go away with the wind to your land,
You must leave....

Birsaite song

The Birsaite Movement (*Ulgulan*) of 1895 was millenarian in form, and agrarian and anti-colonial in character. It was also messianic. Birsa, the leader, acted as a divine messenger and later came to be seen as the deity himself on earth. The revolutionary spirit that usually animates millenarian movements was broken in the Birsaite Movement when it failed to attain its aims and repression had destroyed the movement's organization. The Ulgulan formed part of a long tradition of protest and of a chain of suppressed uprisings. Since the end of the eighteenth century Chotanagpur had shown signs of agrarian unrest. Movements of protest and actions of 'social banditry' were developed by the adivasis of the area, sometimes united in pan-ethnic fronts. The period between 1780 and 1833 was one of intense agrarian protest.[17] Towards the mid-nineteenth century, the *Mulkui Larai* ('the fight for the land') or Sardar

[16] Later on, the strongly anti-British Sapha-Hor Movement of 1942–43 became involved in the Indian national struggle for independence (K.K. Datta 1958: 185 ff.; Mac Dougall 1977).

[17] 1789: Mundas rose against the new alien landlords in Tamar. 1796 and 1798: peasant protests among the Mundas of Rahe and Silli. 1807: agrarian unrest in Tamar. 1831: Mundas, Oraons and Hos participated in the Kol Movement around

Movement started, a legalist struggle that was to last for almost 40 years.

The deterioration of the relations between the adivasis and the missions established in Chotanagpur began when the missionaries started to show interest in the lands of the converts. Other factors included the growing intolerance of the Lutheran church, the persistence of land alienation, forced labour and continuous rent increases. All this led the Mundas to organize themselves to fight for land restoration (S.P. Sinha 1959: 393; Zide and Munda 1969). The adivasi *sardars*, mostly Christian, undertook the laborious task of sending petitions to the authorities and collecting funds to pay for the legal procedures at the Calcutta courts. The government did not listen to these petitions. Even S.C. Roy considered the Sardars to be 'unscrupulous agitators', their claims 'extravagant' and their petitions 'recklessly rabid' (1912: 281). The claim that seems to have particularly incensed the colonial government was that Chotanagpur belonged to the Mundas, that the Hindus had no right on these territories and, consequently, that no rents would be paid.[18] After legal actions repeatedly failed, the Sardars concluded that the path of legal protest was closed. The idea of establishing an independent government began to take shape. By then, close to the end of the century, the adivasis of Chotanagpur were looking for a leader who could organize them in their struggle for independence.

The Birsaite Movement of 1895

The Ulgulan revolved around Birsa, a young Munda who came to

---

the question of land grants (S.Ç. Roy 1912; 1961: 287; Elwin 1945: 258; Hallet and Mcpherson 1917: 31–35). Representatives of various adivasi communities gathered at Lanka (Tamar) decided they 'should commence to cut, plunder, murder and eat...' (testimony in Elwin *ibid.*: 259). The movement suppressed, the South West Frontier Agency was established, Doranda transformed into a military cantonment, and the zamindari police system reinstated.

[18] See the petition addressed by the chiefs of eight *parganas* and 'fourteen thousand Christians' to the Commissioner of Chotanagpur, in S.C. Roy *ibid.*: 282–83, where it is said: 'If Chota Nagpore does not belong to the Mundas, it belongs to none....' Some missionaries like F. Nottrott and F. Dedlockes aided in the incarceration of some Sardars. The confrontation with the missions escalated resulting, for instance, in the Oraons establishing independent churches in the jungles.

be seen by his people as the New King and by some Indian nationalists as a patriot. He belonged to a poor peasant family from Chalkad, was converted to Christianity and educated for some years at the missions where he acquired some knowledge of English. Birsa was excommunicated by the Lutheran missionaries, possibly because he was a Sardar sympathizer and because of his position on the land rights question (Zide and Munda 1969: 39).[19]

Several extraordinary events came to indicate in the eyes of the people and of Birsa himself that he had been chosen by Sing Bonga, the supreme deity, as his divine messenger and that he was endowed with miraculous powers. The Birsaites started protest actions which resulted in the refusal to transplant rice and the abandonment of cultivation. They organized a movement for non-cooperation against the landlords of such proportions that the administration feared it could result in food scarcity and famine.[20] Birsa began to announce the destruction of the world, an apocalypse from which only the Birsaites would be saved. The end of this world being imminent, agricultural work and cattle were abandoned, and savings spent.

Three phases can be detected in this movement (Map 8). In the first, during the first months of 1895, religious elements predominated. The second, lasting to the end of 1900, can be called the agrarian–political phase and included efforts at collective self-assertion (1898 and 1899). From February to October 1901 came the period of disintegration of the movement.

Birsa was imprisoned in 1895 but the movement continued its course underground with the help of the Sardars.[21] The presence of the Sardars remained constant in the Birsaite Movement. The colonial administration clearly detected the merger of the two

[19] He participated in the agrarian struggle and, consequently, was marked by the police as the instigator of the peasant protest march in Sigrida in 1894 in demand of a reduction in the forest tax.

[20] A serious food shortage overcame Chotanagpur in 1895 and 1896. Important insurgent centres (Khunti, Sisal and Basia) were affected by famine. Later, the climax of the protest in 1898 and 1899 coincided with a famine in Ranchi and Palamau and the 1898 cholera epidemic.

[21] At the same time, there was a new wave of conversions to Christianity—symbol and part of the culture of the colonizer—between 1895 and 1897, possibly as a way to avoid harassment by the authorities and for other practical reasons. Zide and Munda (1969) suggest that the critical situation resulting from the 1896 famine was used to force conversions in exchange for food aid.

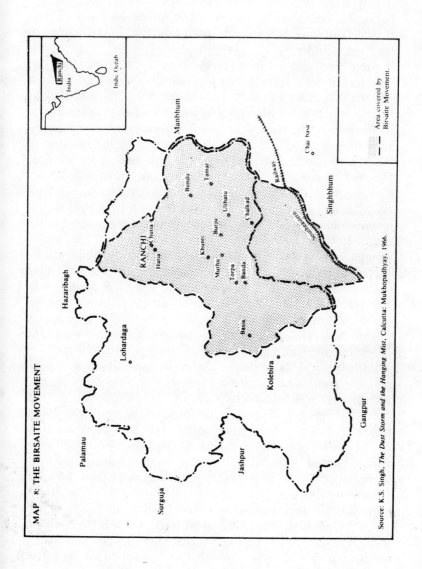

MAP 8: THE BIRSAITE MOVEMENT

Source: K.S. Singh, *The Dust Storm and the Hanging Mist*, Calcutta: Mukhopadhyay, 1966.

movements and was consequently alarmed at the danger to 'law and order' from the collaboration of Sardars and Birsaites, who were seen respectively as 'agitators' and 'false prophets' (Document in K.K. Datta 1958: 99). This alliance appeared as a threat precisely because it embodied the union of two forces: elements of class struggle and the ethnic struggle, both expressed in the defence of land and territory.

After Biras's release from jail, the Birsaites reaffirmed their cultural identity with visits to the temples of Chutia and Jagarnathpur and the fort at Naw Rattan. They believed that these landmarks had been built by the Mundas, who were later forced to leave them by the *dikus*. The visits were aimed at recovering sacred possessions thought to be in these places and honouring the ancestors of the Munda people. The Birsaites were also looking for a copper plate in Chutia where Munda land rights were said to be recorded. The grounds for identifying these places as part of the Munda heritage seem to be fictitious. Whatever the historical basis of this identification, however, the Birsaites were challenging the dominant sectors by appropriating their cultural symbols. They did so by undermining one of the most salient features of Hindu culture, its religion epitomized in the temple, which was also a status symbol of the landed rich (Roy Chaudhuri 1965b: 142–51; R. Guha 1983). The visit to Chutia resulted in the defilement of images and the desecration of the temple. The impact of this defiance via appropriation was reinforced by the destruction of a sacred symbol of Hindu culture. The form (aggression, re-appropriation) and content (defiance of the established order) of these actions were combined in symbolic collective actions, as it is common in peasant insurgency (see Hobsbawm 1963: Ch. IX). Symbolic action embodies codes—of conduct, of strategy, of perceiving reality—that remain private to its users. This is the 'language' of the *oppositional clandestine culture* of the subaltern classes (Devalle 1985a). Collective symbolism and ritualized actions in peasant movements reinforce the 'complicity' that underlies the cohesion among those who participate in them.

After these visits, the Birsaites considered themselves to be prepared for offensive action. The visual symbols of war then proliferated. A landscape of red flags rose at Dombari Hill announcing the beginning of a bloody war that was to engulf all the *dikus*, *thikadars*, *jagirdars*, rajas and Christians. After a Birsaite meeting at Simbua, Queen Victoria was burnt in effigy, and the raja and the British were symbolically destroyed in the angry felling of a plantain tree. The missions in Singhbhum and Ranchi and the houses of converts became the first targets in the wave of attacks and arson in late 1899. Significantly, violence broke out on Christmas Eve, a choice of date that gave the actions the symbolic meaning of overturning the meaning of that day for the Christians: peace. The symbolic was, however, also well rationalized. The Birsaites considered that: 'They have suffered in the hands of the Christian priests who destroyed their caste [*sic*] by converting them to their religion....' (*cit.* in K.S. Singh 1966: 88). This perception was compounded by distrust of the missionaries regarding the land question.

By 1900 the attention of the Birsaites turned to the Hindus and the representatives of the colonial order. Armed confrontations ensued, among them the attack at Etkedih on the Deputy Commissioner and the takeover of the Khunti police station, both visible symbols of authority. With the launching of counter-insurgency operations, the Birsaites had to resort to defensive tactics culminating in the retreat into Sail Rakab Hill. They took their families and food with them and prepared for a prolonged siege.[22] Sail Rakab and Dombari Hill were to be the final sites where protest was silenced in a massacre that was subsequently officially 'forgotten' to avoid inquiries into the role of the army and the police. The people's collective memory, however, did not forget. The images of death in Dombari Hill were kept alive in oral history.[23]

Less than a month later, Birsa was again arrested. He died in jail shortly after, in dubious circumstances. When taken to prison he assured his followers he would return one day to establish the promised kingdom, and gave the British only 10 more years to live. Officially, the political character of the movement was never

---

[22] Until that moment the movement had been in control of 1,024 sq. miles of hilly terrain with forces that contemporary sources establish at 15,000. The confrontations at Etkedih, Khunti and, finally, Dombari Hill, happened in rapid succession in less than a week. The Khunti incident convinced the colonial authorities that general insurgency obtained in the area between Khunti and Bandgaon.

[23] For instance, a Birsaite song says:

Oh, Birsa!, [your] followers fell on the milk-like land.
They were overrun on the cream-like land.
Little children were trampled upon...
Oh, Birsa!, your people mourn.... (cit. in K.S. Singh 1966: 121).

acknowledged, although it was labelled 'a conspiracy'. Birsa was brought to trial as a common criminal and not as a political prisoner. Following the suppression of the movement, Birsaism was reduced to the life of a sect, preserving only the religious elements and circumscribing the Birsaites in a new but closed society. This was an introvert response that attempted to create a new world through segregation.

Birsa's promise to return was not forgotten, and some continued to wait for his second coming. Songs are still composed in Birsa's memory,[24] and even today the search for a leader by part of the Munda *intelligentsia* evokes the image of Birsa: 'A mystic leader, like Birsa, a man that with simplicity can dominate the minds of the powerful, somebody like a saint who cannot be corrupted' (a Munda intellectual).

While the people involved in the Birsaite Movement did relate their struggle to the struggle for national independence,[25] the Indian Nationalist Movement did not embrace foci of anti-colonial resistance such as this one. This was not completely the case' however, of the Tana Bhagat movement among the Oraons (possibly starting in 1914 and crystallizing in 1915) which had religious connotations, was of an anti-colonial character, and rose against the unequal land and revenue system, colonial authorities, missionaries, landlords and usurers. Its followers played an active role in the first non-cooperation movement of 1921. The Tana Bhagats advocated active—and not only passive—protest: from halting cultivation and the payment of rents to the destruction of government property. One of the salient features of the movement since its inception was its emphasis on obtaining social equality *vis à vis* Hindus and Christians, and the attempts it made to revalue Oraon culture, attempts that were partly frustrated by the Oraons' absorption of Hindu practices.

[24] Note, for instance, the song in Mundari composed by Ram Dayal Munda (1967):

Looking for you again,
Muchia Chalkad is asking for you...
Dombari Hill is searching for you...
with the [metallic] sound of arrows and axes.
The rumbling of guns is searching for you.
Bows and arrows touch and jingle
for our mother country....(My translation).

[25] This is reflected, for instance, in the relation established between the role of two leaders, Birsa and Gandhi, evidenced in some later local songs, and in comments made to me by some advasis.

The Millennium's Promised Land

The Ulgulan of 1895 took the form of a millenarian movement with messianic elements, characteristics that were also present in the Santal Movement of 1855. Millenarian mass movements have often arisen among the underprivileged in critical situations (*cf.* P. Worsley 1970: xi, with N. Cohn 1962, 1970). Scholars like G. Balandier (1955), V. Laternari (1965), E. Hobsbawm (1963) and P. Worsley (*ibid.*), consider these movements to be antecedents in the formation of a political consciousness. The revolutionary spirit in millenarism is embedded in the concept of a better world to be attained through a complete structural change. Reformist tendencies can arise at certain junctures in the development of a millenarian movement. In the Ulgulan, this tendency appeared after its suppression, as a kind of compromise with a world that at the moment proved impossible to radically change.

Hobsbawm defends the utopianism of millenarism as 'a necessary social device for generating the superhuman efforts without which no major revolution is achieved' (*ibid.*). Millenarism does not, however, offer a remote utopia: for the millenarists problems are to be solved 'here and now' in order to correct and change a concrete situation of which they are aware. Therefore, millenarism should not be seen as a form of escapism from intolerable situations. In the Santal and the Birsaite Movements, the millenarian project had as its final objective the inauguration of a new social and moral order. In the course of these movements, societies that had been dislocated by colonialism reorganized themselves and forged new social projects.

In the millenarian context, time acquires a special meaning. The millennium marks the end of one time and the beginning of a qualitatively different one (Eliade 1954: 376). The arrival of messiahs in the two aforementioned cases indicated the opening of a new era, a time of salvation and renovation. Catastrophes and chaos (conquest, famine and epidemics like that of cholera in Chotanagpur in 1898) were understood as signs of the end of one time and the beginning of a new one. In the New Era, Birsa the messiah was to become the New King. For the Birsaites, 'the land is in the grip of a consuming fire, like dry grass' since 'customs, traditions and our honour have been snatched from us' (*Rogoto Manuscript*, K.S. Singh

1966: 132–33, 151). The messiah had come to correct the situation. Birsa was born 'to sweep the earth clean', 'to light up the land ' (*ibid:* 131, 133).

The New Era entailed an absolute new beginning. For this to happen, a complete process of regeneration had to take place: the elimination of suffering, insecurity, injustice and death. From the dissolution of the old world only 'the chosen ones' were to be saved. It was to them that the New Kingdom, the perfect land, was to belong. For the Birsaites, hope in the advent of a world without oppression was so strong that at least twice in their songs and prayers collected by K.S. Singh the New Kingdom is said to have been already established and forever regained (*ibid.:* 142).

In the yearning for the New Kingdom, the will to recover territory and land converged. For the Mundas, their territory was given to their ancestors by the supreme deity 'at the beginning of time'. It was not merely a geographical place where men lived and worked. It was the only possible place for them to live. In it they could define themselves and their lives in relation to the land as the source of sustenance, in relation to a sacred landscape and to the places in which their history was written. Territory becomes an existential geography. Outside this vital space, existence for the Mundas would have no meaning. The roots of the community are in the land that its members share, a space that becomes the pillar of the social world.

Land–territory appears as the foundation of all the vital manifestations of the community. It relates men firmly to their origins as they are established in their history ('imagined' or 'real'). It gives them a concrete present and a hopeful future, the reassurance of continuity in time and space. This is the meaning of the words of a Munda elder, who said: 'We should not forget our Mari Disum.... This is our land, it has always fed us. Our father was here and [before him] his father.'

All aspects of life are endangered when the relation between land–territory and men is put at risk. The land of the Mundas was in danger when 'others took over our land' and 'when the old social order was displaced'. The Mundas lamented that 'the land is floating away like a rolling tortoise' (*ibid.:* 132). This is why Birsa's call to unite under 'the *khuntkatti* banner' to recover their land and territory was heard by the adivasis of Chotanagpur. A Birsaite song says:

The true word is in the land...
The word of the land is with us....

With that ally they marched forward in search of victory.

Urban-based Political Organizations in the Twentieth Century

Jharkhand is just here in my fist....
Jaipal Singh (according to a Munda)

The twentieth century inaugurates the modality of formal politics in Jharkhand. Its dynamics since the thirties was aptly summarized by a Munda intellectual: 'Leaders have been coming up like mushrooms in each area with contradictory solutions for the different problems, and end up fighting among themselves.'

The development of the urban-based political organizations in Jharkhand followed an intricate pattern of continuous fission that mirrored the cleavages among the emerging strata of well-to-do adivasis and the sectorial interests that guided their proposals. The concern for socio–economic issues often became a mere rhetorical stance in which the only clear statement was the call for a separate state. This demand never went beyond generalities about the possible extension of this state. The question that remained unanswered, except for references to ethnic/regional restrictions, was who was to benefit from this separation and in what fashion. Vague formulations concerning the demand for a separate Jharkhand state marked the inception of the *reformist ethnicist* line that we still encounter in the Jharkhand Party and among sectors of the adivasi petty-bourgeoisie. A feature of Jharkhand's modern political organizations is the distance—formalized by the mechanisms of modern politics and by class relations—established between the 'intellectual–organizer' (Gramsci 1973: 12; 1975) and the predominantly rural masses. At the same time, the 'intellectual–organizer' functions as a mediator between the dominant groups and the state on the one hand, and the subordinated sectors on the other.

K. Gough has remarked that since the twenties, peasant insurgency in India has been coordinated by political parties and has been of two kinds: (*a*) movements for independence or for regional or national autonomy (she gives the Jharkhand Movement as an example), and (*b*) uprisings that have been primarily class struggles guided by the left parties (1974: 1403). The differences between these two, however, are not so clear cut. A variety of positions, ideologies and class interests are found in what has been generally labelled the 'Jharkhand Movement'. There is a multiplicity of projects which are often in open contradiction. The crux of the matter ultimately lies in the class base, the leadership's class links and the interests that have given substance to the various movements in Jharkhand.

From the thirties to the sixties, Jharkhand's political field was dominated by the urban-based organizations. The *reformist ethnicist* project was mostly an urban phenomenon but it had echoes in the countryside.[26] Given the emergence of forceful peasant protests in Jharkhand form the seventies onwards, one is inclined to believe that the political life of the peasantry continued to develop independently of the urban-based projects.

Reformist activities by missionaries and Christian teachers and students were already under way at the beginning of the century. Their efforts centred on organizing the adivasis into cooperative societies and on promoting Western-oriented education and values. They emphasized welfare phrased according to Christian religious ideals of morality and charity. 'Mission culture' led to the formation of 'native' intellectuals of a new vintage. The clearest example of the mediating nature of the relationships established by the ecclesiastic–intellectuals between the superstructural field (providing social models) and the economic domain is the Chotanagpur Catholic Cooperative Credit Society, founded in 1909 by Rev. J. Hoffmann. It has as its matrix a Central Banking Union. A Government Report of 1909–10 commented:

> It is a large centralized society embracing the whole Roman Catholic population of Ranchi...with the object of enabling the members of the Mission to constitute themselves into a system of federated and autonomous societies within the central institution....

[26] Electoral results during those years seem to indicate this fact. See Vidyarthi and Sahay 1976: Ch. VI, VII; Jha and Jha 1964.

The area... is divided into some sixteen circles corresponding to missionary circles, each in charge of a Missionary. The circles again are divided into villages or groups of villages, each of which forms a rural unit.....(*cit.* in S.C. Roy 1912: 320–21).[27]

The Society or the Bank, as it is commonly known, translated into practice the capitalist values of individualism, saving and profit. It supported the model of the farmer–entrepreneur and contributed to the emergence of a rural petty bourgeoisie. Explicitly removed from politics, the rural development projects in operation in Chotanagpur broadly coincide with the line of thought held by the *reformist ethnicists*. These projects are sponsored by the Christian adivasi elite with the support of the Churches. Even though they are not expressed in a global agrarian program, the different organizations act in concert, aiming at the development of capitalist agriculture.[28]

The paradigms of 'tribal' and Christian community together with Western liberal values guide the planning of these programs, the first gradually losing ground and becoming a stereotyped 'tradition' and an obstacle to 'progress'. The promoters of 'tribal entrepreneurship' oppose 'the cultural and mental make-up of the tribal people'—considered a hindrance to development—to the adivasis' acceptance of some 'modern' elements conducive to their successful adaptation to change: formal education, modern employment, migration, Christianity (Bogaert *et al.*, n. d.: 3–4). The promoters of these projects acknowledge certain problems: continuing land alienation, loss of rights over the use of forests, indebtedness to moneylenders and traders, and the exploitative role of the intermediaries in the market economy. However, these problems are isolated from the operation of the economic system that makes possible their existence, thus becoming part of the ethnically-determined 'tribal problem' (see van Exem 1973).

The period of the associations and cooperative societies also marked the intensification of cleavages between Christian and non-Christian adivasis and among people adhering to various

---

[27] By mid-1910 there were already 229 rural units and the Society counted with Rs. 22,845 as capital.

[28] The data on which the analysis of these organizations is based come from interviews, and from the publications and writings of persons connected with these organizations' projects.

Christian denominations. The internalization among the converts of the 'tribal ideology' also dates from this period. Cultural colonialism penetrated via education and Christianity. Schools and missionaries took in their hands the West's *mission civilisatrice* in Jharkhand. In the educational field, several associations were formed like the early Christian Association founded by Lutheran students in 1898 that, when joined in 1918 by the Catholics, amalgamated into the Christian College Union. A Christian students' organization was founded in 1912 by J. Bartholmen, of the Anglican Mission. In the same year, a broad adivasi organization was formed: the Chotanagpur Charitable Association, which represented the first attempt at unity over ethnic cleavages.

The idea that the problems of the adivasis were those of cultural revival and 'backwardness' gave birth in the twenties to the interdenominational Chotanagpur Improvement Society (*Chotanagpur Unnati Samaj*), whose members were mostly Christian adivasis from the emerging educated elite (Anglicans and Lutherans). The thirties saw the emergence of the demand for a separate adivasi state, which was presented to the Simon Commission and the Cripps Mission (Vidyarthi and Sahay 1976: 87). A fissiparous trend gradually became manifest. Some members of the Samaj separated from it to approach the peasants through the Kisan Sabha (Vidyarthi 1967b: 133; Sachchidananda 1976: 13; N. Sengupta 1982c: 28). The Catholics formed the Chotanagpur Catholic Sabha. These organizations finally merged around 1938 into the Adivasi Mahasabha, ancestor of the Jharkhand Party. The Mahasabha remained outside the Nationalist Movement and, in fact, ended up supporting the British.[29]

In 1939, the Anglican Munda Jaipal Singh became prominent in the Adivasi Mahasabha and was later made its Chairman. Oxford-educated and pro-British, he backed the British in the war and was involved in the recruitment of adivasis for their army (K. S. Singh 1977: 321). In this way, the Westernized adivasi elite, not involved in the Indian Nationalist Movement, dismissed more than a century of adivasi anti-colonial struggles. In the end, the

[29] Several circumstances helped to maintain the Adivasi Mahasabha outside the Nationalist Movement. The Congress Party, with its victory in the 1937 elections, was not thought to represent the interests of the adivasis. The nationalists opposed the partition of Bengal and Bihar while the Bengali–Biharis looked for an alliance with the adivasis to support the demand for a separate Bihar.

Mahasabha launched a struggle not against the British Raj but against the *Diku* Raj.[30] Opinions on Jaipal Singh, the most important leader the Jharkhand Party has had, vary from favourable to highly critical. For instance, an Anglican Munda priest proudly told me: 'You know, he was one of *our* boys!' Non-Christian adivasis portrayed him as ' a sophisticated man, who smoked cigars, dressed well and had money...[who] started to drink a lot and to spend on expensive things, habits he had acquired in England'. It was also remarked: 'He was also violent but had to mellow because the people did not follow his violent line. He ended up divorced from the people.' Furthermore: 'He exploited the image of Birsa and his ideas.' According to Sachchidananda, Jaipal Singh acted as if he was the reincarnation of Birsa (1976: 14). He also resorted to invoking the old millenarian dream of the New Kingdom, modifying it to suit a Christian audience: Jharkhand became the New Kingdom of Christ.

Jaipal Singh's political skills are acknowledged by all. Still, his inability to forge a solid front by bringing together the different leaders, the suspicions of corruption against him and the alliances he sought, all undermined his image as a leader in the eyes of the educated adivasis. That is why nowadays some of them openly long for a 'mystic leader' not susceptible to corruption or cooptation. Interviewed people who were critical of Jaipal Singh, restricted their comments to the personality of the leader and the heterogeneous nature of the Jharkhand movement. Comments on wider political issues and on the difficulties the *reformist ethnicist* line has encountered were avoided.

The Jharkhand Party was founded in 1950 as the political wing of the Adivasi Mahasabha with the aim of attracting the people of Chotanagpur and Santal Parganas into a wide regional political organization. From 1952 to 1957, the party dominated electoral politics in these regions. In the 1962 elections, however, it started to decline, a developement that led in September 1963 to its controversial merger with the Congress Party and eventually to the formation of a new Jharkhand Party under the leadership of N. E. Horo. It appears that the change in electoral preferences was due to the activity of several all-India parties in the area and also to the increasing economic gap between the rising elite and the rest of the adivasis. The class interests that guided the party started to come more sharply

---

[30] Understood in its restricted sense of the dominance of non-adivasi 'outsiders'.

into the light. The party did not have an agrarian program, as is still the case, and failed to address the needs of the growing adivasi industrial working force. Furthermore, it accepted landlords and moneylenders as members, and they came to hold important executive positions. This was understood by the electorate as an alignment of the Jharkhand Party with *diku* interests. Moreover, the party failed to win its only explicit and widely accepted demand: the creation of a separate state at a time when India was being geographically reorganized along linguistic and regional lines.

From 1963 onwards, recurrent splits fragmented the Jharkhand Party. The splintered groups did not have major differences in their programs, and mostly emerged out of personal differences among their leaders.[31] Other organizations emerged in the late sixties and early seventies, like the Birsa Seva Dal, the All-India Sido-Kanhu Baisi and the Adivasi Socio–Educational and Cultural Association. The last two were mostly concerned with cultural revivalism and took up a verbal defence of adivasi land rights (Gautam 1978b: 114–15). The Birsa Seva Dal. formed in 1967 as an urban pressure group, focused on the industrial complexes and on the demand for jobs and educational reservations for the adivasis. For a while it may have had links with the CPI (ML). Until 1969, the Birsa Seva Dal was radical and militant. It was directly involved in the re-appropriation of urban lands in Jamshedpur which ended in police repression in 1968 (Vidyarthi and Sahay 1976). The Birsa Seva Dal then ceased to carry out direct actions, retaining only an intermittent influence at Jamshedpur.

The history of fragmentation of the Jharkhand Party and the proliferation of sectorial groups shows that ethnicity has been variously used in the political arena. These uses depend on the class situation, alliances and interests of those who appeal to the ethnic factor in their ideological discourses. In Jharkhand there never has been just one discourse of ethnicity but several, following socio–economic cleavages. In the eighteenth and nineteenth centuries, ethnic assertion responded to a situation of conquest and was an expression of the adivasi peasantry. In the forties,

[31] The All-India Jharkhand Party was formed in 1967 in opposition to the Jharkhand Party's merger with the Congress Party, and was in turn divided as a result of alliances with various Indian parties. In 1968 the Santal Hul Jharkhand Political Party was formed from which the Progressive Hul Jharkhand Party emerged in 1972 (Sachchidananda 1976: 19).

the rising indigenous petty-bourgeoisie resorted to ethnic politics to place itself in a better position and to gain benefits from an established colonial system whose end was mistakenly not perceived as being imminent. Apparently, this elite saw itself as Jharkhand's natural leadership. It took up the task of directing the rest of their communities on the basis of its class position, 'superior' Western education and, in many cases, its alleged 'superior' religious ascription through conversion to Christianity. By stressing adivasi 'backwardness' and not acknowledging existing structural socio–economic problems, this elite fostered a dangerous 'inferiority complex' (Fanon 1973: 59–76).

Meanwhile, Jharkhand's adivasi peasants took to action independently of the elite and the political parties, responding to a situation which turned critical in the sixties and was made worse by the Bihar drought and subsequent famine of 1966. In this context, forcible harvesting by adivasi peasants marked the 1968 season and together with violent confrontations in the rural areas between landlords and peasants, continued to occur in the years that followed.

A Continuing Tradition of Agrarian Protest

The two-centuries-old agrarian-based tradition of protest in Jharkhand constitutes the background to the oppositional expressions and movements of present times, like the grass-roots movement of the seventies. The Santal peasantry figured prominently in the ongoing rural agitation in Jharkhand's Santal belt of recent years. Press reports and comments during interviews indicate the development in the sixties and the seventies of a repeated pattern of forcible harvesting of paddy on alienated lands in Santal Parganas, Dhanbad, Giridih and adjacent regions of the West Bengal countryside. These seasonal actions of protest well preceded the emergence of the Jharkhand Mukti Morcha (JMM) in 1972. The JMM, in fact, came to lead an already mobilized peasantry, providing organizational elements.

In the seventies, agrarian protest combined with the struggle of the colliery workers in Dhanbad. The worker–peasant alliance that emerged included both adivasi and non-adivasi components. The coming together of the workers, the Santal peasants and the non-adivasi peasantry crystallized at the end of 1972 in the linking of the struggles of the Shivaji Samaj, formed in 1970 among the Kurmi peasants (officially defined as 'a detribalized backward caste'), the JMM, mostly among the Santal peasantry, and the Bihar Colliery Kamgar Union (BCKU). This coalition operated under a triple leadership comprised of the Kurmi lawyer Binod Bihari Mahato, the Santal leader Sibu Soren, and the Dhanbad trade-unionist A.K. Roy of the Marxist Coordination Committee (MCC). In 1973, the Shivaji Samaj was replaced by the Morcha led by Binod Bihari Mahato, Sibu Soren and Sadananda Jha. Significantly, Sadananda Jha was not a Jharkhandi but came from North Bihar. A young trade-union leader in Dhanbad, he was murdered in 1973, possibly by the collieries' muscle-men. Jha's commitment to the Jharkhandi workers' struggle, his being an outsider, and his death, condense the spirit of the emergent movement in Jharkhand in which class solidarity and alliances strove to supersede narrow ethno/regional cleavages. The Kurmis of the Shivaji Samaj as well as the adivasi peasants had been struggling for the restoration of lands alienated by landlords and moneylenders. Under the JMM they concentrated on this issue and on the situation of the sharecroppers and agricultural labourers.

It was around 1971 that Sibu Soren began organizing the people in Tundi (Dhanbad)[32] to demand a better deal for the agricultural labourers and the sharecroppers. At that time, the forcible harvesting of paddy had already become a consistent feature of the agrarian scene despite continuous police and landlord repression. This form of protest was tapped by Sibu Soren and the JMM from 1972 onwards. The JMM movement spread to Santal Parganas, Giridih and Hazaribagh. The years between 1973 and 1975 were the most intense and violent in the struggle carried on in the form of forcible harvesting, the *Dhan kato andolan* ('Recover your paddy'), which involved adivasi peasants as well as other rural poor. These years of unrest in the countryside did not go without a loss of lives when arrows had to compete with the guns of the Central Reserve Police, the landlords and their guards.

In the same period, the early seventies, the independent trade-unionists from the collieries, led by A.K. Roy, engaged in a

---

[32] Tundi: a development block in Dhanbad district, in the Chotanagpur plateau region of South Bihar, comprising 296 villages. Santals constitute nearly 49 per cent of Tundi's population.

struggle against the coal companies in Dhanbad and Hazaribagh on the issue of compensation and rehabilitation of displaced peasants. The years 1973 and 1974, when forcible harvesting gained momentum, were also the peak years of the worker–peasant alliance. During 1974 and 1975, while popular protest was underway and A.K. Roy, Binod Bihari Mahato and other Jharkhandi leaders were in jail, Sibu Soren entered into a compromise with the Congress(I). By then he seems to have become valuable in the eyes of the Congress(I) for maintaining the Party's base in Bihar and containing the rural movement and the worker–peasant alliance. This, however, did not forestall Soren's imprisonment in 1979 under Bihar's Maintenance of Internal Security Act (MISA). A year later, already an MP, Soren joined hands again with the Congress(I).

In 1978, under the Janata government, the demand for a separate Jharkhand state was put forward on a United Front basis. Nine parties and organizations formed the Front's committee: the Jharkhand Party led by N.E. Horo, the MCC led by A.K. Roy, the JMM with Sibu Soren as General Secretary, the CPI(ML), the Birsa Seva Dal, the Jharkhand Muslim Morcha, the Hul Jharkhand, the Revolutionary Socialist Party of India and the Congress(I). Why did the idea of an United Front emerge? It appears that the strength of the adivasi grass-roots movement 'caught the attention of some political parties', although in various ways and for different reasons. According a political activist, 'When the [grass-roots] tribal movement reached its climax in 1974–1975 many parties became interested in gaining influence over it. They needed the tribal leadership.' The combination of political positions and diverging aims doomed the Front to failure. On the part of the Jharkhand Party—according to one of the representatives of the *reformist ethnicist* line—there seems to be a miscomprehension of ideological differences as well as of the modalities of social protest. The Party avoided a dialogue with the other local organizations of the United Front since 'we are going to have problems with the communist friends. They will support the demand for a state, but one should not believe them. It is a trick, tactics…'.

Unrest in Santal Parganas continued well into 1979, marked by violent clashes between peasants and landlords.[33] That was also

[33] H. Dhar (1980a) provides a chronology of events during that year in the district. The incidents ranged from demonstrations against land eviction; CPI(ML)'s demands

the time when two factors contributed to affect the course of the grass-roots movement: a state policy of containment, and the participation of new social elements in the movement. By 1979 it was clear that the mass movement in Jharkhand had become the target of state policies, first of containment and then, of overt repression. The then Chief Minister of Bihar considered the movement as the product of 'anti-social' and 'anti-national' elements that had to be curbed or suppressed. The policy of containment and conciliation was reflected in the appointments as Commissioner, Tribal Welfare Commissioner and Deputy Commissioner of persons (generally from the ruling Janata Party) with a sympathetic attitude towards the rural poor, particularly towards the adivasis and dalits. This policy crystallized in plan proposals and the allocation of resources for economic development which, in fact, only partly reached those who were supposed to benefit from them.

But economic populism was not effective enough. State repression then attempted to attain what populism could not. The Central Reserve Police, the Bihar Military Police and the Bihar Armed Police were given a free hand. They did not act independently but in collusion with moneylenders and landlords in Santal Parganas and with forest contractors in Singhbhum. Indiscriminate arrests of people in the rural areas, the plunder of villages, molestation of peasant women, and killings of protesters became commonplace, transforming parts of Jharkhand into areas under siege. As in former troubled times, adivasi peasants fled their villages to avoid violence. For instance, in March 1980, the combing operations of the Central Reserve Police in the villages around Pakaria (Godda *thana*) resulted in the exodus of more than 15,000 adivasis to the Sundarpahadi hills, where they remained for weeks under starvation conditions (*EPW* 1979a: 650). The common experience of resorting to fleeing and hiding in moments of peril is condensed in the words of an adivasi peasant: 'When they come, we go away.... There is no more to do....' In addition, by 1980 the Bihar government had divided the district of Santal Parganas into five, and Chotanagpur into eight new districts, thereby fragmenting the areas that have traditionally been the strongholds of Jharkhand movements.

---

for a better share for adivasi sharecroppers and minimum wages for the agricultural labourers; 'harvest clashes'; JMM's protests against atrocities committed against adivasis; incidents of rape of Santal and harijan women by policemen and 'andlords; and CPI(ML)'s demands for the implementation of the Act against moneylending.

Originally a peasant organization independent from formal politics, at the close of the seventies the JMM increasingly attracted well-to-do Jharkhandis and elements of the adivasi elite with a political profile that set them close to the *reformist ethnicist* position discussed earlier. At the same time, popular agitation began to be contained in formal politics. The consequences of this, as reported in the press in 1986 and 1987, has been the coming again to pre-eminence of the demand for a separate state to the underplaying of concrete socio-economic issues. By the end of the eighties, the *reformst ethnicist* tendency practically came to dominate the political panorama. Attention was diverted from a combined ethnic–class struggle to focus primarily on the demand for a separate state and calls for cultural revivalism. 'Reformism' in the JMM crystallized on 22 June 1987 in the formation of the All-Jharkhand Students Union (AJSU), officially a front organization of the JMM but in practice independent from it, having as its aim the attainment of a Jharkhand state by the end of 1988.

Two elements come to notice in the development of Jharkhand's grass-roots movement of the seventies: first, the JMM came to lead an already mobilized peasantry; second, an alliance between peasants and workers was temporarily attained. Besides, the ethnic question introduced a further element of complexity at the political level, adding to the major problem of the articulation of the peasants' and the workers' struggles. The question of the posssible alliance of peasants and workers poses a special problem: combining their interests, demands and modes of political struggle, their different 'rhythms (or cycles) of poltical protest' (Post 1979), and making both sensitive to each other's problems. In perspective, and with the added element of ethno–regional differentiation, the success of the grass-roots movement in the seventies was remarkable. Two facts account for this: the composition of the labour force and the efforts that the trade-union leader A.K. Roy made to articulate class and ethnic factors. In the rural areas, the movement's ideal of self-sufficiency at all levels—economic, legal, educational, administrative—favouring cooperation and not competition, the opposition it presented to social sectors like the landlords, and the militancy of its followers, made the project 'subversive' in the eyes of the state. Peasants involved were in fact rejecting subordination and paternalism. Ironically, these were two of the weapons the state used to defuse the movement.

Organic continuity is not a normal part of peasant political action, which is usually localized and limited in time-span according to a world-view centred in the community or the region. The motives that animate rural protest are specific, and are mostly related to the need to have land and to work it for a living, or at least for survival. However, hopes of establishing a more general just order are not absent from the peasants' goals (Devalle and Oberoi 1983). This utopian universality contributed to the 'open' nature of the grass-roots movement. This 'openness' that prevailed until the early eighties, seemed to have derived from a formulation of the Jharkhand question in combined class and ethnic terms.

The development of political processes in Jharkhand appears linked to one of two 'traditions': the agrarian, and the more recent, urban. Although the ethnic element has been and is present in both, these 'traditions' diverge in their nature and aims which reflect their different class contents. It is in the course of the present century that ethnic discourses in Jharkhand start to multiply, accompanying processes of class differentiation and the evolution of the project for an Indian nation–state.

Appendix

CHART 1

Resistance to Colonial Conquest in Jungle Mahals and Dhalbhum Preceding the Bhumij Movement of 1832–33*

Area	Year	Events / Causes
Parganas between Dhalbhum and Barabhum (extending to Panchet, Patkum and Singhbhum)	End of 1769	Reaction against British military operations. Zamindars opposed to taxes. *Chuar* activities Armed encounters
Social unrest		
Dhalhum or Ghatsila	1773–74	Agrarian tensions. Opposition to the British. Jagannath Dhal attempts to regain the title of raja.
	1777	Jagannath Dhal reinstated pays tribute to the British.

Chart 1 (Contd.)

Area	Year	Events / Causes
Social unrest	1795–1800	British revenue system and re-placement of authorities resisted. Dissatisfaction of the *ghatwals* with new police system.
	1800	Loss of lands. Debts. Rebellion of Baijnath Singh, *sardar ghatwal*, in Dampara.
Barabhum estate Well established Bhumij state Social unrest	1798	Problems related to the succession to Raja Raghunath Narain. British intervention. Antecedent of the 1832 Movement.
Patkum estate Well-established state. Persistent Social unrest	1774–75	Opposition to the British. Famines. Tax increases.
	1792–1807	Continuous unrest. British pressures. Resistance to taxes. Problems with the succession of the raja. Opposition to the zamindars allied to the British and to non-adivasi moneylenders. Raja murdered in confrontation with Bhumij leaders. British military repression.
	1832	Dissatisfaction of the *ghatwals* with new police system.
Bagmundi estate	1798–99	Non-adivasi authorities rejected. Opposition to the sale of the estate for revenue arrears. Violence against non-adivasis. Indebted rajas and *mankis* lose their lands.
Koilapal *Jagir* populated only by Bhumijs Social unrest	1783–84	General unrest.
	1798–1810	Internal problems. Activities of Bir Singh followed by 500 *chuars*.

Chart 1 (Contd.)

Area	Year	Events / Causes
Shamsundarpur and Phulkusma Social unrest	1799–1809	Major *chuar* rebellion. Confrontations of the zamindars with the British. Debts. Opposition to moneylenders.
	1832	Dispossessed zamindars ready to revolt.
Raipur Social unrest	1794–1799	Estate sold in arrears. Zamindars instigate unrest. *Chuar* offensive actions.
	end 18th c.– 1809	Agrarian tensions. Fields abandoned. Conflicts with the police. *Dikus* attacked. Zamindar-*sardar* alliance.
	1810	'Bandit' chief Baijnath Singh is sent to prison.
Manbhum Social unrest	1832	Raja related to Ganga Narain supports his claims as raja of Barabhum.
Midnapur	1799	Major *chuar* rebellion against 1793 regulations. Military repression. *Sardars* and *paiks* try to regain their service tenures backed by the population.
Kasipur Bhumij *pargana* in Panchet	1832	Chief Anadlal Singh, in danger of losing his land grant, joins the raja of Panchet.
Ambikanagar	1832–33	Zamindar hostile to British rule. Problems of succession.
Panchet Established estate	1770	Great famine.
	1771	East India Company collects sizeable revenue. Disturbances.
	1774–75	New attempts to increase taxes. Rebellion against British control. Migrants enter the area. The raja, indebted, loses power. Disturbances due to imposition of taxes and non-Bhumij officers.
	1793	Permanent Settlement. Sale of lands to pay taxes.

Chart 1 (Contd.)

Area	Year	Events / Causes
Panchet	1795	Raja indebted. The estate put up for public auction.
Established estate	1797–98	Disturbances. Cultivation abandoned. Sale of lands. Refusal to pay revenue. War against the 'foreigners'.
	1798	Bengalis who had bought land and their employees, killed. Dissatisfied *ghatwals* plan to rebel.
	1799	Lands restored to the raja.
	end 18th c.	*Diku* merchants and adventurers enter the area.

* On the basis of data provided in J.C. Jha (1963).

CHART 2

PROTESTS THAT PRECEDED GANGA NARAIN'S MOVEMENT

Year / Area	Dhalbhum or Ghatshila	Barabhum	Patkum	Jhalda and Panchet	Bagmundi	Koilapal	Shamsundarpur and Phulkusma	Raipur	Manbhum	Midnapur	Kasipur	Ambikanagar
1769	■	■	■	■					■			
1770	■	■	■	■					■			
1771	■	■		■		■						
1772	■	■		■		■						
1773	■			■								
1774	■		■	■								
1775	■		■	■								
1776	■		■									
1777	■											
1778	■											
1779												
1780												
1781				■								
1782				■		■						
1783				■		■						
1784												
1785												
1786												
1787												
1788												
1789				■								
1790				■								
1791												
1792			■									
1793			■		■							
1794			■					■				
1795	■		■					■				
1796	■		■					■				
1797	■		■									
1798	■	■	■			■		■				
1799	■	■	■	■		■	■	■	■	■		
1800	■	■	■	■		■	■	■	■	■		
1801		■						■				
1802		■						■				
1803		■						■				
1804		■						■				
1805		■						■				
1806		■						■				
1807		■						■				
1808		■	■					■				
1809		■						■				
1810	■	■						■				
1811		■				■		■				
1812		■				■		■				
1813		■				■		■				
1814		■				■		■				
1815		■				■		■				
1816		■				■		■				
1817		■				■		■				
1818		■				■		■				
1819		■				■		■				
1820		■				■		■				
1821		■				■			■			
1822		■				■			■			
1823		■				■			■			
1824		■				■			■			
1825		■				■			■			
1826		■				■			■			
1827		■				■			■			
1828		■				■			■			
1829		■				■			■			
1830		■				■			■			
1831	■	■	■	■		■	■	■	■	■	■	■
1832	■	■	■	■		■	■	■	■	■	■	■
1833	■	■	■	■		■	■	■	■	■	■	■

5

Social Imagination and Practice

We are all equal...

An adivasi intellectual

We put red and green on the fields....

A Santal peasant

The discussion on culture, community and supporting traditions that follows seeks to provide elements for the comparison of ethnic discourses in Jharkhand stemming from different class situations and social experiences.

Chotanagpur, the cradle of the *reformist ethnicist* movement, is that region of Jharkhand where the influence of Western education and mission Christianity has been sustained and strong. These two factors have been instrumental in the development of an urban and rural adivasi petty-bourgeoisie. Some of its members, mostly as a consequence of the prestige obtained through education and, in some cases, conversion, came to form an elite attempting to perform the role of 'educators' (in Gramsciam terms) for the rest of their communities of ethnic ascription. In this elite, the Mundas and Oraons—ethnic macrogroups in the region who consider themselves on top of an ethnic ('tribal') hierarchy—are substantially represented and perform a leading role.

The adivasi petty-bourgeoisie has reformulated the basic ideology that shaped the political line initiated in the thirties. The proposals of the Jharkhand Party of recent times are inscribed in this political tradition. Although different sectors of the indigenous petty-bourgeoisie may differ on formal points in their formulation of a Jharkhand project, for analytical purposes and considering the commonalities in their perceptions of social reality, in the resulting political proposals, and the common class situation of those involved, at a collective level their position can be called *reformist ethnicist*. The trajectory followed by the reformist ethnicists is one of political compromise sought through the introduction of reforms within the existing socio-economic and political framework. This path has avoided any substantial questioning of the present system and, in general, a direct confrontation with the state and the ruling classes, except on the question of a separate territory. The reformist ethnicists see as their task 'to make the Government aware of the [adivasis'] problems... so it can solve them'. At the same time they complain about 'too much spoon-feeding'. In addition, the state is perceived in terms of dominance: 'The Government denies us our rights: to have a Jharkhand state that we could organize'. That is to say, a right to a territory and to self-determination. The question of leadership ('organization'), however, remains to be clarified. The adivasi petty-bourgeoisie believes this to be its role, it acts as spokesman for 'all the tribals' and has a leading role in social welfare and cultural groups, associations and projects.

By contrast, the question of the adivasis' rights is understood at the peasant level as a denial over territory and over land as a means of production. What is the reformists' solution to this situation? A Jharkhand Party spokesman argued that: 'Nothing is possible without power. That is why we want a provincial state within the Constitutional framework.' This old demand of vague contents seems to be a magical formula. The unanswered question, whose importance the reformist ethnicists do not seem to consider, is precisely what will be the nature of this state. One of the Jharkhand Party leaders told me matter-of-factly: 'We have to define this state.' This definition has been pending for some 30 years. Substance can be given, however, to the reformist ethnicists' proposal of a Jharkhand state by disclosing the ever present element in their political discourse: the separate state phrased primarily on ethnic (or lately, regional/national) grounds, underplaying basic socio-economic issues. This position has been gaining strength since the eighties, once the adivasi grass-roots movements were contained.[1]

The reformist ethnicist position repeats the old ideological discourse synthesized in the exclusive demand for a separate state, making extrapolations of past socio–economic structures into the present, and interpreting the present through a 'nostalgia of the past'. Those in that position often tend to define themselves through the eyes of others (the tribal construct), always within the limits permitted by the hegemonic sectors. Ultimately and most probably unwillingly, their position has confirmed the state ideology and helped to reproduce the adivasis' dependency. The most recent focus on the 'nationality question', if conceived in wide terms, may provide an opening for the consideration of the Jharkhand situation also in socio–economic terms (see D.N. and G.K. 1989: 1505). The reformist ethnicist discourse, although being the one most widely heard, is not the only one to have been formulated in Jharkhand. Subtle voices, and more than voices, actions, reveal at the grass-roots level different conceptions of the self, of culture and of the Jharkhand community. The grass-roots expressions of the seventies, on which the main data that sustain the following analysis is based, are now considered politically to have been 'a temporary phase'. Nevertheless and importantly, these expressions form part of the long agrarian tradition of protest in Jharkhand. It is most probably this age-long collective lived experience which has been the main element that supported the formulation of Jharkhand identity among the labouring people in the seventies.

Imagining a Community

Jharkhand as an Imagined Community

The reformist ethnicists' conception of a Jharkhand community takes as its starting point an ideological colonial legacy perpetuated by the indigenous intelligentsia: the tribal construct. Government

[1] Of late (1987), reports on recent adivasi political activity seems to indicate a strengthening of the *reformist ethnicist* line, with a strong emphasis on cultural revivalism, as expressed in the position of adivasi students from Ranchi University (*The Week* 1987: 34–40).

and academic advocates of the 'tribe' in India have thus found an unwilling ally in the adivasi elite. This elite has repeated the official 'tribal' discourse, finally legitimating the tribal construct as a social reality. The words 'tribe' and 'tribal' and, more importantly, references to attributes associated with the 'tribals'—'backwardness', 'weakness' and 'ignorance'—were frequently used by members of this social sector during interviews. This perception is reinforced by a feeling of helplessness and dependency verbalized in constant appeals. In the words of an adivasi intellectual: 'If only the Government knew about us, it could help us. The Government would [then] solve our problems.'

There is, however, an awareness that Government paternalism alone will not really solve all of the adivasis' problems. As expressed by a Jharkhand Party spokesman, 'if we, the *tribals*, do not stand with all our strength, politically and socially, we will not be able *to save ourselves*'.

The roots of the adivasi petty-bourgeoisie's ambiguous perception of its 'tribal' identity are easy to detect. The actual culture of this social sector and, particularly, its Christian elements, is a mixture of some old elements detached from its living indigenous social roots, and newer alien elements. This sector's phrasing of its identity according to the 'tribal' model helps to reproduce the ideology of 'tribalism', a mechanism through which the indigenous elites seek a share in power over their own societies by using a pool of common traditions and cultural codes (see Mafeje 1971). The adivasi elite is precisely the most vocal adivasi sector in proclaiming its 'tribal' identity. The 'tribalist' ideology permitted the adivasi elite to enter the political arena and dominate certain fields like that of education, for instance, through the channels provided by the missions, also promoting the tribal construct.[2] The adivasi elite's self-definition as 'tribal' helps push underground the class affiliations, privileges and ambitions of its members, and contributes to present social conflict in Jharkhand only in terms of ethnic confrontations.

The members of the adivasi elite acknowledge that they belong to subordinated ethnic groups and claim solidarity with the lower

---

[2] The Christian Churches' attachment to the tribal construct appears to be related to the conception of missionary activity as being *at the same time* a 'civilizing' mission. This conception translates in the concentration of mission activities in education and in the diffusion of (Western) values and forms of behaviour. A 'civilizing' effort has to have an 'object', which the tribal construct readily provides.

ranges of their own societies *on ethnic grounds*. This is, however, a temporary solidarity—a contingent brotherhood—conditioned by their perception's narrow 'ethnic' angle. This solidarity is used to confront the Indian dominant sectors which are also perceived not in class but in ethnic or regional terms. The contingent brotherhood thus breaks down when the class interests of the elite take precedence or when a class consciousness develops among the subaltern sectors of the dominated ethnic groups. This is precisely what happened when the grass-roots movement gained strength in the seventies. The words of the Jharkhand Party leader are illustrative: 'The Mukti Morcha people continued with the [forest] protest and stopped our discussions with the Government. We suffered due to these "friends". Due to them our movement is discredited and suspected by tribals and non-tribals' (1980). On the other hand, the fragility of the reformists' Jharkhand brotherhood was clearly understood by JMM activists: 'The Jharkhand state is conceived as a broad alliance of all the classes in the region. In Lalkhand [Jharkhand's socialist version] this alliance will be impossible' (1980).

Of late, the Jharkhand Co-ordination Committee (JCC) has phrased the issue of ethnic oppression in terms of the opposition nationalities-'mainstream' (D.N. 1988: 1985–87; JCC 1987: 32–34). The JCC's *Draft Declaration* takes care to underline that 'the question of nationality is not linked with caste-system or race' but with 'the development of a composite nationality' (JCC *ibid.*: 34), and takes into account economic and human rights issues. Despite the JCC's words against economic exploitation, it is still to be seen in which way ethnic and class dimensions will be linked and expressed at the practical level of socio–political struggle.

The adivasi petty-bourgeoisie, particularly in the Chotanagpur area, presents two non-integrated levels of social consciousness. First, they are aware that they belong to subordinated ethnic groups and present a muted resistance to subordination. Second, as a transitional class without a defined class consciousness, they act as a dominant sector *vis à vis* the lower sectors of their own ethnic groups. These non-integrated levels of social consciousness produce serious conflicts of identity and an unclear formulation of a social project. In not acknowledging the class character of exploitation and its links with ethnic differentiation, the adivasi petty-bourgeoisie has tended to accommodate itself to the expectations of the ruling classes:

thereby its constant insistence on 'a dialogue with the Government' and on not openly contesting the state.

A song composed in the seventies by an urban adivasi intellectual in the hope that 'one day it may become Jharkhand's anthem', illustrates the extension of the reformist ethnicists' imagined Jharkhand community. Unity and consensus are the dominant themes. Some of the song's lines read:

> *They speak the same language...*
> *in a united Jharkhand...*
> *Hindus and Muslims*
> *Adi dharmi[3] and Christians,*
> *Sikhs, Jains and those of other faiths,*
> *they all can live here*
> *in a united Jharkhand...*
> *Mundas, Oraons, Santals,*
> *let them go forward together.*
> *Kharias, Hos, Paharias,*
> *together with the Sadans*
> *in a united Jharkhand...*
> *All are pained in one pain.*
> *All are happy in one happiness.*
> *For us only one destiny is written by the Ordainer*
> *in a united Jharkhand...*
> (From the author's manuscript in
> Nagpuri, following his oral translation).

In this text, nobody is excluded from the Jharkhand community on the basis of language, religion or ethnic ascription. The scope of the Jharkhand community described in the song seems to respond to the political need to surpass a narrow 'tribal' conception of the proposed state by including the Sadans. The Sadans are 'the old *dikus*', Jharkhandis that have not been catalogued as Scheduled Tribes and who immigrated into the region in early times. As a young adivasi intellectual explained to me, 'the old-established friendly *diku* can stay... ', adding, in what seemed a practical compromise, 'we must have the *dikus* [in Jharkhand] since they have money and could corrupt the leaders'.

---

[3] *Adi dharmi*: 'those whose *dharma* is the orignal one', the adivasis who follow their own religion.

The broader scope of the proposed community also appears to have responded to a situation in which other political movements had come to dispute the reformist ethnicists' monopoly over the Jharkhand project. The song dates from the mid-seventies, precisely when the JMM movement based on the peasant–worker alliance was gaining strength. We note, however, that social differences that may shatter the ideal Jharkhandi unity are not mentioned in the song–anthem. Therefore, the sharp contrast between the reformist ethnicists' and the grass-roots' conception of Jharkhand remained unchanged.

The reformist ethnicists' statements in interviews regarding the scope of the Jharkhand state are often contradictory. In one breath, a spokesman of the Jharkhand Party said:

> The idea of a separate state must be implemented for the *Jharkhandis*, *tribals and non-tribals*. This population forms *a nationality*. Our opponents—the landlords, the contractors—say accusing us: 'This demand is a tribal demand. With a separate state all the outsiders will be thrown out.' This is not true…On the question of a separate state *all the tribes* are united. *The tribals want to be a polity*….

Jharkhand's imagined community stretches and contracts, within limits, in the reformists' minds: it shifts from 'the tribals' to 'all Jharkhandis'. What moulds their conception of a Jharkhand community? The major formative element appears to be the tribal construct. By accepting this construct the adivasi petty-bourgeoisie unwillingly accepts the racist derogatory stereotypes and the attributes of weakness and backwardness it implies as a basis to formulate its identity. The results are serious contradictions in this social sector's self-perception.

'Mundas sing to remember themselves who they are,' an adivasi intellectual explained to me. 'Social' tunes, however, differ according to the voices that utter them and those who listen to them. By no stretch of the imagination are those who sing in the fields while working 'remembering themselves' in the same way as the family of an adivasi professional that, being Christmas time, sang gospel songs in English, to the accompaniment of a tape-recorded guitar, under the shade of a plastic Christmas tree. This last instance illustrates the degree of deculturation of the adivasi petty-bourgeoisie.

Even a superficial situational comparison provides a picture of the enormous class and cultural gaps existing in this social sector's imagined Jharkhand brotherhood: the human voice in chorus *versus* a tape-recorder; music for work *versus* music for leisure; the fields *versus* the living-room; nature *versus* the consumer's market tree.

At the level of self-definition, this example shows the different ways identity is expressed by different social sectors. Those singing 'work songs' provide a succinct self-explanatory statement about who they are. The professional's family felt instead the need to verbalize its identity, as if they had to justify their behaviour. When asked about dancing, for instance, the answer was: 'We are born knowing how to dance. Music is in our blood. My wife knows the dances...but she does not dance in public! We know the things of the past. We keep them.' At that point of the conversation, an assorted lot of broken ornaments and the remains of an arrow wrapped in a bundle were taken out of a trunk. Although this example comes from a Christian family, the situation it describes refers generally to the adivasi petty-bourgeoisie's self-perception and attitudes. These attitudes have to do more with the ambiguous class situation of the petty-bourgeoisie and its identity than with religious ascription.

The weight of the tribal construct on the reformist ethnicists' formulation of Jharkhand also bears on their self-perception. Consequently, they catalogue their own societies according to the superiority–inferiority paradigm the Indian hegemonic sectors employ in their classifications. This was evident at a meeting of members of the adivasi petty-bourgeoisie in Ranchi (all of them Mundas), discussing the formation of a cultural society.[4] The initial defensive attitude of those present towards me broke when it was finally acknowledged that I (a yet uncatalogued being) belonged to 'this Ote Disum' (this world). I was somehow 'catalogued' in a satisfactory manner. The following dialogue ensued: 'We are all tribals,' a school teacher explained. 'However, the primitive tribes [the Bir Hors and Asurs] are more backward than the tribes themselves.' At that point, a young man asked me: 'Where you come from, are there tribes like us? Are there primitive tribes?' I

---

[4] There were a dozen people present, including professionals, a clerk, a petty-zamindar, the landed *pahan* (religious leader) from nearby Hatia, a retired army man, and a retired Christian priest. The age of the participants varied from 22 to 70 years. The discussion was conducted in Mundari, sometimes shifting to English.

tried to explain that our 'cataloguing system' is somewhat different, that there is no such thing as a 'primitive'. Disconcerted looks. Another person inquired: 'Do they speak many languages? How do they preserve them?' And yet another: 'What do they work in? Do they use the bow and arrow? What do they hunt?' I explained that Mexico's indigenous people are mostly peasants, and re-frained from saying that, if they possess weapons, they would probably be some old firearms, not necessarily used for hunting but for protection.

The issues raised at this gathering, similarly expressed on other occasions, show that the adivasi petty-bourgeoisie tends to see the 'tribal community' in terms of the official evolutionary continuum. In this continuum, the Munda elite consider their group more advanced and other ethnic groups 'backward' and 'more back-ward'. The questions on the characteristics of other indigenous groups referred only to ethnic markers (language; material cul-ture) and to stereotyped images of the unchanging 'tribal' (the bow-and-arrow hunter). There were no questions on the situation of the indigenous peasantry they were asking me about. On the other hand, the audience was rather surprised at the absence of 'primitives' (of a cataloguing continuum) in my part of the world.

To speak of a complete internalization of an imposed dero-gatory image among the decultured members of the petty-bourgeoisie when they conceptualize their collective identity is erroneous. They are aware that ruling-class control is exerted over the adi-vasis *as ethnic groups* through cultural hegemony. This is reflected in the constant preoccupation with the preservation of their langu-ages, the need to prepare school text-books and to find the best teaching methods (issues discussed at the above-mentioned meeting). However, these activities are thought to end up being conditioned to the Government willingness to fund them.

Image of power and subordination are constantly evoked, princi-pally through the stereotype of the 'inferior' and 'dependent' adivasi, showing the pervasiveness of cultural hegemony over the adivasis as ethnic groups. However, stereotypes are never blindly accepted by those on which they are imposed. In fact, there seems to be a 'make-believe' game going on. The rejection of the derogatory image by the adivasi elite is never explicit. On the contrary, what is explicit is their assertion that adivasis are indeed 'backward' (thus inferior, primitive, ignorant). There is, nevertheless, a muted protest, mostly individually expressed, accompanied by a feeling of impotence that is translated in perceiving the efforts to eliminate the stereotypes as a waste of time (refer to Chapter 6).

'Tribes': India and the West

The term 'cultural colonialism' has been applied to the acceptance of exogenous cultural elements and values in situations of subordination, a mechanism through which the 'centre' expands its hegemony over the 'periphery'. In Jharkhand, especially in the urban areas, the members of the adivasi elite function as bearers of exogenous cultural values. Their influence, however, is relative since their audience is restricted by class barriers. They appeal to the same class sector to which they themselves belong, attempting in the process to extend their influence to the rural areas through development and educational programs.

On the one hand, the members of the adivasi elite feel proud of their Western education and values; on the other, they earnestly pursue cultural revivalism. This contradiction is reflected in the case of a young non-Christian reformist ethnicist leader, urban-based, educated and with long periods of residence abroad, who remarked: 'The educational system takes you gradually out of the village. Suddenly, you are out of it. To belong to the village one must be in it. How can we preserve our culture otherwise?' Jaipal Singh was possibly the best example of this contradiction.

The younger elements of the adivasi petty-bourgeoisie are educated within the assumptions of both the tribal construct and Western values. Somehow, these two diverse paradigms—Western and 'tribal'—do not clash, possibly because they are compartmentalized. Their self-definition, however, seems to continue to be locked within the tribal paradigm. How does this paradigm relate to the Hindu and the Western paradigms? A leading non-Christian adivasi intellectual defined 'the tribals' in this way:

The tribals feel *they belong to India*. We consider ourselves *equal to the Hindus*. We don't have any caste. *We are all equal*...Tribal society is becoming *similar to the highest stratum of Hindu society* in education, marriage patterns, even in dress. The tribes are *more universal* because of their free and fearless outlook; they are *closer to the West. Westernization* tends to level up people. *Christianization* has led to a loss of identity. Christianism regiments society all over the world. By converting to it, the adivasis come to resemble the Hindus: their emotions are not expressed in normal life....

Endogenous values—equality, freedom, strength—are praised in this and other similar statements. A Christian adivasi leader highlighted five major qualities of 'tribal life': 'equality, dignity of labour, common ownership of the means of production, dancing and singing to make life livable, and efforts towards community welfare'. These traits are included in the Rousseauian stereotype held by some defenders of 'the tribes'. In the words of a European priest established in Chotanagpur, 'tribal society' is 'egalitarian, based on consensus, (formed by) good, simple and honest people'. However, he felt the need to add, 'tribals are not children, they are free men'.

Coming back to the first statement, emphasis is laid on the equal standing of the adivasis and the higher Hindu castes, despite the caste system being rejected. Even more, 'the tribes' are described as universal, all-embracing...'like the West'. We encounter here still another construct, a product of a colonized perception of the world: the universal West, source of equality. Christianity is not seen as part of the Western heritage but as an autonomous power-ful ordering system, as restrictive as the caste system. The counterpart of the West is India, the actual starting point for comparisons. India is straightforwardly equated with the caste system, Hinduism and inequality. Therefore, the point of reference is Hindu India. Had this interview taken place today, it would have shown an awareness of the rising Hindu fundamentalism evident in India in the eighties (Devalle 1985b).

Contrary to what the 'emulation' and 'Hinduization' theorists maintain, the adivasi intellectuals perceive Hinduism and Hindui-zation as the greatest threat their societies face. Hinduism has been present amongst them for a long time, possibly making the adivasis more sensitive to the present Hindu attempted all-India hegemonism. There was genuine alarm in the words of a Jharkhand Party leader when he said:

The majority of the tribes are very Hinduized. The Bhumijs are totally Hinduized and have associated themselves with the Hindus. Those in the Government belong to Hindu society, so the Bhumijs want to be related to the ruling classes. I have said to them: 'You have become Hindu! You have lost your identity!' I tell those tribals who are not Christians: 'You are now free, but if you become Hinduized you lose your status and *you become slaves in a society that has already made millions of slaves*....

The rejection of caste, a very volatile political issue in caste-ridden Bihar, is one of the clearest statements in the adivasi elite's definition of its identity: Rev. N. Mintz (Oraon), has probably been the most virulent adivasi denouncer of casteism in the Chotanagpur region:

The 'cowdung culture area' of the north has systematically penetrated into the fertile central tribal belt with all its anti-social and anti-human activities. The tribals were exploited socially and economically in the past. But the present exploitation is of the mind and the heart of the tribal communities in the central tribal belt. The expansion of schools and colleges, even universities, as bearers of corrupt ideas and attitudes are a means of intellectual exploitation by the people of the 'cowdung culture area' of the tribes of this region.... (Mintz 1979).

We observe here an understanding of Hindu cultural hegemony. However, by concentrating on the caste issue as solely a cultural problem, attention is diverted from the existing class relations expressed in caste terms, since these are considered a phenomenon of the past. Yet, at a meeting dominated by 'tribal administrators' (some of them adivasis), it was enough for Rev. Mintz to raise the issue of caste and of the exploitation of the adivasis, for him to be vehemently accused by several of those present of... denouncing casteism in Bihar! He was asked 'to leave politics aside', and the audience was exhorted: 'Let us forget the moneylenders, exploitation, missionaries, politicians, and let us do something together. This Ranchi will show the path'. The participants in the meeting found comfort in nationalistic outbursts that piously camouflaged the realities of inter-ethnic and class conflicts.

Christianity: a 'Replacement Community'

Another construct of community enters the picture among the converted members of the adivasi petty-bourgeoisie: that of Christendom. It does not form part of the Christian reformist ethnicists' political discourse. For the formulation of their identity, on the other hand, it tends to remain a supportive base, as a 'replacement community'. To be Christian is to acquire a parallel identity by adhering to what is considered to be a prestigious community. Usually, this prestige and a certain social mobility come via education at the missions, processes that began in the middle of the nineteenth century.[5]

Why is Christendom considered a 'replacement community'? It offers a solution to the uncertain identity of the members of the adivasi petty-bourgeoisie. On the one hand, its members distance themselves from the ethnic style of their rural communities of origin by their class situation. On the other hand, they do not fully belong to the Indian 'middle classes' with which they wish to identify. since they are still catalogued in ethnic/racial terms and perceived as 'different', no matter how deculturated they may be. Christianity has provided the converts with a corporate feeling. They believe they belong to a powerful world organization that will lead them to 'progress' and thus, out of the derogatory stereotype. The effects of imagining themselves part of this super-community can be particularly observed in the economic sphere.

Conversion to Christianity has introduced a divisive element among the adivasis. The dissimilarities among the converts of different denominations are constantly stressed. For instance, a Lutheran Munda considered that: 'The Catholic Church is a world organization, a feudal system in which the people do what the pastor says. Protestants are free; they discuss; they have a taste of democracy; they depend on themselves'. Accusations came back from a Kharia Catholic priest: 'The Catholic Church is better organized.

---

[5] Conversions started among the lower and landed (*khuntkattidar*) sectors of adivasi society. The spread of Western education through mission schools and capitalist penetration in the countryside resulted in the development of a rural indigenous petty-bourgeoisie, some of whose elements moved to the urban centres to become part of the social sector ambiguously called 'middle classes' in India (teachers, clerks, technicians, public servants). Conversions also led to the creation of an indigenous clergy.

It is not so divided because it is hierarchical. The Lutherans are too democratic'. Ethnic boundaries seem to have been reinforced inside the converts' community. The Lutherans, for instance, have two religious heads, one Munda and the other Oraon, each addressing his own ethnic community.

From the elite's Christian members' point of view, what results has conversion brought to the adivasis? According to a Christian adivasi political leader: 'Christianism has maintained the tribes' identity. It *solved the tribal problem in India* by giving them a place of honour in the country, in society. This should be contrasted with what Hinduization has done to the tribals.' All the elements pointed out earlier are present in this statement. The elite's Christian adivasis seem to have solved *their* 'tribal problem'. Their Christianity has a dual aim. First, to stop Hinduization since deep down it is identified with *diku* dominance. Second, to acquire a powerful ally:

> It is said that the tribes that go to Christianity are not tribes any more, that they are part of Hindu society. We say, no! After Independence there has been a belief all over India that the tribals are being Christianized for political reasons, that if they convert in great numbers they will be a political threat in the future since *the other Christian countries of the world may intervene* [to back them]. *The Hindu dominator wanted to convert all tribals to Hinduism.* They started schools in Bihar to educate adivasis who would then have a good position as part of Hindu society and act *against* the Christian sector....(*ibid.*)

In this vein, a European missionary flatly stated during an interview: 'Christians in Ranchi District are a political force and the Government cannot afford to antagonize them.'

With reference to the Jharkhand question, interviewed non-adivasis considered that the Lutherans are usually associated with politics, while the Catholics are perceived as 'not interested in Jharkhand'. This seems to be the case in formal politics. In the words of a Lutheran political leader: 'Among politicians, the majority are Protestants. They are prepared to take risks.'

Christendom as conceived by the converted members of the adivasi petty-bourgeoisie, represents another instance of an imagined community in B. Anderson's (1983) terms.[6] As in the Jharkhandi brotherhood of the reformists' political formulation, inequalities among its members are not acknowledged, while differences with those outside the fold are. Thus, an adivasi Catholic priest, referring to bonded labour in Palamau, said: 'The unconverted toiling masses suffer in bondage because of their ignorance.' In this context, ignorance is seen as the cause of exploitation and contrasted to education at the mission schools. The community of the Christians do not acknowledge the roots of social inequality. However, the converted adivasis, acting as a body, have in fact helped to enhance class differences through the selective implementation of development projects.

The Community of Labouring People

The formulation of Jharkhand as Lalkhand ('Red land'), a community of labouring people, guided the JMM in the seventies while it responded to its grass-roots base. The comments that follow refer to the JMM as it then was and not after it underwent the changes alluded to in the preceding chapter.

Jharkhand was initially defined in the JMM's program on the basis that: 'A Jharkhandi is a producer, irrespective of caste, tribe or religion, within the boundaries of Jharkhand' (*cit.* in Iyer and Maharaj 1977: fn. 160). The role played by the social actors in Jharkhand's economic system determined Jharkhandi identity. The regional location provided the context, the *locus* where this community was to develop. It is to be noted that the definition expressed an anti-casteist and non-xenophobic stance, and that it did not follow the usual 'tribal–non-tribal' model adopted in the past by the various reformist ethnicist movements. The early JMM attempted to be a regional class-based and not an ethnic-based movement. The new conception of Jharkhand came to question the ideal of the harmonic brotherhood which the reformist ethnicists espoused. Devendra

[6] The parallel conceptions of 'tribal' and Christian communities are used also by the missionaries to explain the meaning of conversion. For instance: 'Adivasi Catholics do not want to be second-rate; they know the teaching of the church, which completes their ancestral conception of universal brotherhood; they know that her very name implies a need to go to all the nations' (van Exem 1975: 70).

Manjhi (MLA) stated bluntly the aims of the Jharkhand project, still current in 1980: 'We want a Jharkhand free of exploitation, a Jharkhand where those who work will eat, while those who loot will go' (election manifesto for the Lok Sabha). In a similar way, Sibu Soren stated that the Santals were taking back lands and crops that were in the hands of the moneylenders 'not because these are outsiders' but because they were engaged in usury, and that 'those who work the land themselves have a right to keep it'.

If the reformist ethnicist construct of a Jharkhand community is based on the ideal of non-conflictive co-existence of all classes in Jharkhand, the grass-roots movement built up its conception of community by acknowledging the existing contradictions as expressed in class, ethnic and regional antagonisms. For those involved in the movement, being a Jharkhandi came to mean not just 'a way of life' but a 'way of conflict'. Thus, in the already quoted statement of a political activist: 'The Jharkhand state is conceived as a broad alliance of all classes in the region. In Lalkhand this alliance will be impossible.'

The conception of community and collective identity in this case was constructed on the basis of concrete experiences of workers and peasants in and around the Santal belt, with reference not to a narrow perception of the ethnic but taking as referent the regional socio–economic context. In fact, the socio–economic referents came to acquire primacy over the particular ethnic ones, in turn rephrased in regional terms. Jharkhand, defined with social, economic and cultural contents, became more than a mere geographical conception.

The community of labouring people was not just an idea. In the seventies it crystallized in the worker–peasant alliance and joint political actions. This translated, for instance, into the active support given by adivasi peasants to the workers from Bera's colliery (1974) and to those from the Khaskuian and Sijua collieries who opposed the management's 'pressure groups' (1975), by joining the demonstrations of Sindri's retrenched factory workers, and by backing the demands of the railway workers from Gomoh (1975). The workers also made common cause with the peasants in the peak years of the movement between 1973 and 1975 by, for instance, joining in the forcible harvesting operations.

The nature and contents of the community of labouring people was forged in practice. The new leaders put into words a non-verbal discourse that had been already spelt out at harvest time, around the planting of teak, and in the repeated confrontations of workers with the industries' 'pressure groups' (usually called *goondas* or *lathaits*). Signals showing the path ahead were already present when in the early seventies trade-union leader A.K. Roy engaged in a struggle against the coal companies in Dhanbad and Hazaribagh on the issue of the compensation and rehabilitation of peasants displaced by industrial development.

A.K. Roy appeared to be the key leader in explicitly formulating the new community and a new tactics for joint political action which would embrace the miners and the peasantry of the area. From the start, the idea of an alliance to carry forward political struggle was conceived as one between labouring people and not as one limited to any specific community or ethnic cluster. The ethnic question was, nevertheless, considered. A political activist explained in 1980:

At the beginning Roy did not feel [the need to consider] it [the ethnic question] ideologically. Afterwards, he entered into a close relationship with the tribal leaders, especially with Sibu Soren and Binod Bihari Mahato.... Then came the peasant–worker alliance when the tribal movement reached its peak and the question of a separate state emerged. Roy had ambiguous feelings. He thought of Lalkhand. Could it be possible in the tribal areas?....

The linking of the peasants' and workers' political actions was formalized in late 1972. The composition of this new coalition (adivasi peasantry, non-adivasi peasantry, miners) was reflected in its triple leadership. In organizational political terms it meant an alliance of the JMM with the MCC. The new conception of Jharkhand was put into practice by both the JMM and the MCC combined. However, it was perceived by the Jharkhand Party and by the new *ethnicists* in the JMM as only the making of A.K. Roy and the MCC.

By a combination of circumstances, I arranged a meeting with A.K. Roy at the end of 1980. We began to talk about other peasants and workers, about Latin America, what was being done and what could be done there. Then I heard about the formation of the worker–peasant alliance in Dhanbad, the difficulties of this task, the oppressed nationalities question, and the linkage of the class and ethnic questions. In his words:

> Jharkhand cannot just be separated. It should be liberated [since] it is the home of a majority of downtrodden people and oppressed nationalities. They are socially and economically exploited and are set in an area that in its turn is exploited as an internal colony....
>
> Casteism has turned into open racism. Take the case of Gua. Repression there could proceed with impunity because it was launched against a tribal agitation. Or think about the atrocities committed against harijans[7].... The present system injects communalism at every level....
>
> In Dhanbad the non-tribal workers were mobilized in support of the tribals. The working class first acquired a consciousness of itself as a class, regardless of ethnic differences and avoiding communalism. A bond was built between the workers and the rural poor, who are the vast majority in Jharkhand. Then the workers came in support of the oppressed nationalities in their process of emancipation....
>
> The struggles of the working class cannot succeed unless they take into account the aspirations of the oppressed nationalities, the tribals, the dalits, the socially downtrodden....

The nature of the grass-roots Jharkhand project emerged in sharp contrast to the reformist ethnicists' proposal. In Roy's vision, this project formed part of a wider conception, beyond Jharkhand's geographical boundaries. He talked about the need to develop the concept of 'Indianism', in which the emphasis was to be put on both class issues and on the situation of the many 'nationalities and subnationalities of India'. In this way, 'Indianism' appears as an alternative to the state-ist conception of the nation in India,

---

[7] In one of his published articles, A.K. Roy compared the situation of internal colonialism in India with the South African case, a point that the left criticized. He wrote:

> Here belated capitalism, social unevenness and regional disparity combined together have created a phenomenon of internal colonialism in the pattern of South Africa or pre-liberated Rhodesia... In South Africa, the rulers and the ruled are separated by colour, in India by physical work though colour prejudice is also there in social life (A.K. Roy 1983: 7).

where state and nation have been conflated into one single over-powering entity.

Contrary to the criticism made by some observers (Chakraborty 1982), neither Roy nor the MCC working together with the JMM ignored the class character of exploitation in Jharkhand. In fact, the conception of Jharkhand as Lalkhand tended to emphasize the class factor. The ethnic factor was often defined in the course of interviews with MCC political activists as a strategical element: 'The question of tribal identity is more important in strategical terms (mobilization, solidarity) than class'; 'It is said that tribals follow a leader and die for him. This happens not just because of the leader's charisma, but due to the strong unity of the community. This is what makes them act together'; 'The tribals are determined to struggle to the end, together'.

In other interviews the situation in Jharkhand was approached in more holistic terms, avoiding the 'class only' path that has usually taken the left to failure in rural areas: 'The tribal and the class questions coincide [in Jharkhand]. The struggle in this case is one that does not accept any compromise.' The Government, on the other hand, judging by its response to the movement (cooptation, repression), paid keen attention to the combined class/ethnic struggle, visualizing it as dangerous.

If we compare the conception of the community of labouring people to the reformist ethnicist conception of Jharkhand, we see that the terms used to define the first of these were reversed and enlarged. In the conception of Jharkhand as a community of labouring people, the old demand for a separate state lingered in the background and, until the later changes operated in the JMM as a *formal* political organization, it remained there. On the other hand, Jaipal Singh and those who came after him were and are still struggling primarily for a territory. In their project, the bulk of the Jharkhandis are absent as social agents. The grass-roots Jharkhand movement, on the other hand, was aimed at a *political* Jharkhand by means of mass struggles for concrete economic and social ends. The labouring people of Jharkhand seemed unwilling to wait until the separate state became a reality, especially as this has proved to be a utopia hard to attain. That is why in the early JMM and the MCC view, and particularly in that of the latter, Lalkhand, meaning the economic and social transformation of the peasants' and workers' situation, came first. The aim was 'a liberated Jharkhand', not merely 'a separate Jharkhand'. Sibu Soren himself used to be unconcerned about the moment of the separate state's birth: 'I do not care if I do not live to see [a] Jharkhand [state]. I care much more about us as human beings'.

Building up Lalkhand fused two struggles: the one against class exploitation and the other against 'national' oppression. At the concrete level, the situation of the majority of the Jharkhandis—particularly of the adivasis—matches the political combination. An awareness of the double-facedness of the phenomenon was certainly already there in the seventies. Otherwise it is not possible to explain the following and success of the movement in that period. 'They call us *junglee*,' a Santal peasant told me defiantly, 'and take away what is ours: the land. I may be a black Santal, but I well know [which one is] my piece of land.' Identity consciousness is present, the narrow and prejudiced 'tribal' definition is questioned ('black' but not gullible), and an ethnic cum socio–economic profile comes to the foreground. Thus, oppression is experienced in a comprehensive way: as being an object of racism, as belonging to a subordinate ethnic group and as being a dispossessed peasant.

Jharkhand's community of labouring people became endangered by the early eighties not by ethnic divisiveness but by the increasing institutionalization of the JMM, the effects of state policies of containment and repression, and a change in the ideological correlations emerging from class differences present in the movement's new social composition. All these factors seriously undermined the unity achieved among Jharkhand's labouring people. This change in the JMM was symbolized in the demands made by its newly included reformist elements in 1980 that 'the green flag cannot go with the red flag' (Dhar 1980b: 1299), the first being that of the JMM, the second that of the MCC, both together symbolizing the worker–peasant alliance. During the 1986 Jharkhand Divas annual celebration, in which the reformist ethnicists were conspicuously vocal, the green flag flew alone (*India Today* 1986a: 3). Meanwhile, Lalkhand remains as a community for peasants and workers to shape. Judging by the past history of Jharkhand, the green and red flags may yet fly again over the harvested fields.

The bonds among those constructing the community of labouring people were not only 'acted out'—as in the peasants' and workers' political actions of mutual support of the seventies—but also 'felt'.

To the question of what peasants and workers have in common, usual responses were: 'What happens there [factory, collieries] is not different to what happens here [rural areas]. We are always working for somebody else and getting little...'; 'He may work there [industry] but comes from my village... [Therefore] we know him...'; 'The landlord and the mine-owner are the same. We [who work] are the same...'. Jharkhand peasants have frequently had the experience of wage labour in non-agricultural work, usually temporary and not conducive to their transformation into a true industrial labour force. Given their mobile location in the forces of production, peasants and workers are aware of their mutual grievances. As it happened in the mid-seventies, this awareness can be politically mobilized.

Class oppression is not perceived by the peasants and workers of Jharkhand in the abstract, as a product of a well-articulated system of modes of production in the countryside, or as derived from industrial capitalism in the coal-mines or the industrial complexes. Peasants concretely experience the loss of their land, the pillage of the products of their labour, the consequent deprivation and hunger, and the terror of the landlords' paramilitary groups. Workers have had to face the inhuman time–work–discipline for the sake of increased production, ruthless retrenchment from jobs, the lack of labour protection and rights, and maiming and death at the hands of the management's muscle-men (see A. Sinha 1982a: 111–34). These circumstances are reflected in the succinct statement of an adivasi peasant with wage labour experience in the industrial setting: 'After working all day at the mercy of somebody else, we find our stomachs empty.' Whether the reference was to agricultural or industrial work, it did not seem to matter much in terms of results and the situation of helpless subordination. At the base, in Jharkhand the interests and demands of peasants and workers coincide regarding fundamental needs and rights. Their life experiences provide the grounds for a common dialogue.

Oppression, exploitation, ill-treatment and violent death is something that both peasants and workers understand. Underdeveloped capitalism has not succeeded in setting up barriers to separate the social sectors into rigid class categories. The worker–peasant alliance materialized largely due to the composition of the working force in the collieries, made up of people of rural origins who maintained strong links with the agrarian context. Furthermore, a considerable number of these workers were of adivasi peasant origin or belonged to the Scheduled Castes, a fact that facilitated the understanding of the combined nature of class/ethnic oppression. 'The miners in the lowest ranges are harijans and tribals,' explained a political activist. 'In this area, almost all the harijans are of tribal origin, like the Bauris. Detribalization here is relatively recent. In a way, they are one and the same people.'

At the same time, a problem arises in the Jharkhand context with the working force in the industrial organized sector which has come from outside the region and was hired under different labour conditions. Holding more than 50 per cent of the industrial jobs, they have gradually acquired the status of a labour aristocracy. Paradoxically, their situation is at the same time privileged and uncomfortable, for they hold prized jobs but are simultaneously despised for being outsiders by the Jharkhandis. This is indicated by the derogatory term *Bhojpuri*—often applied to the muscle-men—used to denote people who will not side with the interests of the Jharkhandis, and who lack sensitivity towards their problems. One may compare the new derogatory term *Bhojpuri* with the old one *diku*. Common to both is the alien nature of the subjects thus named. However, while *diku* makes sense only in relation to the 'tribal–non-tribal' dichotomy, *Bhojpuri* belongs to the realm of class, despite its 'regional' connotation.

In this situation, the new labouring community was confronted with two different political problems. In the case of Jharkhandi peasants and workers the issue was to present a joint platform and to surmount the immigrant workers' segmentation along ethnic or regional lines. This task was made rather difficult by the interpretation of the Jharkhand situation in the media as an issue between 'immigrants and locals'. In interviews with political activists, it was stated:

> The worker–peasant alliance was not so successful in places like Ranchi or Jamshedpur where many of the workers are outsiders [because] there the contradictions between skilled and unskilled workers are used by the management to divide them. The union of all the workers is absent in these places [Ranchi, Jamshedpur].

On the other hand: 'It was different in Dhanbad. Roy could even unite the workers that came from outside against the moneylenders, who equally exploited the workers coming from Bihar and West Bengal.' Furthermore, in a complex situation where class and ethnic identities so interplay, Roy's success was viewed by political activists as 'particularly important considering the background of failures of the tribal leadership that take into account only tribal unity, and that of the leftist leadership that only considers class'.

The situation, however, changed considerably after the BCKU became a recognized union and tended to concentrate on the workers' problems. The former combined ethnic–class, peasant–worker grass-roots project seemed to have been relegated for the moment to be a chapter in the social history of Jharkhand's labouring people. In this social history, the definition of who is a Jharkhandi ('a producer....[in] Jharkhand') stands as a political formulation. Interpreting this formulation, Nirmal Sengupta defined the implicit self-perception of the labouring people in the region by considering them to be 'the destitutes of Jharkhand' (1982a).

Culture at the Cross-Roads

The Conception of Culture and Efforts at Cultural Development Among the Adivasi Elite

The reformist ethnicists devote a great deal of their efforts to the promotion of cultural revivalism. What does this revivalism imply? To be revived, a culture has to be dead or dying. A culture dies only when those who live it die, is destroyed by external forces (ethnocide), or when the culture's links with the material conditions of existence are severed. The last seems to be the case of the adivasi petty-bourgeoisie whose constituents have experienced changes in their class character and passed through a consistent process of deculturation.

Cultural revivalism takes as its point of reference a culture that has been fixed at an idealist plane. This is the field from which the reformist ethnicists take the material for the invented traditions that help them to forge their identity, legitimize their leading role and back their struggle for political power. Cultural revivalism is an effort at social engineering when searching for legitimation.

The adivasi elite's efforts in this respect are immense given that they partly live within borrowed cultural frames stemming from Western education and, in many cases, from mission Christianity models.[8] They are, however, sincerely concerned with preserving the culture of their communities. This culture is nevertheless conceived as an idealized ('traditional') one. The transitional class nature of the adivasi petty-bourgeoisie may be made accountable for this sector's extreme susceptibility to the influence of dominant ideologies. Education, the means to acquire prestige, respect and authority, has become the channel for the socialization of the members of this social sector into (dominant) extraneous values. The culture they live has been moulded by these values.

The following statement, given in the course of an interview with a Jharkhand Party leader, illustrates the adivasi elite's conception of culture and resulting cultural distortion:

I organized a cultural society for the Mundas with young artists.... Through this organisation I wanted to say that all this culture can and should be *preserved*, also in an urban setting. In this new setting we try *to present it to a new audience*. In the *akhra* one dances to *enjoy, not to perform*. Therefore, for the dances [in a performance] I thought of a uniform [trousers for the boys and saris with blouses for the girls] *so they will not be ashamed*. Otherwise, they would be *naked*....

For the creators of these dances, adivasi peasants, dance is never a performance but a collective activity in which men and women, young and old, participate, only acknowledging the authority of the *pahan* and the elders. This point was firmly stressed by adivasis in the countryside: 'We dance for ourselves. Nobody can ask us to dance for them and then sit and watch us.' The dancers *are not* naked. Educated adivasis, particularly the converts, have acquired Western puritanical values, filtered through the missions. They seem to consider Western dress (usually used by men of this sector) as a mark of 'civilization'. The usual way of dressing of the adivasi peasantry is perceived as so inadequate that the existence of clothes is denied: they are 'naked'. The educated adivasis, not necessarily the dancers, feel ashamed.

[8] One must note that in the case of a few reformist ethnicist leaders of recent times, Western education means university training in Europe or the United States, often updated with visits to these places.

Another element enters the picture: culture as a commodity. Dances are planned for commercial shows, euphemistically called 'folklorical ballets' the world over: sterile and expurgated samples of popular culture. One clear instance of this kind of performance, taking place with official blessings, was observed at the opening of a meeting of local applied anthropologists in Ranchi. Although without a commercial purpose, this performance in fact was 'selling' something: a version of 'the traditional tribal culture'. The participants in the meeting were received by girls dancing a 'tribal dance', well wrapped in new saris. The leading (non-adivasi) anthropologist was greeted *as if* he were the *pahan*, an unlikely role that he seemed to accept naturally, as a person conscious of his authority over a community to which he did not in fact belong. The anthropologists and administrators present celebrated the performance as if it were an everyday event, thus becoming accomplices in the distortion of popular culture. It is in ways such as this that those in a position of power can invent 'tribal traditions' for the 'tribals'.

Some educated adivasis are aware of the consequences of deculturation. This shows, for example, in the attitude towards dress. But this awareness refers to deculturation produced by Hinduization and not by Westernization. The referent not to be imitated is the model of Hindu prudery. An elderly adivasi man considered that 'sometimes they [read 'we'] ill-define pride: covering the body from head to toe, hiding the women or not educating them. Hindu women are dirty, they do not take off their clothes when they bathe'.

The educated adivasis are earnestly occupied in the promotion of Jharkhand's vernacular languages, succeeding, for instance, in starting an extensive language program at Ranchi University, and in engaging adivasis from their own ranks to develop a common literary language. The multitude of Jharkhand's ethnic groups implies the existence of a host of languages. An additional common language for cross-communication and a common script for the existing ones would be advantageous. Already Sadani or Nagpuri has been spontaneously gaining use as a *lingua franca*. The educated adivasis' efforts to maintain their languages—important identity markers—are a form of legitimating their ethnicity. This is mostly reflected in the literary field (poetry, fiction, drama), in works published in papers, magazines and books. Thus, the first issue of

Johar was launched at the end of 1980 in a limited edition of 150 copies. Its (adivasi) editor described it as a 'tribal magazine' and 'a literary forum'. It is published in Mundari, Santali, Ho and Khariya. The journal is financially sponsored by the Government, but it is a group of Mundas around Ranchi that is mostly responsible for its publication. Another important issue that has been raised by the educated Mundas is the production of school text-books in Mundari and the need to consider new teaching methods. The Horo Cultural Centre has already prepared text-books to be used at the intermediate and bachelor levels at Ranchi University. However, to my knowledge, the question of rewriting their own history, usually considered by the *intelligentsia* of subordinated ethnic groups as a vital issue,[9] has not as yet been broached by the adivasis.

Another project is the Horo Cultural Centre, established at Jade village (Horo Senra Samaiti or Horo University),[10] dedicated to the Munda community. Dr. Hans, its founder, explained: 'My dream is to have a Munda University here, for all the Munda branches. I have launched the word *sasankir* for "culture", and it has been accepted. The people are very happy. They ask: "Is it going to be our Nalanda".'

This centre was planned to lodge a library and what Dr. Hans described as a 'village university'. The project attempts to direct the efforts at cultural maintenance to the rural areas. Two aspects of this strategy should be noted. First, it is planned as a cultural centre for one of the major ethnic groups in the Chotanagpur area. Second, the project possibly shows an elitist conception of culture (revealed, for instance, in the idea of a library), despite it being called 'a village university'. One may consider, however, the future reach of the efforts at cultural development, for instance, the spread of a new written (in this case, Munda) tradition outside the urban areas and the centres for formal education. At the same time, one cannot but compare the spirit of this project with the new uses the JMM attempted to give to the *akhra* as a venue for basic teaching, open to everybody.

[9] For instance:
Until now the colonizers have spoken for us...We are beginning to use some of [their] weapons: paper, and through it we declare that we are tired of oppression, and that we wish to spread our culture and to write the history of domination. This time it will be written by historians from the dominated sector (Jiménez Turón, Ye' cuana [Venezuela], 1979: 201–06. My translation from Spanish. Original in Yecuana).

[10] 'Horo University' means University of the Munda People.

There is an element underlying the adivasi elite's efforts at cultural development that should be mentioned: an uneasy mixture of pride and shame when 'using' their 'ethnic' culture, that I attribute to the already mentioned class/ethnic contradictions present in their identity's formulation. Their concern about their languages has two aims: one, to preserve them; the other, to upgrade them, to make them 'literary' and written, to make them 'civilized', according to the dominant canons that oppose a written to an oral tradition. At the same time, some of the educated adivasis feel uncomfortable when using their own languages. On different occasions I heard comments by educated adivasis like the following: 'They [read "we"] feel shy to speak their own language' (A Munda. His wife even refused to speak Mundari to him in private); 'At home, in the urban areas, mothers speak to their children in Hindi because there might be other people around and they would feel shy.'

The use of the pronoun 'they' and not 'we' in these and other quoted comments (English was used) is worth noting. The educated adivasis put distance between themselves and their ethnic identity. Their 'we' side prefers to speak Hindi or English, the two hegemonic languages, as repeatedly observed in the urban environment and particularly in Ranchi, a local centre for the diffusion of cultural hegemony. Thus the insistence: 'our people will have to learn to speak Hindi' (comment made in English). The 'we' side is uncomfortable with ethnicity (the distanced 'they') and feels ashamed of revealing it by speaking in the vernacular.

Shame created by deculturation spills from the urban to the nearby areas. For instance, according to an elderly Munda, in the villages around centres like Ranchi, 'the people now feel shy to dance at night, and with the coming modern culture have begun to forget their own. They now dance only at festivals. The flutes are gone now.'

Invented Traditions In Cultural Revivalism

Cultural revivalism provides legitimating support to the reformist ethnicists' ideology. Part of Jharkhand's history and cultures have been selected and reformulated to legitimize a political discourse based on ethnic referents and to call for a broad ethnic solidarity. Images of the past, not the flow of history, have been chosen by the reformists and often institutionalized. The ensuing invented traditions are concerned with establishing a continuity of the political discourse with the past and not with an understanding of historical discontinuities or the presence of social contradictions.

The image of Birsa, for instance, has been abstracted from the past, and its symbolic contents institutionalized in a statue erected on the road to Khunti. The statue as such is not a creation of the reformists, but a product of official populism. It is also not unique in the region.[11] The symbolism of these statues—particularly the one at the outskirts of Ranchi, the stronghold of the reformists—goes beyond the initial populist gesture. Birsa has been hailed by the reformists as the symbolic representative of the people of Jharkhand and of the ideal of good leadership, a connotation that was not lost on Jaipal Singh when he tried to act as a second Birsa.

As a point of reference with the past, the symbol attempts to unite all the adivasis in the tribal brotherhood. The status fixes Birsa beyond time and beyond the social context in which the leader of the Ulgulan once operated. He has become the official, institutionalized, 'father' of Jharkhand. Significantly, the statue depicts Birsa in the pose shown in an extensively reproduced old photo: with tied hands while being taken to prison. The statue's pose was criticized in the local press (NR 1980a), but only by a Bengali resident, since a statue depicting a free Birsa was considered to be more appropriate. Did the original populist gesture inadvertently help 'to fix' a symbol of the adivasis as a people in bondage, thus creating a permanent reminder of what is still to be done?

The detail of the tied hands has caught the attention of all. Dr. Hans, himself a Munda, told about a play he had written in one act around the imagery of the statue. The play was performed with great success in the villages in Mundari. The author's description of its plot was very succinct: 'Birsa is tied with ropes. Then culture comes and cuts the ropes. With that, the Mundas are liberated.' In this context, culture means education, and liberation means abandoning 'tribal backwardness', a product of ignorance. The educated adivasis' self-perception following the tribal construct is

[11] Statues like this—probably cast of the same mould—in bronze, started to crop up in the seventies and the eighties, possibly as a conciliatory move by the government after years of rural unrest in the region. In 1984, a new Birsa statue rose near Rourkela, accompanying the opening of a cement mini-plant at Mandikubar village (Orissa) (*The Stateman* 1984b).

reflected in the play: the adivasis' situation derives from deficiencies in their own societies (ignorance). The play fits well with the reformist ethnicists' discourse; it does not intend to question the status quo, since there is no mention of the need of any social change, except for education.

Other possible meanings of the Birsa statue as an anti-colonial symbol, a political statement of opposition and struggle by a 'freedom fighter of Chotanagpur' (as the press now qualifies Birsa), are not generally perceived. In addition, the Munda intellectuals seem to monopolize the image of Birsa. From this, two results may ensue: the weakening of the ideal of 'tribal' brotherhood, and the reinforce- ment of the Mundas' feelings of superiority over other local adivasi groups.

For the reformists, the links Birsa establishes with the historical past are tenuous. This is a highly idealized past of freedom and economic independence until the *dikus* came. The historical context on which the past as invented tradition has been built is not always known to the bulk of the deculturated adivasis. This was noted, for instance, at a gathering of urban-based educated adivasis. It was commented that I had gone to Chotanagpur's 'deep country' and reached Dombari Hill. Dombari Hill, where Birsa fought his last battle, is a very precise historical landmark in Chotanagpur's history, the theme of many old songs. Neither the name of the place nor my mention of some of Birsa's deeds seemed to provoke signs of re- cognition. It appeared as if it was the first time they were hearing the story of the Ulgulan.[12].

The lament of one of the elite's elderly members sums up a feeling some have of losing touch with their ethno–cultural roots: 'Some- times we talk of going back to Mari Disum, the old land, the original village [in symbolic terms], but now people are forgetting it.' Ethnic identity is becoming elusive for the members of the elite. Their des- perate efforts at capturing their identity translate into the invention of traditions: an ideal past with not many historical referents and a fixed 'traditional culture', very much in line with Hobsbawm's analysis (*loc.cit.* in fn. 12). These traditions may help the elite attain a certain social cohesion in the political arena, but can never encompass more than a small part of the ethnic style that was their source.

[12] One may then say with E. Hobsbawm that, 'Movements for the defence or revival of traditions... common among intellectuals...can never develop or even preserve a living past... but must become "invented traditions"' (1983: 8).

Symbols, once institutionalized, tend to change their meanings. The bow and arrow (*a'sar*) are held as symbols of adivasi culture. However, while proudly carried by adivasi peasants in their marches, at the homes of the urban petty-bourgeoisie they are not usually displayed but stored out of view. Some were amused to show me how to handle them, although they no longer had any use for them. On more than one occasion, what was brought out of the cupboard were broken remains: a bow without a string, an arrow partly broken. The bow and arrow is a powerful but, for some, a risky symbol. It is a symbol of struggle and not of compromise. As such, it does not fit comfortably in the reformists' repertoire.[13] For the elite, the bow and arrow symbol has become a depoliticized ethnic marker. The Bihar Government's 1980 ban on the possession of bows and arrows made an adivasi politician complain:

> The already dehumanized tribals were now being subjected to a process of 'detribalization'... The association of bows and arrows...started at birth itself when the placenta was cut by an arrow. The custom still prevails in the interior areas. Bows and arrows [are] an integral part of tribal life...(*NR* 1980d: 1)

The symbol of struggle disappears to become an element of 'tribal life' in the 'interior areas', reinforcing the 'tribal' stereotype.

Through cultural revivalism and invented traditions, the reformists codify and fix ethnicity, following their class needs, interests and cosmovision. They may not necessarily use their version of ethnicity to increase their power, but they certainly use it to legitimize and strengthen their position as the heirs of 'true tradition'. As such, they become their ethnic groups' official interlocutors in the eyes of the state and the ruling sectors.

[13] At the end of the sixties, for instance, the Birsa Seva Dal used the slogan *Jharkhand Larke Lenge Teer Ke Bal Par* ('Jharkhand will be won by a struggle with the force of arrows'). Sachchidananda says that this proposal 'was not relished by the old or new Jharkhand leaders' (1979: 253). It seems it was not so much, as Sachichidananda believes, because it pointed at a 'tribalist' conception of the Jharkhand state, but because the Birsa Seva Dal was becoming radicalized ('passing into the hands of the Communists'), and was a potentially disturbing element for the reformist ethnicists' attitude of political compromise.

The Forging of Heroes at the Grass-roots Level

Two leaders led the development of the JMM in the seventies:
Sibu Soren and A.K. Roy. Of them, popular imagination created
different images of the leader–hero.

A Santal from a village in Hazaribagh, Sibu Soren is the son of a
school-teacher—a familiar 'intellectual' figure in rural unrest—
who consistently opposed the local moneylenders by organizing
the adivasis against them. In the end, the school-teacher was
murdered by the moneylenders, the crime remained unpunished
and Sibu Soren and his family were harassed. Soren was fifteen at
the time, had to leave school and go to work as a labourer. He continued his father's task of opposing the moneylenders. Initially,
Sibu's entrance into the political arena was as an 'avenger' (Hobsbawm
1976). This attitude seems to have subsequently changed when he
realized that 'it was all of us, the Santals, who were being exploited,
robbed of our land, our crops, even our women...and we did not
complain'. For almost 20 years he was engaged in organizing the
Santal peasants to get their lands back. In 1972, with the birth of
the JMM–MCC coalition, he tapped the forcible harvest protest to
launch a campaign on that basis. It appears that his main concern
has always been his own community, the Santals who, in his
words, 'walking on a land of theirs, rich even in uranium, go
around naked'. In the seventies, Soren and the JMM supported
the ongoing struggle for the forests of the adivasis in Singhbhum.

Sibu Soren's effectiveness as a leader of a grass-roots movement
made him valuable in the eyes of the Congress(I) which started
moves for a convenient rapport with him. It was then that what
have been qualified by some observers as Soren's 'mistakes'
began. In consequence, his image among some political activists
was tarnished. However, during interviews, MCC activists avoided
making direct criticisms of Sibu Soren. They stressed at the same
time that he was 'undoubtedly a grass-roots leader that rose from
the base'. It was also said: 'he has a vague idea of ideology'. Despite
his increasing involvement with institutional politics, he still showed a
distaste for it in the early eighties. A point came in Sibu Soren's
career when he was labelled 'a government extensionist agent'. On
this issue, the MCC remained silent.

The fate of adivasi leadership is commonly perceived as sealed:
its inevitable cooptation by the state in a process in which 'the first

step is to make them MPs...'. Cooptation needs identifiable subjects. When, in the eyes of power–elites, grass-roots leadership becomes 'visible' as representatives of oppositional forces, cooptation may be used as a defusing mechanism. The institutionalization of grass-roots leaders by absorbing them into party politics performs this role. In this way, by becoming involved in a different mode of political struggle, these leaders can be 'lost' to the movements they represent. But cooptation is not, as commonly argued, the natural fate of the 'tribal leadership' in India: it is a general feature of the present Indian political system. Despite the fact that in the seventies Soren was drawn into the regional worker–peasant movement, his permanent loyalties have remained with the Santals. This may be explained by his personal history: family experiences, class extraction and the social and cultural milieu in which he lived. Later changes in JMM's ideological stance have also influenced his present 'ethnic only' position, now prevalent in the JMM.

Soren has usually been described by the Weberian term 'charismatic' with its somewhat elusive meaning. This charismatic aura, frequently used as a handy explanation for his mass following, was created on the basis of the peasants' perception of Soren the leader as a kind of supernatural hero. Extraordinary powers were ascribed to him, like riding on a motorbike over water or his ability to appear as four or five Sibus, all alike, working here and there simultaneously. Peasant heroes tend to become omnipresent. They are everywhere and nowhere, a characteristic with a practical side in times of danger (anonymity, mobility, hiding). Often too, they become immortal. After they die, they remain as a lingering presence in the peasants' landscape. They will always return, it is believed, although in another shape. It is not yet, however, Soren's turn for immortality; it may never be. The press came to consider in 1987 that despite AJSU '[having] snatched the leadership...from the older JMM', Soren was 'still the most respected figure in all tribal land' (*The Week* 1987: 34, 37). Nevertheless, it is difficult to deduce from these comments how peasants do perceive Soren now.[14]

A.K. Roy has been the other main political figure in Jharkhand's

---

[14] At the end of the seventies it was considered that Soren was already alienated from the peasantry. He was then forced by circumstances to retreat to Pokharia (Tundi), restricting his activities to a handful of villages (Maharaj and Iyer 1982: 200).

grass-roots movement. He has also been described as 'charismatic', on the basis of the admiration the coalminers feel for him. A mechanical engineer in Sindri, described as a 'declassed professional', he became the leader of the workers' movement at Dhanbad coalmines. He is highly respected by the workers, who call him Roy Babu, as an honest and committed leader. His integrity is acknowledged by all. Advisors to the collieries' management, for instance, although not agreeing with Roy's political views, spoke of him with respect: 'He is the only one who could achieve an alliance between peasants and workers in Dhanbad. He is articulate and has a logical mind.' At the same time, they compared him with Sibu Soren, whom they considered without hesitation 'a criminal... after all a tribal engaged in illegal activities like stealing crops'.

The contrast between the two leaders was established by these advisors on several planes: ethnic ascription (Soren being 'a tribal', therefore likely to engage in 'criminal' activities), class situation (Roy being a professional, educated and therefore 'logical'), and political strategy (Roy's known, therefore understandable, practices: trade unionism, alliances *vs* Soren's involvement in informal popular protest).

In the workers' eyes the contrast was in turn established between Roy and the leaders of corrupt unions and contractor gangs. At the collieries, Roy was perceived as a liberator: 'Before Roy Babu formed his union here [Beda], the *goondas, mahajans* and officers tortured us. We then chased the *goondas* and *mahajans*. Now we are free....' (*Indian Express* interview with a miner, 1979. *Cit.* in A. Sinha 1982a: 125).

Aside from his capacity to guide them in their struggle, what makes Roy extraordinary in the workers' perception has been his total commitment to them to the point that they could say: 'He is one of us...He lives like we do...When we have trouble, he is with us.' That he lives 'as they do' contributes to the image of the leader that renounces the benefits of his class and sacrifices all material comforts he could otherwise be enjoying. This spartan way of life followed by Roy could be observed in the course of interviews with him. To the general impression gained from how he lives, the 'charismatic' element adds up when he speaks, in a soft voice and in a patient, convincing tone (a characteristic that others have observed and is part of his 'special' image). In this, he is contrasted with leftist union leaders of the organized sector who 'talk much and loud and in the end do little'.

Alongside the leaders turned into heroes by the people, there are also the martyrs, like trade-union leader Sadananda Jha, killed in the early seventies, and political activist P., killed in the early eighties. The first was a young man, the other a verteran activist. Both, however, were non-Jharkhandis and were related to the worker–peasant alliance and the class/ethnic-based ideology of the early JMM. That is to say, they were connected to that 'tribal–worker struggle' which has been perceived by the state as 'dangerous'. What is common in the people's perception of leaders as extra-ordinary individuals, making them into heroes and martyrs, is that these leaders share their lives and that they are *with* them, even in death.

The Drums of Harvest

The trajectory of agrarian protest in the Santal Parganas–Dhanbad area proved a fertile ground for the emergence of the JMM. Tundi, a block in the Chotanagpur plateau bordering Santal Parganas became the site where the early JMM tested the new Jharkhand community, capitalizing on the already existing experience in agrarian protest. Presently, half the peasants in Tundi are Santals. The majority of them have become landless in a context in which land alienation and indebtedness have been rampant. Santal peasants have been the main protagonists in the increasing instances of the forcible harvesting of paddy.

In the background of present-day agrarian protest lies a long struggle for the restoration of alienated lands and a history of administrative indifference. The 1969 amendment of the Chotanagpur Tenancy Act, 1908 provided for the restoration of all 'tribal' land alienated in the preceding 30 (in scheduled areas) and 12 years (in non-scheduled areas). Legal provisions, however, were not translated into practice.[15] Faced with this situation, the task of recovering lands fell to the peasants themselves. For this purpose, they used an

[15] R.N. Maharaj and K.G. Iyer mention that, in the sixties, before the villages of Tundi became the theatre of operations of the JMM, the Santal peasants of these villages had suffered massive land alienation through mortgage for loans, on interest rates ranging from 150 per cent to 600 per cent. Land passed into the hands of the moneylenders who did not invest to improve agriculture since their aim was to extract the produce of the land and labour. Usury reduced Santal peasants to become sharecroppers or bonded labourers (1982: 173–74).

indirect path, the only one they considered viable: to seize the crops they had planted, 'to take at least part of what is ours', and since 'we cannot walk away with [take back] our land, we then take what the land has given to us [the crops]'. This appropriation of crops was seen by the peasants as a right: 'We go [to the fields] to take what is ours'. In this way, forcible harvesting began in Bihar in the shape of peaceful collective actions and turned into 'harvest clashes' (as reported in the press) only when landlords and moneylenders retaliated and fired on the peasants.

Forcible harvesting takes place in an organized manner. The groups of harvesters range from a hundred to a thousand people. It is a community affair: women, men, children, young and old, join the 'team'. A whole village or groups of villages participate. It usually begins with a march in broad daylight towards the fields to be harvested. The men carry their bows and arrows for self-defence against wild animals and, increasingly in the course of time, to defend themselves from landlords who begin attacking them while attempting to harvest. Hundreds of people may march to such harvests at the sound of drums. The continuous beating of drums marks the rhythm of the advancing crowd. The drum 'talks' to the Santal peasants. As one of them said, 'When the drums call, we gather, we go to harvest.' Even when in broad daylight, the sound of drums together with the rather solemn behaviour of the crowd, contributes to create an eerie atmosphere and, according to non-peasant informants, great alarm in the landlords towards whose disputed lands the people advance.

Forcible harvesting is guided by the peasants' decision to collect the product of the lands they have tilled, lands whose control they have lost through illegal alienations. These alienations resulted mainly from indebtedness (non-registered, impossible to redeem, high rate interest loans). Moreover, reduced to sharecropping, peasants often do not receive the right share of the produce of the land they have cultivated. The state and part of the media declared these actions to be criminal offences. But in the peasants' view: 'We are not stealing'; 'This is our paddy'; 'Is it a crime to retrieve what has been robbed from you?' The peasants' perception of justice is also revealed in the fact that forcible harvesting took place only on illegally alienated fields (see 1973 and 1974 cases in Maharaj and Iyer 1982: 180–87).

Increasing in frequency and extension, actions of forcible harvesting began to be recorded in Bihar and parts of West Bengal by the police and the press in as early as 1968. With the creation of the JMM, forcible harvesting was embraced into the *dhan kato andolan* as part of its program of restoration of illegally alienated lands and became widespread. By 1973, harvesting operations spread from Tundi to other blocks in Dhanbad with adivasi populations. Later, Santal Parganas and Hazaribagh became involved in the protest. At the same time, legal actions were undertaken to demand the implementation of existing laws like the Bihar Debt Redemption Ordinance. The 1974 and 1975 harvest seasons turned violent. The rising tide of committed harvesters was increasingly perceived by landlords and moneylenders as a threat that would become difficult to contain. Armed clashes began to occur with disquieting frequency. As the harvesting campaign gained momentum, so did the efforts of the landlords, moneylenders and the local administration to crush the movement. The landlords reinforced their paramilitary groups and let them loose on the harvesting peasants.

Forcible harvesting involved not only Santal peasants but other rural poor, Kurmis and dalits amongst them, and received the additional support of the workers, as in the case of those from Bera colliery harvesting paddy together with the peasants in 1974 and 1975. Those were the high years of the worker–peasant alliance when solidarity on a class basis and across ethnic demarcations was enhanced. Repression, too, strengthened rather than curbed solidarity: protest marches gathering thousands of peasants came to complain before the authorities for the killings taking place in the rural areas (*ibid.*). In the language of the early JMM, hundreds of villages had been 'freed' by 1975 through forcible harvesting. In Sibu Soren's words, these areas were 'liberated from the *dikus*'.

Forcible harvesting continued unabated in the years that followed. Paddy fields were transformed into battlefields during harvest season. At the end of 1980 the press still continued to report instances of forcible harvesting which had spread by then into West Bengal. For instance, under the title 'Steps to Prevent Harvesting Clashes', the *Patriot* (1980: 4) published then Bengal Minister Jyoti Basu's declarations pointing at 'adivasis from Bihar under the leadership of the JMM...stealing paddy from the fields'. The news talked of harvesting on 'lands belonging to some villagers' and 'on a disputed plot of land'. It was accompanied by a photograph of peasants with the caption 'Peasants peacefully harvesting paddy'. Nevertheless, it was also reported that in four days at least 47 people had been hurt 'by bullets and bombs [*sic*]' during clashes between landlords and sharecroppers. The police, in turn, stated that harvest clashes that year were 'a real headache'. There were exceptions among Government officials, such as Dhanbad's Deputy Commissioner S., with whom I had the opportunity to talk. He showed a slightly paternalist attitude towards the adivasis, but at the same time acknowledged the objective causes of their situation. Unlike other Government officials, he visited the JMM headquarters in Tundi and assured the JMM that land restoration would proceed according to the law. He informed the peasants about the provisions of the Debt Redemption Ordinance, and did not take measures to stop forcible harvesting but ensured that the operations took place peacefully (for instance, setting tripartite committees [officials–adivasis–landlords] to settle disputes. See Maharaj and Iyer 1982).

Forcible harvesting attempted to answer the question a Santal peasant left hanging in the air: 'What is then left to us?...' In the peasants' logic, the risk of facing the landlords' guns and arrest by the police does not measure up to the threat of hunger, deprivation and continuing dispossession. These peasants have 'nothing to lose and everything to gain' (Fanon 1983: 47) in a situation that may have reached the point of 'no possible coming to terms'.

Culture: a New Morality?

The early JMM made use of existing indigenous elements to address the community's needs. At the same time, it sought to create a 'new man' through the introduction of a new moral code, partially based on a modified version of the past. The past acted as a legitimating agent.

Considerable efforts were made at evolving a feasible educational system, independent from governmental assistance and funding. The traditional *akhra*—'dancing place'—in every village where the movement was operative was transformed into the *akil akhra*—'the place of knowledge'. This type of school functioned during the night since the youngsters and anyone else who wanted to attend were usually working during the day. Significantly, lessons were given in Santali, the everyday language of the pupils and a vital anchor for their cultural identity. This early stress on language–identity seems to have weakened later on, at least in Soren's view. By the early eighties Soren reluctantly admitted that Hindi may have to remain the main educational medium. This position may aid in the reproduction of Hindu–Hindi cultural hegemony. The *akil akhra* appears as much humbler but at the same time more suitable than Chotanagpur's 'village university'. Children from the lower castes would also flock to the 'school' and join the adivasi students. Education was elementary but nevertheless provided the villagers with defensive elements against moneylenders and traders who wanted to cheat 'ignorant' peasants.

The issues that became more problematic in the early JMM program were those that involved a moralizing intention: the attempt to create a 'new man' through coercion more than conviction. These issues revolved around the areas of pleasure and the situation of women. The JMM approached the issue of the adivasis' liquor consumption with the powerful slogan *Kalali Toro, Jharkhand chhoro*: 'Smash the liquor shops. Quit Jharkhand'. Liquor consumption in Jharkhand had indeed become a fostered vice, reinforcing mechanisms of social degradation. For instance, it helped maintain the adivasis indebted in the industrial complexes where meagre wages went rapidly into liquor shops.[16] On the other hand, for the adivasis, liquor is associated with social (communal drinking) and religious (propitiation of deities) occasions. This aspect seems not to have been considered by the JMM. The community's social pressure acted effectively in the countryside to curtail liquor consumption drastically. It was the women's participation that made the campaign successful. They took to it with great zeal, since prohibition for them meant, among other things, more resources for the household. The method they used was to shamefully expose the drunkards before the community. As a result of the campaign, liquor shops disappeared from the areas where the JMM operated. The anti-consumerism campaign led to the saving of scarce resources and the avoidance of heavy debts. However, the campaign led to a disavowal of collective pleasure on the basis of economic rationality. Anti-consumerism was also put into practice in the celebration of marriages. The high expenses derived from bride-price, gifts and celebrations were cut down. Other controversial JMM reforms were those related to the situation of women, on

---

[16] As shown by N. Sengupta (1982a: 27), liquor consumption in Jharkhand means big business and good revenue for the Government.

which Radha Kumar has already commented (1982: 203–09). The JMM favoured monogamy, and condemned polygamy and divorces that it considered groundless. Young women were not allowed to work as maids 'for *dikus*' since this was acknowledged to be exploitative and conducive to concubinage and prostitution. As stated in interviews, the refusal to send women to work as maids, which was thought to encourage their reincorporation into the agrarian economy and assure their respect, resulted in an attempt to introduce attitudes alien to the adivasi perception of women's roles. In this way, 'now it seems *immoral* if a woman goes out of the house'. At the same time, women's organizations like Mahila Shilp Kala Kendra took to teaching them new skills. However, it was considered that A.K. Roy 'was the only one who really backed the women's organizations'.

The JMM of the seventies appears to have aimed at introducing a conception of morality alien to adivasi peasant society. For this purpose the JMM sometimes used invented traditions. In one instance, contrary to the practices of adivasi society, JMM activists claimed that monogamy and restricted divorce were part of adivasi 'traditional' society (*ibid.*). Apparently, the JMM started inventing adivasi traditions for the adivasis' consumption. At the same time, it ignored a lived ethnic style and its supporting past as expressed in religious and social celebrations, forms of marriage and divorce, and the way criminal acts like rape were understood (whereby women are not stigmatized). Some of the early JMM social reforms were pushed forward by force or threat, like the anti-liquor campaign. Possibly, important indigenous elements which could have served to maintain the vitality of adivasi society and its specificity, and helped in strengthening solidarity (collective festive consumption, confidence brought by properly propitiating the deities, the women's equal status), were sacrificed for the sake of economic imperatives. By contrast, the reformist ethnicist project seems to have given more importance to 'the things that make life enjoyable'.[17]

Social imagination translates into social practice. Sometimes,

[17] Some analysts, while discussing the present JCC umbrella organization, have pointed at several important issues that the movement has disregarded: the inequality of women in relation to property rights, necessary changes in customary law, and the women's and youth's practical exclusion from the formal political life of the village (D.N. and G.K. 1989: 1506).

like in the case of the grass-roots movement of the seventies, social imagination projects itself beyond what the actual circumstances permit. Social imagination is nurtured by 'pasts' that are partly 'invented', partly remembered by collective memory. Culture enters as a central element in shaping the social imagination of a people and their discourses about what they *were, are* and *want to be.* These discourses are many, conditioned by specific historical and socio–economic circumstances and, more often than not, enter into contradiction with each other. All these discourses are, nevertheless, expressions of a society's vitality, of the continuous re-examination and reformulation of the *meanings* a society has for its different members. The variety of ethnic discourses in Jharkhand and their changing nature are a proof of the vitality of its people's social imagination, of them acting upon history in many different ways.

Part Four

THE DYNAMICS OF
CULTURAL STRUGGLE

6

Culture of Oppression and Culture of Protest

*Culture is the vigorous manifestation on the
ideological or idealist plane of the physical
and historical reality of the society that is
dominated or to be dominated....*
                    Amilcar Cabral, Return to the Sources

Bihar has been described as a 'near-lawless state', an example of
'the culture of torture', an 'area of darkness'.[1] Violence in Bihar
marks the prevailing social order and has become a signifying system:
a language, some of its codes open, others concealed. There are
other facts of a different nature in the context of this area of India.
Some of these facts are somehow less tangible or easily acknowl-
edgeable. Of them, it suffices to mention one that overrides the
picture: the subaltern sectors' collective will *to live*, not just to
survive. This is the most significant and basic manifestation of a
culture of protest, the other side of pervading oppression. Survival

---

[1] *Link* 1983: 10; 1986: 9; *EPW* 1980b: 1993–94; *India Today* 1986b: 40–43.
Although Bihar may be taken as an extreme example, similar processes have developed
elsewhere in India since the Emergency, in a variety of socio–political contexts.

is taken here in its most plain meaning: physical survival under specific conditions of subordination. It is interesting to note here what V. Das says while commenting on Saadat Hasan Manto's stories on communal riots: '...death is the unmarked category; it is all-pervasive and unproblematic. In contrast, life needs to be explained...' (1985: 7–8).

The concepts *culture of oppression* and *culture of protest* that are introduced[2] in this study will prove helpful in grappling with the nature of ethnicity in Jharkhand, a region where class exploitation and ethnic subordination coalesce, and where a dialectical movement develops between continuous efforts to make hegemony effective and visible and clandestine efforts to contain and contest it. A brief section will be devoted to the situation as perceived by the observer. This is a datum to be taken into account. It may help in understanding to a greater degree, how the people that live day by day in such a situation experience it, and how they deal with it. When approaching the issues to be examined in this chapter, the questions of *feeling* and *experience* will be kept in mind. In doing so, faulty objectivity is not being advocated but the 'recovery of subjective experience' (Samuel 1981: xviii ff.).[3] Unavoidable elements of subjectivity must be acknowledged in any social analysis. Facts speak—can be translated into a discourse—having the observer's as well as the 'observed's' *Erlebnisse*—lived experiences with a past and a present—as vehicles.

Culture

Culture is understood here in its deepest meaning, as foremost and always social, forming part of everyday social reality and closely linked to material life. It is shaped around the synthesis of the collective consciousness of a people, a class or a social sector, a synthesis by which their perception and representation of the social and natural totality is organized in each historical moment. Taking

[2] The role of culture in situations of domination has already been discussed in Devalle 1985a: 32–57, where a *clandestine culture of protest* was conceptualized.

[3] Feelings and experiences, in their actual manifestations, are objective. Feelings can order social behaviour, although they have their source in a subjective appreciation of reality.

place in concrete, flowing historical contexts, this constant exercise in synthesis is likely to produce changes in the consciousness of the particular people, class or sector in its thrust to organize social relationships and the relationships between men and nature, be it by preserving them as they are presently lived or by altering them radically. As such, then, culture far exceeds the empiricist's limits that restrict it just to its material expressions or to the external symbols of identification. The materialist position understands culture as 'a whole social order'. R. Williams (1982) has discussed the evolution of the concept of culture in the field of the sociology of culture to finally concentrate on the present convergence of the idealist position—emphasizing the role of a 'spirit informing a whole way of life'—and the materialist position, into a conception of culture as a 'signifying system' that operates in all forms of social activity. The utilization of this combined perspective has widened the analysis in the field of cultural inquiry.

In the discussion and analysis of data that follow, culture will be understood as a comprehensive field, embracing all that is produced with the hands, the mind and the 'heart', not in isolation but in close relationship with the social 'body', 'mind' and 'heart'. That is, culture is conceived here as a *way of life* moulded by social and economic forces, entailing *a whole social order* which involves a set of *signifying practices*—the languages in which a cosmovision supporting a social order is expressed—and *a way of feeling*—the subjective experience of the social that allows one to link, in Samuel's words (1981: xxxii), 'the individual moment with the *longue durée*' [4].

In examining the process of dominance and subordination one must also consider the question of the reproduction of hegemony and how this is negated.[5] In brief, hegemony is a whole social process in which specific and dominant meanings and values are organized and expressed in practices, and incorporated into a social order. Hegemony is related to questions of the distribution of power. It acts on the whole level of living, being 'in the strongest sense a "culture"... which was also to be seen as the lived dominance and subordination of particular classes' (Williams 1978: 110). Hegemony

----

[4] I am indebted to Jorge Galeano for his comments on the importance of this element: *feeling* as constitutive of culture.

[5] The concept of hegemony is used following Antonio Gramsci's formulation (1973), in essence going back to what is expounded by Marx in *The German Ideology* (Marx and Engels 1965: 61).

is therefore an uneven process in which the discontinuities emerging from an attempted hegemonic inclusivity over the whole area of lived experience, set limits to these attempts, thus leaving spaces free to be conquered by counter-hegemonic forces.[6] Gramsci considered hegemony (consent) and coercion to be interdependent, and the use of coercion as being determined by the nature of the consent that had been achieved. The relationships between hegemony and coercion are complex and can be approached not in the abstract but by setting politics in a historical context. Coercive ways may be used while attempting to establish consent or to reinforce a weak hegemonic order.

We observe in Bihar that the achievement of hegemony has been sought through the operation of a *culture of oppression* and that, at the same time, counter-hegemonic practices have become integrated into a *culture of protest* in opposition to the first. None of these two cultural formations are like *any* other culture, given that they evolve in very specific historical situations, are in mutual dependence and develop dialectically. In both cases these cultures are manifested in *explicit* modes as well as in *concealed*, often *clandestine texts*. In the present context, a *concealed* or *clandestine social text*[7] refers to those values, symbols, and ideas about the world and society that have a social meaning and are communicated, principally through codes exclusive to the class or social sector concerned, providing background support to their *explicit* expressions. Ingrained in the *concealed* or *clandestine texts* are the lines for potential action. *Explicit* as well as *concealed texts* have to do with power; both are purposive and are translated into social practices. The cultural formations of oppression and resistance are treated separately in the present chapter to facilitate the presentation of data. But both cultures should, however, be considered side by side, interacting, as two voices in counterpoint. It must be noted

---

[6] In E. Genovese's words: 'Hegemony implies class struggles and has no meaning apart from them... It has nothing in common with consensus history and represents its antithesis—a way of defining the historical content of class struggle during times of apparent quiescence' (1976: 77–98. Cited in E.P. Thompson 1978: 163, fn. 60).

[7] I first developed the concept of *clandestine text* in 1981 (Devalle 1981; 1985a). Shortly after the publication of my second article I came to know J. Scott's (1985) conception of 'hidden transcripts' that share some aspects in common with my own conceptualization of these *texts*. These *texts* are conceived here as being part of social and political processes. Contrary to Geertz's metaphor of culture as a text, culture is understood here as reality, i.e., linked to material social processes.

that only parts of the culture of those who are dominated are structured into a *culture of protest* and develop in direct response to a
culture of oppression. 'Resistance', on the other hand, should not
be understood in its original limited sense of 'the resistance of the *parti-
san*' (like during the Second World War). In situations of oppression, a
great part of culture continues developing as *lived culture* in the
frame of social and political processes, with its own motivations,
continuities and contradictions. As such, this vitality of the cultural
field in the context of domination may be seen in itself as the most
significant act of resistance and defiance to an attempted hegemonic
order.

Feeling: The Sensing of the Social Phenomena

*I became aware of everything, as if terror could make oneself
conscious of every moment and, at the same time, as if terror
had an autonomous inertia...*
>   **C. Monsivais**. Interview with *Proceso*, Mexico,
>   23 September 1985.

*Like a text, human action is an open work, the meaning of
which is 'in suspense'... Human action...is opened to anybody
who can read...*
>   **P. Ricoeur**, 'The Model of the Text...'

Culture is dynamic, continuously constructed at the quotidian
level, and related to social and material processes implying forms
of practical consciousness. How, then, can one free events and
experiences from the fixed forms they are made to adopt as 'facts'
in common scientific discourse? How can one capture the social as
it is actually lived by the observer as well as by the protagonists?

By the 'sensing of the social phenomena' I refer to what Raymond
Williams calls 'the undeniable experience of the present' facing 'all
that is present and moving, all that escapes or seems to escape
from the fixed and the explicit and the known, [and that] is grasped
and defined as the personal: this, here, now, alive, active "subjective"'
(1978: 128). This experience not only has *per se* as much value as
any other quantifiable and catalogueable fact, it is instrumental—as

Gramsci remarked—to avoid falling into 'the intellectual error...[of] believing that one can know without understanding and even more without feeling and being impassioned (not only for knowledge in itself but also for the object of knowledge)...'. (1973: 418).

In Bihar, the moment when fieldwork took place was not favourable to inquire and look into social and political phenomena. In retrospect, one can think of few moments appropriate for that purpose. When in the field, signals were sent to me to remain passive. Even after I had returned to Delhi, a local administrator from Bihar, apparently alerted by some grapevine, sought me out and commented to me: 'You talk little but you see and hear too well.' 'Seeing', 'listening', 'getting to know', are not healthy activities in Bihar. References to this fact were often made to me during my fieldwork in the form of advice or warnings. What was it that everybody was afraid would become known? Warnings came sometimes in the shape of casual anecdotes, with the implicit intention of protecting the observer's safety, as in the following comment made to me while in one of Chotanagpur's villages: 'You remind them [the peasants] of Miss X [a British young lady, possibly a missionary]... They took you for her. She was killed. It was said that it was a passionate crime. The fact is that she knew too much....' The ground for this confusion was my showing interest in them and a feeling that, somehow, I 'knew' (what the situation was). It is important to note that the common people regard this kind of 'knowledge' as dangerous, and feel concerned about those who seek 'to know'.

With respect to those who wielded power, what could be clearly felt was their need to demonstrate this power in the form of arrogance, scorn for others and authoritarianism. This circumstance was reflected in an incident in which a pass given to me by the Commissioner was withheld by one of the local notables during a period of curfew. I was finally forced to use the pass under rather uncomfortable circumstances: at night, crossing the fields during tight curfew and with riots going on in the area. At night, a little piece of paper could not have made much difference. The stage of nature: darkness, a sense of helplessness in lonely surroundings, united to the social *text*: the very tangible presence of violence, were elements that can provoke fear (not as an individual psychological event but a social event). At that moment, I took the incident of the pass only as an annoyance. Fear reached me much later during the derailments and disturbances on the road to Patna, on another, quite different night, and later still, in November 1984, when what I had perceived before in Bihar was magnified a thousandfold in Delhi and across North India.

As long as the origins of fear are traceable, personalized, it is easy to fight it. It is when it comes to be perceived as 'an autonomous force', as Carlos Monsiväis observes (1985), that it successfully permeates the social fabric and the collective psychological realm. When oppression evolves into a social order structured with forms, patterns, designs that seem invisible but are implacable, and is accompanied by specific practices, fear—the soul of subordination—installs itself in quotidian life. The social field thus becomes governed by the rules of violence—physical and psychological, open and subtle, not occasional but persistent, repetitive. Finally, fear may develop into something 'learned', 'natural', a part of the process of socialization.[8]

The Bihar stage was filled with the constant interplay of practices of dominance and subordination in daily life, feeding servile attitudes, the treatment given to the lesser people, the shouts, the commands, the expressions of petty power, the racist scorn in daily conversations and attitudes, the insidious crushing of self-respect. The way in which many of my interviews were arranged and conducted also reflected the social climate. Many interviews were anonymous, unexpected, at odd hours and usually took place with great precautions. This happened not only in Bihar but in Delhi as well when the interviewees were people active in Bihar oppositional politics. In these instances, care was taken to ensure my safety. In such a climate, certain attitudes start developing. The observer begins to 'speak little', to look and listen intently. But what happens to people that daily live in such a social environment?

The signs of resistance were more subtle than the reality of oppression, but they could still be read: the silence of contempt, the unspoken distrust, the endurance and the preservation of vitality in a social environment of constraint, the desire to approach the observer under the cloak of anonymity and the insistence on the need 'to make people know (what is happening)' (sometimes an explicit request, but always an implicit one). Besides such signs,

---

[8] Other elements also contributed to create in the observer a first impression of Bihar's social stage, for instance, the disclosure at that moment of the Bhagalpur blindings (Kamath 1981: 17; *EPW* 1980b: 1993–94; *TI* 1981b: 3; *IE* 1980a and b).

there were the open actions that will be discussed in the course of this chapter and the omnipresent attitude of resistance permeating life.

A Culture of Oppression

A great part of politics and law is always theatre....
E.P. Thompson, 'Patrician Society, Plebeian Culture'

Terror, counter-terror, violence, counter-violence: that is what observers bitterly record when they describe the circle of hate, which is so tenacious and so evident in Algeria....
F. Fanon, The Wretched of the Earth

A *culture of oppression* can be defined as the aggregate of dominant meanings and values, accompanied by practices in which violence and coercion enter as significant constitutive elements in the reproduction of the hegemonic order, by which the powerholders aim at maintaining and strengthening their superordinate position.[9]

The expressions of this culture in the public domain are usually abundant given that its force resides in making these expressions widely known to the subordinates.[10] This extensive appropriation of the public domain by the powerful stems also from the necessity to limit the use of this field by the powerless. It is in this realm that the *theatre of power* takes place, pushing the subordinate classes' 'text' of protest underground. In situations of domination–subordination, where a structured *culture of oppression* prevails, the *theatre of power*—so aptly analyzed by E.P. Thompson (1974: 382–405)—may develop into a *theatre of terror*. The *theatre of terror* has several characteristics, mostly defined by their extreme nature: to cause terror, not just fear of authority; to be repetitive, not finite;

[9] For a different view on violence, *cf.* Riches 1986: 1–27.
[10] This is observable in the frequency of atrocities against labouring dalits and adivasis reported in the last decade, presented to the crowd as instances of 'exemplary punishment'.

pervasive, not localized; inculcating self-derogation, not just compliance. Terror as a mechanism to enforce subordination does not stop at being only part of a 'theatrical style of dominance' but usually gives way to an actual *practice of terror*, experienced by those who are its targets as *reality*. The *theatre* and the *practice of terror* attempt to pervade the whole area of lived experience in order to make it lived dominance and lived subordination.

The case of the Gua killings on 8 September 1980 illustrates the dynamics of a 'theatrical style of dominance' and its transformation into a *practice of terror*. A procession of adivasis, wishing to submit a memorandum to the Forest officials, was allowed to march into Gua and hold a public meeting organized by the JMM. Gua had already been sealed off by the BMP. When the police arrested two of the leaders and attacked the multitude, the adivasis answered by shooting arrows, killing two policemen. The police fired, killing some and injuring others. The injured were taken by their companions to the hospital where police forces were already waiting. The wounded and those who had carried them stopped near the entrance to the hospital. The police lined them up and shot them.[11] The Gua story concludes with instances of the *practice of terror*: the killing of the *innocents* at the doors of the hospital performed as exemplary punishment (assumedly in retaliation for the death of policemen during the confrontation). The symbolic meaning of the *punishment inflicted on the innocents* should be noted. This punishment stresses before the subaltern classes the unlimited reach of the violence inspired by the powerful's wrath. Terror comes to be seen as a force that nobody can contain. It is perceived by its 'objects' as unending and beyond human control. People in the Chotanagpur/ Singhbhum area commented to me: 'Death, raids, attacks on women...and death, raids and attacks on women again. Nobody sees [takes notice] and it will never stop...'; 'We are killed and robbed. It happened yesterday, [it happens] today, [it will happen] tomorrow....'

In Bihar, the dominant order appears to rest on physical power (coercion, punishment and terror), and on cultural hegemony

[11] The incident took place shortly before I arrived in the field. Therefore, it was possible to collect enough material to reconstruct the events on the basis of comments and information collected in the course of interviews, supplemented by data collected by journalists. See also PUCL Report 1979; *EPW* 1979b: 940–43; Devi 1981b: 1595–97; Pardesi 1980).

(enforcing a socialization into subordination). Of the unedited discourses that back the *culture of oppression* as it operates in Jharkhand, I concentrate on the following: the conceptions of (*a*) superiority–inferiority; (*b*) dominance–subordination; (*c*) violence as a 'right' of the powerful and construction of an 'object' of violence; and (*d*) a perception of the subordinates as dangerous.

Conceptions of Superiority–Inferiority and Dominance–Subordination

The adivasis, particularly the majority in the lower economic range, are conceived as *inferior*: biologically, in intelligence and achievements (people seen as 'naive', as 'children', as the stereotype of the gullible 'savage'), and culturally (people seen as beyond the pale of 'high culture', in other words, not conforming to the dominant cultural values).

The adivasis are called *junglee*, 'people of the jungle' or 'wild', a term close to the pejorative 'savage'. They are referred to by the racist name *kaliparaja* (from the Sanskrit *kali* = black, and *paraja* = born of another, a member of another community, alien, different). The colour question is present although not always made direclty explicit. Self-devaluation in racist terms has been internalized as, for instance, in the following remarks: 'What can I do? I am just a black Santal' (a peasant); 'Would you marry a Munda youth... even if he is a bit dark?' (a Munda woman).

Non-adivasis talked of the adivasis as 'simple' and 'naive', adjectives that in the present context are not eulogistic. Such terms go well with the pseudo-scientific 'primitive', still in vogue among the anthropologists working in the area (but not exclusive to them since this is an all-India phenomenon among anthropologists and administrators). Another accompanying adjective is the well-known and officially sanctioned 'backward'. For instance, I was told on different occasions: '*Primitive* tribes are more *backward* than the tribes themselves' (an educated adivasi); 'There are tribes in an *extremely underdeveloped stage*' (Government officer); 'We are dealing with one of the *most intractable problems* of India' (an administrator on the 'tribal problem'); 'They are *simple* because *they do not understand* the economy. They do not understand what is surplus capital. They start to want things and have to enter the money economy. But *they do not become aware* of what,this economy is all about'; 'The *main problem* of the tribal people is their *traditional* background' (development officers); 'India is an anthropological *museum!*' (a local anthropologist).

Simple, not able to understand, in a 'lower' stage of development, backward, they are seen by the state and its agents as the most difficult problem for the administration, a problem that is considered to be the adivasis' own creation, the result of 'their traditional background'. If there were not adivasis, there would be no problem. In this context of discrimination and condescension, the anthropologists' image of India as a museum sums up a generalized perception of its indigenous peoples: constructed and catalogued as specimens belonging to a remote era in society's evolutionary process.

As an example of undervaluation, a portrait of adivasi women is instructive. Non-adivasi women considered that, 'Adivasi women are free and naive! They are ignorant and so they are abused'; 'They [the adivasis] are exploited by other people because their women are free and the men are weak.' On the marriage of a European with an Oraon girl there was the following comment by the wife of a development officer: 'She used to work in the fields of the mission. He is very rich. She does not know English and likes status symbols given that she lacks any education. She is a mercenary. She is very confused.'

Economic exploitation and sexual abuse are directly ascribed to the 'innate' features of the adivasis. 'Ignorance', 'weakness' and 'freedom' make an awkward combination to express something like 'these are not our values', therefore 'these are the consequences' or 'it is their fault'. When the adivasis change and move into forbidden grounds, the image is not any more flattering: ignorance again, confusion and deceit, as in the case of the Oraon girl who from field-hand tried to become 'a lady'. As already pointed out, the adivasi women's 'naivete' and 'freedom' were given as an argument to justify their prostitution around the industrial complexes. Prostitution, a phenomenon with deep socio–economic roots, is understood as an 'accident' resulting from the irresponsible nature of the adivasis.

Instances where the concealed texts of superiority–inferiority were made explicit could be observed at a workshop organized by the Bihar Tribal Research Institute. This was an opportunity to witness a mini-social drama: The Government, the scientific establishment, i.e. the total local body of applied anthropologists, and the Church with missionaries representing every denomination operating in the area, were conspicuously present. Around the table there were adivasis and non-adivasis, a fact not obvious at first sight. Most of those present wore Western clothes; few wore Indian garments. Those adivasis who were part of the round table—part as well of the elite of 'the educated'—all were in Western clothes; their identity was disclosed only if by chance they mentioned their names. However, this way of dressing did reveal the class position of those who wore them and a 'style' that broadly identified them with executive positions (as in Government).

I chatted with the leading anthropologist before the proceedings began. He asked me about the Lacandons in Mexico: 'Are they primitive?' I did not understand what he really meant. Another participant informed me that Bihar is an amazing treasury of 'tribal relics'. The proceedings then started with talks about the 'need to attain the psychological integration of the tribals into the mainstream'—a 'sacred' mainstream that anthropologists apparently believe should 'not...be violated by research' (Sengupta 1986: 5). Some of the applauded conclusions were: 'Some of the groups called "backward" are really backward'; 'As "primitive" sounds harsh for people [who are] more or less like us, I suggest the term "primary group"'; and 'Development must be imposed without waiting for them [the adivasis] to decide', as this was considered to be 'a sacred national task'.

The only adivasi speaker, an elderly priest high in the Christian ecclesiastical hierarchy, spoke with deference and only referred to the need to preserve cultural traits and languages. The response of the Government representative was quick and reassuring: 'We are careful to preserve traditions, customs and culture. We have the rich traditions of the tribal people... Culture has to be dealt with. From a nationalist point of view we need to see that this happens.'

Then, after much serious talk, the 'light show' started. A mini-drama on the themes of superiority–inferiority and dominance–subordination was staged: Four adivasi boys, very young, from the Bir Hor, Savara and Asur groups, had to perform as 'samples', literally, before the audience. The boys were poorly dressed, with bits and pieces of cheap and worn clothes. Standing huddled together at one side of the table on the dais, they looked shy and uncomfortable. They were made to say their names and ethnic group, and made to give a prearranged and monitored speech in Hindi—with a Hindi teacher sitting at the table constantly correcting them in whispers. The short and forced speech finished, the audience relaxed and smiled, as if these boys were three-year-olds reciting a poem in front of visiting relatives. The boys were not allowed to participate in the discussions being held *about them*. Moreover, to close their brief appearance, one of them, the Bir Hor boy, sang a song. Some of its lines said:

> *Everything is changing except the Adivasis.*
> *The Americans have gone to the moon,*
> *and the Adivasis are only crawling about...*

The boys dismissed, the audience was asked to rest and have some tea.

What are the *texts* that can be read in this brief social drama? First, what about the actors? On the one side, the carriers of the dominant ideology, the 'intellectuals of the superstructure' in Gramscian terms, were all present, physically as well as symbolically—Government, Science, and the Church, accompanied by the 'intermediaries': members of the educated adivasi elite. They differentiated themselves from the rest of the actors by their dress, position in the room, attitudes, form of speech and the language they used (English). Regarding clothing, it is to be noted that in only two cases did it reveal a different identity: the Ramakrishna Mission representative in yellow robes, and an administrator cum anthropologist considered to be 'more progressive', in a Nehru jacket. In this context, one may see these clothes as expressions of tradition and nationalism.

At the other end of the stage were the adivasis. They were represented first through the constant translation into speech of the tribal construct (the symbolic), and second, in the brief performance of the four adivasi boys, which served to reinforce the construct. Their appearance and behaviour contrasted sharply with the audience's. They conformed to the stereotyped image of 'the tribal' as 'primitive': poor, foolish, childish, clumsy, ignorant, subservient, with an 'inferiority complex', and in constant need of guidance (monitored speech, repeated unasked for help, relief of the audience when they 'could make it').

The verbal discourses during the meeting showed the strength of scientistic constructs in legitimizing the superiority–inferiority hierarchy, as reflected in the adjectives being used ('primitive', 'backward', 'tribal', etc.), the ideas that the indigenous people are 'relics of the past', and that some are 'people like us' (while others implicitly are not). The defence of the hegemonic order (dominance–subordination), sometimes euphemistically phrased as 'the national task', permeated the discussions and revealed itself, for instance, in the conception of the indigenous people as 'objects' of development and policies in general, with no right to give an opinion or to decide about their own lives. The intention to 'deal with culture' (like a process to be externally controlled) and the emphasis on 'psychological integration' fall within the same parameters.

The presentation of the four boys before the audience is a whole *text* in itself, that of dominance–subordination in its explicit mode. The boys were brought in, 'used' for the show and dismissed, after being treated with condescension and not with equality (exclusion from the proceedings to the extent that they were not allowed to remain in the room).[12] Regarding the boys, the *text* reads somewhat differently: their shame of themselves and their apparent acceptance of their discriminated condition and subordinate status.

From this general assignment of innate inferiority to the adivasis stems the view that these are people who should occupy a *subordinate position*, a subordination in which they should and will inevitably remain (a view that shows in the comments made about the Oraon girl quoted above). This belief in the marginality of the adivasis is in turn translated into social practice. First, in its 'benevolent' form characterized by paternalism, charity and unasked for guidance. Secondly, in its authoritarian form, in the practice of psychological and physical violence.

'Tribal' is immediately equated with low social status. This is the perception that supports the perpetuation of the image of the adivasi as the ideal *coolie*, that is, fit to serve or to perform tasks that are related more to strength and endurance than to the use of skills. Thus, for instance, it is common to see teams of adivasis dragging long two-wheeled carts with heavy loads, pulling rickshaws, or doing menial jobs in houses and offices. There were opportunities to observe them in their assigned subordinate roles in situations

[12] The way I recorded my impressions at that moment (an association with Columbus' times) in my notebook seems to provide an appropriate parallel: some 'specimens' were brought to 'Court' to prove their existence and the success of 'conquest'.

where authoritarianism and servility interplayed. For instance: Prof. Y rings a bell for his adivasi servant to pick up the phone, the pen that is exactly in front of him on the desk, or just to make him come in for nothing. Somehow the scene evokes the 'crawling' in the Bir Hor boy's song quoted above.

Besides, adivasis are thought only to be suited to till the land and work in precarious mines. I have already commented on how prejudiced stereotypes and assumed 'traits' ascribed to the adivasis are used to maintain them in the unskilled positions in the industrial sector, and how these constructs have helped create 'labour-supplying areas'.

Violence as a 'Right' of the Powerful and its 'Object'

Violence has acquired for the dominant classes in Bihar the weight of a 'value'—the normal condition of life necessary to maintain the existing order—legitimized as *the 'right' of the powerful*.[13] Meanings, even those with an already disturbing implication, are further twisted and charged with an additional load. In this way, from being a symbol of potential violence, the gun becomes a symbol of the violence of the powerful. In Bihar, the gun 'has a caste' (not just as applied to Uttar Pradesh: castes with arms, but in the general sense of 'the "caste" of the armed ones').[14]

Violence has meaning only if it has an *object*. Values of inferiority–superiority easily provide this object. In the evaluation of inferiority, first comes the idea of servility and naivete. Then the process of dehumanization begins: adivasis are seen as ignorant and primitive ('like children', a common remark made by non-adivasis), but able to stand hardship. When violence enters the picture, the process of construction of the object is completed: poor adivasis become objectified, a dehumanized target, a mass without identity. The result of this process of objectification of the victim is reflected in

[13] See, for instance, Home Commissioner Arun Pathak's statement: 'Why are you [Government officials] wasting time on improving the lot of the tribals?... Crush them... Frame their leaders and put them behind bars' (Pardesi 1980: 7).

[14] See the data on licensed and unlicensed arms and the social sectors that have access to them in *Link* 1981: 16–17. The existence of private militia in the rural areas at the service of landowners has been widely reported (*F* 1979a: 7–8; *Link* 1983: 9–10; *EPW* 1986: 15–18). The group that has access to firearms and can arm a body of men with the purpose of controlling other social sectors, is part of the 'caste of the armed ones'.

all its crudity in the *practice of terror*. When alluding to some of these violent incidents, like the Gua killings, the view was expressed that the lives of the adivasis are worthless. For instance, 'Well, yes, *some* tribals were killed'; 'After all, it's *inevitable*. *How* does one maintain *order* otherwise!' ; '*What* could the police do with that *mob*! *As usual*, a bullet is fired, *there is* anger, *somebody* always dies.' (Various comments recorded in the Chotanagpur/Singhbhum area.)

The victims are not clearly identified; they are just a vague 'somebody'. Violence is seen as a normal part of life (it is 'usual'), as an autonomous force (it is 'inevitable'), and its agents usually remain concealed in speech by the use of the impersonal ('there is...'; '... is fired'). The legitimacy of this 'upper' violence is also clearly reflected in the 'hows' and 'what elses'.

Perception of Subordinates as Dangerous

Observing the practice of violence by the powerful in Bihar and its stimulus, and considering the systematic nature of dominance–subordination, one recalls J. Scott's suggestive idea of the development among the powerful of a 'structural paranoia' (1986: 5), in circumstances when the subordinates' thoughts and intentions are perceived as difficult or even impossible to grasp with certainty and, one may add, when coercion is widely used in the organization of consensus. We observe the existence of a behaviour and feelings of omnipotence in conjunction with a fear of retaliation (see Klein 1960).

For the powerful, the mass without faces becomes an eerie blank page, pregnant with concealed threats. Thus, it was said to me about the 'nature of the tribals': 'When they cannot bear it any more, they turn to violence and to the bow and arrow... This is a problem in the control of people.' Subordinate sectors are perceived through 'paranoid' optics as deceitful and *dangerous*. This perception is reflected also in the language used in the press, i.e., 'a frenzied mob of Adivasis', or just 'the mob'(*TI* 1981c: 5; *NR* 1980e: f.p.), that anonymous, feared 'monster' that the assertive presence of the subaltern classes, everywhere and in all times, has become for the powerful.[15]

[15] At the same time, the subaltern classes can use to their advantage the menacing presence of the crowd and the anonymity it provides, as part of a strategy of popular action, a point already noted by E. P. Thompson (1974: 401 ff.).

Violence begins to appear in the minds of the powerful as legitimate tactics of self-defence. In the case under study, this 'structural paranoia' reveals itself in the awe evoked by the arrow, mainly because it kills silently. The 'hidden hate' of the adivasis is feared because it can strike unexpectedly, much like the arrow does. I was told: 'They [the adivasis] are dangerous, violent... Oh, yes!, we have guns, but they have arrows and, you see, arrows come silently and then...[a gesture of slashing down and a sibilant sound].' For the rural powerful arrows have become, and may have always been, something to fear and, at the same time, a justification for arming themselves, allegedly against the unpredictable insubordination of the subaltern classes. As was said more directly on one occasion: 'One needs to watch them quite closely. Who knows what is in their minds, what will they do....'

It does not seem incorrect to consider the ban on the possession and carrying of bows and arrows and the requirement of licences to carry them imposed in Bihar by the State Government, a result of this 'structural paranoia'.[16] Other, more powerful weapons—guns particularly—were not banned at the same time. On the contrary; in moments when confrontations became acute, the Government found it natural that 'landlords and rich peasants...formed [armed] groups to protect themselves and their interests' (*F* 1979b: 4). The ban against bows and arrows was clearly not intended to curb the incidence of violence in the Jharkhand area. Violence continued coming from other quarters altogether: firing incidents by the police became commonplace as was the general exercise of physical violence against adivasi labourers.

The way in which this 'structural paranoia' is aroused, the mode in which tenuous hints of the subalterns' *texts* are read, was well registered by a reporter: 'Tribal drums in Mayurbhanj, Purulia, Palamau or Raigharh no longer weave dance patterns in the air. Their sound is one of defiance....' (*TS* 1980a: 5). In Beldiha village (Santal Parganas), the *dum-duggias* were beaten to warn the villagers that the troops of the Central Reserve Police and the Bihar Military Police were surrounding the area. The sound of the drums was reason enough for the police to open fire.

[16] *NR* 1980c; Link 1982c: 12; a ban still in force at the time of field-work.

A Culture of Protest

We had attacked, we the slaves; we, the dung underfoot; we, the animals with patient hooves....

A. Cesaire, Les Armées Miraculeuses

If one were to search for a common heritage among the indigenous peoples everywhere—those who have come to occupy subaltern positions in the course of conquest and of the process of state formation—we will find as a commonality long histories of resistance and protest guided, primarily, by the will to survive physically as well as socially. This is not by any means a monopoly of indigenous peoples but part of the life of all subaltern sectors. There is, nevertheless, a difference: in the case of the indigenous peoples the dimension of historico–cultural (*ethnic*) identity, tends to give extra meanings to resistance.

The dominant populations have usually depicted indigenous peoples as not having a history previous to the moment of conquest/domination. This conception has inspired the official versions of 'national' history (history as told by the 'winners', elite history). Despite the smothering blanket thrown over it by official histories, the history of the indigenous peoples is kept alive in a collective memory expressed in oral history, in aesthetic forms, and in the shared activities of daily economic and social life. Culture becomes the privileged means to interpret social reality and to communicate this interpretation despite the situation of confrontation, violence and repression.[17]

As domination is not only exerted economically and politically but also culturally, the struggle against it is also launched at multiple levels, employing every possible mode of willed action. Thus, cultural notations and activities may become impregnated with political meanings. Therefore, we see the formation of *cultures of protest* which are not only active in open revolt but operative in the consciousness and in actions of opposition developed by the subordinate sectors in everyday life.

[17] Carlos Guzman Böckler, for instance, shows the ways in which the Guatemalan indigenous peoples have elaborated their strategy for resistance (1975: 102).

The message of protest becomes clandestine by the force of circumstances, is grounded in a collective memory and expressed in codes specific to the subordinate social sector. These codes effectively protect the contents of the message of resistance as well as the intention of purposely defensive and offensive actions. When the channels for the open expression of social protest, popular grievances, aspirations and opinions are absent or blocked by force or law, the communication, the exchange of ideas and the preservation of a collective memory may develop, for instance, in the aesthetic realm, one of the various fields that can substantially remain under the control of the subaltern classes.[18] The forms in which a *culture of protest* is manifested are many. The message in each form reflects the particular ways in which domination has taken place and is continuing in the society that produces such a rebellious culture. What needs to be analyzed further is this potential for rebellion. There is no inherently or perpertually rebellious culture. Culture *becomes* rebellious. Explanations should be sought by looking at the ways in which social consciousness develops given existing socio–economic contradictions and oppositions.[19]

What realities can be 'read' in the language of resistance and protest being spoken in Jharkhand? The following discourses of resistance could be detected in Jharkhand: (*a*) the urgency to assure physical and social survival; (*b*) the value of justice; and (*c*) the careful preservation of 'coded' social spaces (*zones of resistance*). These discourses in turn do have explicit expressions which, despite their often apparent 'failure' at the practical level, are effective: the expressions of an oppositional culture provide substance to the challenges to the existing hegemonic order.[20] A Santal peasant described such moments of resistance while talking of forcible harvesting as 'tiny, tiny steps on the land', and its effects as 'an arrow that flies high and far'.

At this point one has to ask: what do these concealed and explicit

[18] Cases from Africa and Latin America were discussed in Devalle 1985a.

[19] As Thompson remarks: 'It is not sufficient merely to *describe* popular symbolic protest...it is necessary also to recover the significance of these symbols with reference to a wider symbolic universe, and hence to locate their force, both as affronts to the rulers' hegemony and as expressions of the expectations of the crowd' (1978: 155, fn. 43. Italics in the original).

[20] I agree with C. Pelzer White on the importance of considering the question of the effectiveness of popular everyday resistance, underlined in her critique of J. Scott (Pelzer 1986: 50–51).

modes of the *culture of protest* in Jharkhand oppose in the concrete? They oppose and question the dominance–subordination paradigm and its expressions in social practice. The existing social order, which is maintained by force and therefore has minimal legitimacy, is considered to be expressed by its agents. These agents are resisted and, often indirectly, fought: individuals as well as institutions. Comments recorded in the field refer to 'those who rob', 'the ones who do not work' (landlords; often *dikus* in general), those who 'when they come, they kill' (police; landlords' armed men), those of 'double-speak' (usually those in position of authority exercising it through imposition and authoritarianism), the 'bloodsuckers' (exploiters in general, seen by Sibu Soren as 'the enemy') and, as previously discussed, the bearers of Hindu culture.

Preserving Physical and Social Survival

The urgent need to assure physical and social *survival* is a common denominator in all modes of resistance. In different ways and from different political and class angles, the adivasis acknowledge that their survival is at risk. In interviews with some of their leaders (already mentioned in the previous chapter) this perception was made explicit: 'If we, the tribals, do not stand with all our strength, politically and socially, we will not be able to *save* ourselves'; 'If you become Hinduized you lose your status and you become a *slave* in a society that has already made millions and millions of slaves'.

Among the adivasi peasantry, the menace to survival is perceived in a much more direct way: 'When they [the police, the forest officials] come, we leave, we go to the forest and wait'; 'To see [know] is no good' (comments recorded in the Chotanagpur/Singhbhum area); 'They [the landlords] take our paddy and leave us hungry. Then we die...[That is why] we have to take our paddy back [reference to forcible harvesting]' (a Santal peasant).

In a situation of perceived and experienced threats to survival, a great part of resistance is kept concealed or disguised from the eyes of the powerful by means of the age-old mechanism of dissimulation. One important expression of resistance is, paradoxically, the use of silence: expression through non-expression. Silence can be of enormous effect in the staging of the *theatre of the powerless*. For instance, the impressions I recorded of peasant marches (as those of forcible harvests) and the accounts of the slow and silent procession proceeding to Gua, illustrate the *text* of silence. Drums were certainly sounded, but somehow this merely served to emphasize the absence of the human voice. We should also remember that the frightening quality of the arrow resides in its silence and in the silence of the person who shoots it.

Silence is a component in many of the attitudes and actions of resistance that aim to avoid frontal opposition. It is present in the attitude of feigned servility and acceptance of authority and in 'behind the back' gestures. For instance, a small incident took place at the house of a middle-class Bengali in Ranchi: M. shouted to his servant (a young adivasi boy) to bring water to wash his hands. He snatched the towel from the boy's hands. Something was not to M.'s pleasing. He threw back the towel, slapping the boy's face with it. The boy did not utter a word. Other people present did not pay any attention either to the incident or to the boy as he left. One could follow him with the corner of the eye as he went beyond a small partition open on two sides. He left the jug, stood still with the towel in his hands, threw it on the ground, started wiping his feet on it, and finally stamped on it. The gesture would have angered his master had he seen it, especially considering the association, common in India, between feet or shoes and insult. This incident can be easily explained as the reaction of a servant who dislikes his master. Although the unequal relation of master and servant is enough to account for the 'behind the back' behaviour of the boy, more meanings are in fact implicit in it. We refer mainly to the aggregate of inferiority/subordination traits ascribed to the adivasis discussed in the former section. The attitude of servility is maintained in front of the master, but it does not last behind the curtain.

In the same way, other gestures made 'behind the back' take the form of concealed insults (for instance, rickshaw-pullers spitting—not because of betel-chewing—after certain passengers get down from the vehicles). Also, explicit comments such as the following are made 'behind the back': 'They [the *dikus*] are dirty. They do not take off their clothes to take a bath. They do not clean their tongues.' This may be taken as an expression of adivasi ethnocentrism, but it certainly returns the insulting adjective 'dirty' with which adivasis are very commonly qualified.

Then also, there is an interesting addition to silence: laughter.[21] Concealed laughing and satire lie beneath some of the expressions of contempt with which the authorities' attitudes and ideas are judged. For instance, the case of the two Ho teachers laughing (instead of seriously complaining) after witnessing the humiliating treatment given to one of their people at an official meeting. Their dismissal of the incident as 'just a show', precisely took away strength from the demonstration of superiority that 'show' was intended to be.

The spitting behind the back of some people (usually Bengalis or Biharis, who are considered as part of the *diku*, alien, super-ordinate world) in urban areas of Jharkhand, may be related more to satire than simple insult. Spitting (accompanying betel-chewing) is associated with urban Hindu employees and seen as one of the markers denoting petty power. On one occasion, the depiction by some adivasi sweepers of a fat, lazy, betel-chewing petty-bureaucrat, sitting at a desk and passing his time trying to hit with precision the spittoon, was the cause of much laughter. In the satirical description, gestures ended up assimilating the figure of the lazy, fat bureaucrat to the object of his attention: he came to closely resemble the 'round, dirty [vessel], sitting still in a corner'. The caricature was a quite effective way of demystifying images of authority.

In the rural areas, different metaphors are used to draw caricatures of the powerful. The image of ineffective, lazy but prosperous authorities ('those who do not work', usually described as 'fat', with 'big round bellies', as often indicated by gestures) popular in urban areas, is replaced in rural areas by one of 'those who rob' and, at the same time, are dangerous. Often, these objects of satire are identified by the name *diku*, used in its dual meaning: alien/exploiter. A common simile, recorded also by other observers, is that of the *diku* as a greedy cat, always coveting the food of others and sometimes becoming aggressive—'showing the nails'—to get it.

I recorded an interesting story in Chotanagpur's 'deep country' which had to do with elephants. There was plenty of laughter among the listeners when it was told. The script included the healthy element of 'laughing at themselves' that Genovese has pointed out.

[21] E. Genovese already noted its value in his study on slavery in the North American South: '[The slaves] by laughing at themselves...freed themselves to laugh at their masters... Oppressed people who can laugh at their oppressors contain within themselves a politically dangerous potential' (1976: 584).

The story was told after I inquired about the low and precarious huts that could be seen in the fields:

> These are for us to watch for incoming [wild] elephants. They are dangerous; they come in big herds; they are big and step on everything: people, fields. They can kill. The worst of them are the mad elephants. They are like the *dikus*: they come from beyond the village and like to steal. They make people run away.
> They come and start looking for the liquor that is stored in the houses, smelling with their trunks. They may break the roof in order to put the trunks inside and thus get the liquor. They always get what they want. A lot of damage is done. If they are mad, it is better to get out of their path.
> Once X [one of the villagers] was dead drunk, walking unaware in the fields. An elephant smelled the liquor inside him and followed him. The elephant was upset because this jug [the drunken man] did not seem to have an opening [to take the liquor out]. The elephant got mad, picked up X and started shaking him to see if the liquor could come out. Not a drop was spilled and so the elephant, being so upset and liquor-less, decided to leave X on top of a bamboo tree. There we found X, still dead drunk [laughs]. This is the story of the *diku* elephant who thought himself more cunning than drunken X, but left without a drop of liquor and could steal nothing [more laughs].

In the course of the story the metaphorical elephant, the *diku*, gradually takes precedence over the real elephant. This superimposition of the two texts occurs in the description of the herd of wild elephants coming into the village, the need to watch their approach, and how they do not stop before fields or people (the exercise of power), the destruction they cause and the fear they arouse, thus making people flee (the impunity of the powerful), their greed to take away food (liquor, although in this case it may also mean joy and rest). Moreover, the elephant acted precisely like a *diku* does in the eyes of the adivasi peasants: trying to squeeze the poor peasant to get at least a drop of what he may have and may be hiding.

The audience laughed at the poor drunken fellow, at the ridiculous sight of him walking innocently or stupidly when menaced by the elephant/*diku* that followed him, at his maltreatment and at the elephant finally leaving him on top of a tree in a most dishonourable situation. The villager had to be rescued from the tree, still drunk, but he still remained in possession of what was his (the liquor inside him = his self, his belongings). Drunken X becomes the hero of the story, he is the one who cheats the mighty elephant. Thus, by laughing at themselves, at the image of weak, drunk, gullible men they are thought by the powerful to be, the adivasis can laugh at the foibles of the powerful.

There may be another hint in the story that would point to the need to preserve 'coded spaces': the acting foolishly on the drunk man's part stands for dissimulation. The story of the elephant is in itself an example of the use of concealed, coded *texts*, hidden beneath the 'pages' of a different and open *text*. The story was obviously not new. It had been told before, but the laughter still occurred. The story was a fable with a message which was reinforced through repetition. Given the adivasi's creativity in oral literature, one has grounds to believe that while traditional metaphors like those of the cat and the elephant continue to be used over and over again, new ones also come into being.

Concealment and dissimulation through silence tend to stress the negative, these being defensive methods that, while effective in maintaining the subalterns' spirits high and their pride protected, do not pose a real threat to power. On the contrary, at least on the surface, these methods seem to imply the acceptance of the established power (silence and satire are 'within the rules'). This acceptance promotes the continuation of a 'theatrical style' of power and not its disassembly. However, when protest becomes explicit and politically phrased, the silence and laughter of the powerless may prove to be reservoirs of strength which can be channelled into positive political action.

In this light, silence can be an effective addition to the *theatre of the powerless*. While embedded in action, silence itself makes protest explicit and the presence of the powerless visible. The huge procession at Dumka on the occasion of Jharkhand Divas in February 1980 gives a good example of disciplined silence. According to reports, while the Santal marchers were being insulted by shopkeepers and some passers-by (*dikus*, according to the Santals), the marchers did not utter a single word nor did they return the insults. Boycotts are another, somewhat similar addition to the *theatre of the powerless*, a sort of silence by means of absence. Such silence by absence has often been used as a means of exerting some political pressure as, for instance, in the 1980 boycott of the officially organized annual Santal Hijta fair (*F* 1980a: 8).

Silence and satire can certainly make the powerful uncomfortable. In a situation of social violence like the one that prevails in Bihar, however, this uneasiness of the powerful is caused mainly by the subordinates' silence, since satire tends to remain more of an underground *text*. This uneasiness may ironically bring more wood to the fire of the powerful's 'structural paranoia'.

The Value of Justice

A strong sense of *justice* and the realization that legal avenues to find redress are of difficult access, are themes frequently expressed by adivasis when they refer to their situation. Some of these comments have been quoted in previous chapters while discussing the unequal socio–economic order in which adivasis are placed and their political views.

In Jharkhand, the combination of a sense of justice, the experience of injustice and blocked legal paths inspired the big rebellions of the past. On those occasions, the extreme nature of the situation led to instances of counter-terror, as in the case of the Santals in the middle of the nineteenth century. Counter-terror is not only a show of force and of direct insubordination. It also contains the element of 'making justice by one's own hands', together with the search for satisfaction through vengeance. This is not the usual way in which adivasis make their conception of justice–injustice explicit. Instead, there are reports of cases of what are called 'trials Jharkhandi style' (conducted at the outskirts of the village where the wrong occurred and, in the cases reported, punished by beatings). These reports indicate that the saying 'The wicked must be punished and the good protected', became current in early 1981 among sections of the JMM (*F* 1981b: 6). The saying as well as the setting up of these trials contain elements of the subalterns' counter-terror tactics, the aim being not only to effect justice but to inspire fear of popular wrath.

More than the practice of a new legality, what could be generally observed were verbal, symbolic and practical manifestations of the justice–injustice discourse. Verbal manifestations ranged from the blunt words of an adivasi intellectual: 'We are all equal', which implied 'but we are not treated as such', to the statements in which some referred to themselves as 'victims of progress', 'the under-privileged', 'the uprooted'.

People from the rural areas understood injustice not in the abstract but through the experience of it in daily life. For instance, they said: 'Sand, stone, soil, land, trees, the Government takes it all, and we even have to pay for it. The Government denies our rights.'

At present, the adivasis do not seem to engage in counter-terror. However, a play of veiled menace does take place using a symbolic language. Once again, the arrow provides possibly the best symbolic instrument of justice in a world turned blind and deaf to suffering. That the arrow, besides being a useful menacing symbol, is an effective weapon, is clear to the adivasi peasant since 'the arrow knows where it goes. It is never wrong'. Furthermore: 'They [the landlords] are deaf, they do not understand words. They seeem to see [to have eyes] and still do not understand. They only know to talk the tongue of guns [a roar]. We know the tongue of arrows'. Few are the sounds uttered in 'the tongue of arrows'. In fact, in the areas where the JMM had a following, the provoking of violent incidents was consciously avoided. This has also been the position of the Bihar Colliery Kamgar Union led by A.K. Roy which allowed the carrying of bows and arrows but avoided the use of violent means in the course of political action (A. Sinha 1982a: 126). The presence of bows and arrows in events connected with issues of justice–injustice (processions, protest marches and carried by working teams during forcible harvests), suffices for the message of the arrows to be 'heard'.

The symbolic and practical meanings of the drums are clearer still: they convoke people, they always 'say' something to somebody. To the powerful, the message has always been disquieting: at harvest time, the landlords initially used to flee at the sound of the drums that heralded the approach of peasants, eager to get a just share of the crops. Soon the landlords learnt to answer the warning sound of the drums in 'the tongue of guns'.

Preservation of 'Coded' Social Spaces

The totality of the social field is a potential terrain for formulating resistance and protest. However, the nature and extent (pervasive-ness) of a given hegemonic order set limits to the uses the sub-altern sectors may want to give to this vast field. Therefore, the need arises among these sectors to find and protect (to codify) the most suitable spaces available in the social field as *zones of resistance*. These *zones* are normally marginal to the spaces the explicit play of power relations occupy.

In Jharkhand, the resistance and protest concealed in these spaces are sometimes translated into explicit actions as, for example, forcible harvesting. In other instances, when resistance becomes clandestine, the spaces used are to be found underground rather than on the surface (i.e. in oral history and literature, in the meanings woven in aesthetic manifestations and in collective activities, and in the symbolic realm). What is not directly 'said' communicates in another 'language' much more than what the obvious message conveys. The strength of clandestine protest resides in the way this 'double language' is used.

At least four coded spaces can be noted in the *culture of protest* as it operates in Jharkhand: the production of symbols and meanings; work; oral history and literature; and leisure.[22]

The *production of symbols and meanings* in the cases of the arrow and the drums has been already discussed, and the changing messages conveyed by the use of flags were mentioned in the previous chapter. Let us briefly refer to one of the possible combinations of symbol–meaning–action: purposive collective presence translated into the public political domain and how it comes to occupy a social space. The Jharkhand Divas is a case in point.

Since 1973, on the fourth day of February, Jharkhandis supporting the grass-roots Jharkhand Movement, have been holding annual massive meetings to express their demands. These are always peaceful events. The first Jharkhand Divas, jointly organized by the JMM and the Bihar Colliery Kamgar Union, took place at the Dhanbad polo-ground. The participants were workers and peasants, adivasis and non-adivasis. They demanded a separate state and the return of alienated lands to the peasants, and expressed their opposition to the retrenchment of local coal-miners. On the occasion of the 1974 celebration, 20,000 workers joined a multitude of 40,000 peasants. The main demand at the time was for Jharkhand as Lalkhand. The green and red flags used to fly together on those occasions. They symbolized the worker–peasant alliance as well as

[22] Each one of these coded spaces deserves close examination and analysis. This task will be hopefully attempted in the future, in a separate research project. At the present moment, some indications will be given about how these spaces are used.

the combination of regional (Jharkhand) and class (Lalkhand) demands (data collected in interviews; also Sengupta 1982c: 37–38; Iyer and Maharaj, 1977: 75, 79). Subsequent years saw a decline in the workers' participation and, of late, a change in the political contents of the meetings. Although the number of participants varies, it appears to have remained high (30,000 in 1980), and lately to have gone up (70,000 for 1986) (*India Today* 1986a: 3).

The Jharkhand Divas has maintained a number of characteristics through the years: the event is repeated at regular intervals (annual), always on the same day (4 February), at the same places (Dhanbad and Dumka); it used to enjoy a wide participation on class grounds (workers and peasants) and across ethnic divides (adivasis and non-adivasis); it always has the same features (peaceful, bows and arrows, large numbers of participants, speeches), and at least one constant demand (a separate state). This regularity has helped to instal a pattern, resulting in the subaltern sectors conquering certain time and geographical spaces which, in turn, has enabled them to take over momentarily the public scenario.

During the peak years of the worker–peasant alliance, the very presence of workers and peasants together was in itself an explicit message: that of their solidarity and the decision to join their struggles. This message was certainly uttered in a loud voice and was well heard by the authorities. As A.K. Roy put it: 'The authorities are not worried about the workers' movement or the tribal movement, but they are greatly alarmed about the worker–tribal allilance. That is why there has been such a persecution.'

The collective presence that keeps materializing every fourth of February is not perceived as an abstract (faceless) and feared 'mob' but as a *political* presence. The contents of these two 'presences' ('mob' and purposive collective presence) are different. In the second instance, we find explicit political meanings focused with precise aims on the terrain of practice. In this sense, the Jharkhand Divas of the mid-seventies were not expressions of the *theatre of the powerless* but of the real conquering of political spaces by social actors, obtained by means of an 'invasion' of symbols and meanings through actual practice.

The *domain of work*, especially when performed collectively, provides ample scope for the development of techniques of resistance and protest. In fact, this has always been one of the classical grounds where oppositional attitudes and activities have been put successfully into practice. The conflict between the conceptions of time–work in the industrial setting and the attitudes of the adivasi workers in relation to it has been pointed out in Chapter 3. It was suggested that the assumed 'inability' of the adivasis to comply with the time–work–discipline ethos of industrial capitalism, could precisely be a skill: to resist total subordination at least in some minimal space, contesting the control of time and behaviour at the working place.

The phenomenon of forcible harvesting illustrates the potentialities the ambit of work has as a suitable field for the development of a *culture of protest*. To an extent, forcible harvesting is a predictable phenomenon, taking place each harvest season. What is not predictable is the field in which it is going to take place. The combination of both factors: exact timing and unknown targets, assures the effectiveness of this form of resistance since it makes peasants and their demands 'visible' on the social stage. Forcible harvesting is organized on the same basis as any other harvest is in normal circumstances, only that in this case the modality of work is adapted to the needs posed by it being work and a mode of protest.

Forcible harvesting has been labelled a criminal offence by the state and part of the media. Peasants, instead, see it as their right: to collect what they have planted and worked for, the product of their toil. In the background of this attitude is the concealed discourse on justice–injustice: only those plots that a landlord has illegally obtained (contravening old or amended laws) are harvested. The attainment of justice seems to be the main motivation behind forcible harvesting. In the words of a peasant: 'We do not want to harm anybody, we just want our share (of paddy). We have asked and asked, but we were not listened to. We could not wait any longer. We had to harvest our fields and take our paddy.' In the end, the effect is one of open but measured defiance, its righteousness stressed by the peaceful behaviour of the peasants during harvest operations and the open performance of the task during daytime. At the same time, there is a sense of urgency which arises from very concrete needs that have to be fulfilled. As a peasant said: 'They took our land. We work and work. They take our paddy and leave us hungry.'

The public message of resistance and protest that harvest marches and forcible harvesting convey is that of peasant solidarity and discipline, and of the continuity of their demands. These peasant tactics demonstrated that peasants can be the masters of a space: the modality of their work, the actual field on which this work is done, the time during which it is performed, and that they could even momentarily change the conditions under which this work is usually done.

Oral history and *literature* are the subaltern sectors' redoubts of resistance *par excellence*. They are spaces with 'a past', with continuity, based not just on the effects of repetition. Oral history and literature are in themselves links between the past and the present. They record past and present experiences that have often been forced to remain guarded with zeal under concealment.

I have previously quoted the answer a Munda gave to the question 'When and why do Mundas sing?' He said: 'When people have something important to say, they sing. Mundas sing to remember who they are.' For the adivasis of Jharkhand, a *life–song–community–history complex* is practically synonymous with life, both in personal and in social collective terms. There is a saying in Mundari that explains: 'Walking is dancing. Saying is singing' (*Senge susun, kajige duran*). The community is implicit in all references made to music, song and dance, since all these three develop on the basis of collective participation.

The *life–son–community–history complex* embraces the community in its historical depth. This complex is in itself a code, a most complicated one. The fact that literature and history among the adivasis of Jharkhand have remained mostly oral (the writing of literature being recent and partial), helps to maintain the inviolability of the code. The characteristics of Mundari poetry, for instance, are functional in this respect. Mundari makes ample use of parallelism (synonym and antonym), onomatopoeia,[23] metaphors, repetition of words or syllables to obtain rhyme, emphasis,[24] and of the omission of relatives and prepositions. At the same time, to each poem/song corresponds a certain melodic and rhythmic pattern, and both are related to the rhythms of the life of the community.

[23] E.g.: *satob satob*, the noise that people with shoes make when they walk. See the poem 'Hatia village...' later in the text, where the onomatopoeia describes the engineer and technicians at the industrial complexes.

[24] For example, *do*, a particle that marks contrasts (see J. Hoffman *et al.* 1936–50: 1073).

With oral history and literature one enters the linguistic domain.[25] Language can be considered not only as an indicator of identity (in the sense of 'a people that speak the same language'), but also as a wider field in which identity is defined and redefined, reality is ordered, and ways of acting upon reality are communicated. Language does not only refer to the spoken word but to any form of communication. Communication, in turn, is purposive and not simply voluntary, since it takes place in concrete social situations.

On earlier occasions I discussed the possibility of discerning several *texts* in oral tradition.[26] Of them, the following are relevant for the present purposes: an oral tradition on history; an oral tradition on ethnic definition, and an oral tradition of opinion. In the first of these *texts*, key events in the history of the community are recorded. This is the case with the 'songs of rebellion' composed about the peasant movements that swept Jharkhand in the nineteenth century (see K.S. Singh 1966). Other songs are new and closely follow the pattern of the old ones. The history of the Birsaite Movement of 1895 is a theme that is taken up often in modern poems/songs. The following song, written at the end of the sixties, evokes the figure of Birsa:

> *Looking for you again*
> *Muchia Chalkad is asking for you.*
> *Dombari Hill is searching for you.*
> *Is looking for you*
> *with arrows and axes ringing [as they touch].*
> *The rumbling of guns searches for you.*
> *Bows and arrows touch [making a sound]*
> *for our mother country.*[27]

These types of songs that record history are repeated, remembered and reinvented. They are easy to memorize, are usually short (no

[25] In this respect, what S. Varese has to say is suggestive: 'For an ethnic group, the structure of a language plays the role of a *referential matrix*. As an ethnic referent, this matrix is what possibly permits an ethnic group to have continuity' (Varese 1988. My translation from Spanish).

[26] At the staff seminar of the Centre for Asian and African Studies, El Colegio de Mexico (Mexico, 1979), at the South Asia Seminar, ANU (Canberra, 1983) and at the International Congress of Anthropological and Ethnological Sciences (Vancouver, 1983).

[27] R.D. Munda, 'Muchia Chalkad Do', *Seled* 1967:53. My translation from Mundari.

more than four stanzas), and their lines are connected by words that give continuity to the text. Often, the same idea is repeated more than once to strengthen the message of the song.

History is kept in the collective memory of a people. Among the adivasis of Jharkhand, poem/songs are only one of the vehicles through which the contents of collective memory are communicated. Another vehicle is 'telling' history. I had the opportunity to listen to history-telling while at a Munda village at the foot of Dombari Hill, a place where the old millennial dream was buried at the start of this century. Aside from the preservation of history, other elements were revealed on that occasion like the definition of identity and resistance to deculturation.

S., the village headman, was an old man, small in stature, but of great vitality and of difficult temper. He was proud to have worked at Gandhi's side. He was also proud of his family which, having converted to Christianity in 1858, later abandoned it. Unashamedly and laughing, he defined his family as being one of 'petty zamindars.' 'More like rajas' he added. He understood and spoke English well, but insisted on speaking Mundari. As a consequence, the talk became confused and S. increasingly irritated. When his fury subsided, he burst out in perfect English: 'One should speak one's own language! why don't you speak in your own language?' I agreed with him. He should have spoken in Mundari and I in Spanish, a most unpractical proposition. His scolding did not stop there: 'In Mexico they are brown like us. Your colour is wrong. Why?' (I found Mexico rang a bell when I mentioned it. I still do not know exactly why.) I could not give a reason for this 'mistake'. Displaced from my role as observer, I understood how uncomfortable one can feel when observed and asked questions, especially when there are no possible answers. After making his point, S. amicably took me up Dombari Hill and told me his version of the Birsa rising. He must have been a child when the events were still fresh in the minds of the people around him. The story most probably was commented on and told many times in his village, close to the place where the movement was crushed.

Going up Dombari Hill, S. unfolded the detalils of the last chaptei of the Birsa Movement. He pointed at spots on the way, showed me where the Birsaites placed themselves for the siege and from where the troops came, and recounted what happened afterwards. On top of that hill and with the bit of lived history that S. provided,

Dombari looked exactly as the deadly trap it had been 80 years ago: a small plain with a precipice on one side and no possible escape for the rebels and their families who took refuge there. S.'s version did not deviate from the known facts, only some small details were added: that children were killed [there is an old song that recalls the incident], what the people did on the hill, what happened to them and how they felt.

There are in oral tradition *texts* that aim to assert the historical identity of a people. In Jharkhand, through the medium of songs, the themes of self-assertion often refer to land and territory and the rights the adivasis have over them. Old songs tend to stress these aspects (see Culshaw and Archer 1945; K.S. Singh 1966). More recently, a song related to the Jharkhand Party, claims identity in the following way:

> *We are the natives of this country*
> *Yet they are driving us from our*
> *birthplace....*

> (Orans 1965: 109–10)

A wider conception of identity is put forward in a recent poem/ song:

> *In this country we are born brothers,*
> *let us be united in love.*
> *Nobody is in front and nobody is behind,*
> *We are all brothers and relatives.*
> *Do exchange garlands of flowers.*[28]

Sometimes, a concern for the problems suffered in Jharkhand is expressed in 'songs of opinion.' I translated one such song from Mundari. It refers to the effects of industrialization in the area, specifically to the industrial complex of the Heavy Engineering Corporation on the lands of what used to be Hatia village. Some of its lines read:

> *Ranchi road shines!*
> *The steps of the white men sound*
> *as torrential rain* [satob satob].

[28] Composed by Kande Munda (*Hisir* 1967). Original in Mundari and Hindi. My translation.

Hatia village trembles [in the distance while]
The metallic sound [jirib jirib] of the
    workers' tools can be heard...
Ah! from the slopes they did uproot rocks and stones.
They made the god of the mountain [Marang Buru] flee.
When they brutally threw away the guardian god,
Hatia collapsed in the dust like stones
    falling on green leaves ....[29]

In this poem, dispossession and destruction is described as being not only material (loss of land, destruction of the village), but also in terms of social and cultural dispossession.

Another space to be mentioned in connection with the formulation of resistance is that of *leisure.*This is an extremely fertile and flexible space.[30] An important point to remark in the present context is that leisure entails collective activities: dancing with the participation of everybody present (in one way or another); listening to the music and words of old and new songs; sharing food and rice beer. All these elements form part of a specific semantic field. Leisure for the adivasis is a social and not an individual event. The immediate result of such social enjoyment of leisure is an enhancement of solidarity in the community, based on a basic attitude of sharing. It is possibly not a coincidence that the most visible aspects of leisure (mixed dancing, drinking, sexuality) have been precisely those which have been more often questioned by missionaries (on moral grounds) and by the dominant society (through derogatory stereotypes). In the end, such critical attitudes to leisure seem to attempt to undermine the social role of leisure.

To sum up, the development of processes of dominance–subordination and of forces to resist and contest these processes has given rise in Jharkhand to two cultural formations: a *culture of oppression* and a *culture of protest.* These two cultures are found to be operating in interaction and, at some levels, evolving dialectically. In Jharkhand, the dominant values and meanings around which a *culture of oppression* is organized are condensed in discourses on dominance–subordination and on the legitimacy of the powerful's

[29] Poem/song by R.D. Munda (*Hisir* 1967. A complete translation and comments in Devalle 1977b).

[30] M. Orans (1965) has already referred to the 'pleasure complex' among the Santals.

violence, and translated into social practices. The weak legitimacy of the existing hegemonic order and the presence of a complex of resistance and protest have conditioned the nature, use and extent of coercion in Jharkhand. In such a situation, one observes that a measured 'theatrical style of dominance' can be easily replaced by the *practice of terror*, directly experienced by the subaltern classes as lived dominance.

It is especially in situations where domination attempts, using coercion, to pervade all the levels of life of the subordinate classes, that resistance and protest become entrenched, expressed and guarded in the labyrinth of a cultural language. This is a dynamic language, adapted to the circumstances being lived, and may express itself through indigenous symbols or newly generated tropes. In a situation such as the one that has prevailed in Jharkhand, the culture of the subordinate sectors has become rebellious accompanying the development of a social consciousness. The universe of thought and attitudes that rejects the hegemony of the powerful has become structured into a *culture of protest* that supports a social strategy for survival, self-assertion and, ultimately, social reproduction.

Conclusion

Ethnicity, Culture and the Anthropological Quest

For social scientists, ethnicity has been synonymous with Otherness, the unsolved enigma. In an effort to decipher it, many researchers have reduced ethnicity either to a troublesome element in old and new 'melting pots' or to an instrument used in the competitive game fostered by 'social engineering'. There is also primordialist ethnicity, one even closer to a conception of the other as *the essentially different*. The understanding of ethnicity will not come through attempts at deciphering or simplification. It is necessary to rephrase the problem and look at it from angles that have often been underplayed. The present book is an attempt in that direction. From the study of a concrete case, the varieties of ethnic discourses in Jharkhand, I have derived a series of considerations regarding the general study of ethnicity.

History's Open Hand

Ethnicity should be viewed as a process whose meanings can only be understood in context, evolving within the flow of history and according to the particular social circumstances of a given people at different points in time. Moreover, the presence of ethnicity and class together in one and the same social formation adds to the complexities of the processual nature of ethnicity. The articulation and contradictions of these two processes—ethnicity and class—arising in the course of their evolution, can only be apprehended by looking at the historical dimension of the society in which these processes take place.

Classical anthropology has studied people as if their past was not worth exploring. The concern with the 'ethnographic present' has helped foster the myth of peoples with no history. Seen as social atoms with an irrelevant or elusive past, ethnography has given the people it studied the status of objects, of passive elements that left no imprint on history. One of the central aims in the treatment of ethnicity in this book has been to endow ethnic phenomena with historicity and to relate them to the social whole.

Under the influence of the older European schools of anthropology, anthropological training used to be preceded by an acquaintance with history and philosophy, conceived as anthropology's primeval sources. Anthropological research often looked for support in history. Despite the indications of its origins, and the ideas and aims that informed it, somewhere in its development anthropology disavowed its close links with history and philosophy. The various dialogues that can be established between anthropology and history depend on the theoretical position of the researcher in his/her discipline. Philosophy helps to establish the terms in which the dialogue is posed.

Anthropologists have remarked on the potentialities of a cross-disciplinary exchange between anthropology and history but, for the most part, they have rarely translated this appreciation into their research practices. At the most, a perfunctory bow to history is made by reducing historical dynamics to a sober and evanescent background landscape. Despite Evans–Pritchard's urgings in his 1950 Marett Lecture (1961), anthropological studies in the British and North American traditions have remained, if not totally anti-historical, generally ahistorical. Recently, a post-modernist ethnography has developed in the United States with the works of James Clifford, George Marcus, Michael Fisher and S. Tyler, among others. Post-modern ethnography has arrived to the alarming conclusion that neither social experience nor history exist until the ethnographer creates them in ethnographical *writing*, tending to mistake what it *sees*—particularly what it *writes*—with what objectively *is* (see Tyler 1986: 138; *cf.* with Rabinow 1986: 257). 'Post-modern language and the brave new history of anthropological theory and practice', Polier and Roseberry tell us in their excellent critique, 'boldly assert that the material world is imaginary and the imaginary world...is real' (1989: 258). Therefore, up to the present, with the exception of the political economy school, ethnohistory and Marxist studies, most of anthropology has resisted a rapprochement with history. At the same time, something has been happening on the other side of the disciplinary divide. Historians have begun to apply to their research new perspectives resulting from a cross-disciplinary exchange with the social sciences (see discussion in K. Thomas 1963 and Thompson 1972, 1977), but not without encountering resistance from the ranks of the historians themselves.[1] What does history, as a potential partner in a joint endeavour, have to offer? Among other things, one can mention a reciprocal critique of the practice of research, putting the 'ethnographic present' into perspective, providing social phenomena with contextual meanings, and restoring to the societies under study the (social) time depth that ahistorical variants of anthropological analyses have denied them.

In the study of ethnic phenomena in Jharkhand, a historical perspective has helped to detect the course that the process of ethnic conciousness-building has taken in the long duration, and to trace the origins of dominant discourses which use the ethnic theme as a subordinating agency. I refer, of course, to the colonial situation in India, to identities scientists and administrators

---

[1] As E.P. Thompson puts it: 'In some eyes, the "systematic indoctrination" of historians "in the social sciences" conjures up a scene of insemination, in which Clio lies inert and passionless...while anthropology or sociology thrust their seed into her womb. But the encounter between partners is going to be a good deal more active than that; and it is difficult to believe that the complacency of some anthropological...typologies will not be as much shattered by historical examination as the reverse' (1972:46).

constructed and translated into a category of inequality namely the 'tribe', and to the way ethnic differences were phrased during the process of nation-building. The historical dimension thus provided contextual meanings to the analysis of the adivasis' political manifestations in Jharkhand.

By emphasizing the time depth of social processes, the 'ethnographic present' is displaced from centre-stage to become 'a moment' in a processual flow. This shift, instead of diminishing the importance of the 'ethnographic present', in fact enhances its contents. Social phenomena appear not to be 'accidents' in the life of a society. The present ethnic-based political expressions in Jharkhand acquire new meanings when they are related to an adivasi *tradition of protest*. What we can recover from this past of protest represents only the tip of the iceberg. To avoid risky speculations, the study has taken as a vantage point for observation the *times of high density* in the history of Jharkhand's adivasi societies. In those moments, under an increased dialectical tension between socio–economic and political transformation and historico–cultural maintenance, overt collective confrontations with the instances of power come sharply into view. Much else still does not figure in this picture: the silent quotidian resistance as well as the absence of resistance at certain moments, since people cannot live in a constant state of protest. As I have stressed with reference to a *culture of protest, culture* becomes *rebellious at particular junctures and in specific modes*.

There is yet another outcome of the application of a historical perspective to anthropological research. Much of anthropology has conceived of these societies as being without a past, while at the same time it has constructed their present in the image of what they are supposed to have been in the past (usually in the pre-colonial past). Both the past and present of 'object–societies' have been situated at the margins of history. As a result, these societies have emerged as passive 'objects' that are defined only in *essentialist terms*. Among these anthropological 'objects' are the 'tribes'. It is not surprising that societies so de-contextualized often continue to be studied through their languages, material cultural manifestations, religions and customs, without these aspects being related to the social evolution of the societies in which they are present. By restoring historicity to the societies that anthropology studies, their *social* qualities, their dynamism and their presence in the current of social events—all denied by fixed categories and typologies—are acknowledged. E.P. Thompson has said that 'the mind of the historian has been enhanced, his perspectives extended, his awareness of significance aroused, by a reading of anthropology...One hopes that some anthropologists will return the compliment....' (1972: 48). My analysis of ethnicity hopes to return to history a few of the compliments Thompson has paid to anthropology.

Not Objects but Social Agents

For some time a number of social scientists have been trying to develop a dialogue between disciplines, but also to evolve an interdisciplinary strategy that 'consists in creating a new object that belongs to no one' (Barthes 1984: 97–103). This shift in perspective and aims in the social sciences brings us to another of the key analytical issues posed by the study of ethnicity in Jharkhand: the construction of Otherness in anthropological practice and the ways in which social categories have been reproduced by the hegemonic sectors in order to validate structures of inequality.

The conceptualization of societies as 'objects' has been one of the standing issues on the anthropological agenda since the late sixties. In J. Copan's words, it is necessary 'to change...the illusory object that anthropology has constructed up to the present.... To change the origin of the questions we should answer... To talk of *other things in other terms...*' (1974: 142; 33. Italics in the original). The Other must be seen as a social agent and not as an (alien, passive) 'object'. This social agent speaks a language that is 'active, transitive (political)...aiming at transformation' (Barthes 1984: 149. Also Abdel–Malek 1963). Despite J.P. Dumont's assertion that 'the imputed transformation of objects into subjects...has by now almost degenerated into cliche...' (1986: 356), the problem still stands at the core of the discipline. The efforts at solving this problem through reflexivity and dialogical anthropology, have resulted in a new appropriation of the Other (as an 'object') by post-modern enthnographers (see Rebel 1989: 124). Contrary to their alleged wishes, post-modern ethnographers again take up the old situation of advantage of the observer, and elevate the enthnographer to the position of 'author, creator and consumer of the Other' (Polier and Roseberry *op. cit.*: 246).

Can the use of subordinating categories like 'indio', 'racial group', 'tribe', and now 'ethnic', still be considered acceptable? Why are certain societies and not others viewed solely in ethnic terms? Given that systems of ethnic relations are essentially systems of inequality, is this terminology an instance of the 'inequality of languages' (Asad 1986: 141–64) with which different societies are addressed?

In the present study of Jharkhand the category 'tribe', of firm standing in Indian studies, was subjected to critical examination. Historical and ethnographic evidence was brought forward to demonstrate, on the one hand, the methodological weakness of this sociological category. On the other hand, the reasons for the ideological force that this sociological category has acquired are sought in the colonial redefinition of pre-colonial structures of social relationships and, once redefined, in the transformation of indigenous systems into parts of the colonial context. This new ordering of social relationships occurred at the ideological level through the objectification of the indigenous peoples as tribes and through the instauration of a 'natural order of things' in which social relations became ruled by the 'principle' of difference (ethnicity). The adivasis were not only asymmetrically incorporated into a new political economy but also, as representations of Otherness, into a new system of unequal relationships. Through the Census and later, through the Indian Constitution, the objectification of difference (ethnicity) succeeded in becoming an officially recognized paradigm for social classification. This process has also been helped by the acceptance of this objectification as a legitimate parameter to order social relationships by those in a position of subordination. This situation is reflected in the language sometimes used by subordinated ethnic groups, for instance, in the words employed by educated adivasis in Jharkhand to qualify themselves and others with reference to the tribal paradigm. Therefore, *ethnicity can be made to play the role of an autonomous force*, and thus actually help in the reproduction of structures of inequality.

By placing Jharkhand's adivasi societies in historical context and in Jharkhand's present social formation, it becomes evident that *ethnicity cannot be understood unless issues of social differentiation, processes of class formation and the development of class conflicts are considered in the context of their articulation with processes of ethnic differentiation.* Adivasis live in a class society and in an economic formation where the capitalist mode is dominant. 'Tribe', therefore, is an ill-suited sociological category to analyse the structural position of the adivasis in Jharkhand, either in the past or at present. 'Tribe' as a fixed and timeless category, is an in-adequate concept to understand the adivasis as agents in social processes. Situated in a social formation with specific characteristics, the adivasis not only exist in it but also act upon it, as their past and present struggles demonstrate. Our contention is that there were and are no 'tribes' in Jharkhand. What does exist, however, is the construct of tribe which helps in the reproduction of structures of inequality.

To deny the existence of 'tribes' in Jharkhand as defined in anthropological and administrative practice, and to categorize the indigenous communities basically as agrarian in view of their historical evolution, does not imply that dynamic ethnic configurations do not exist in Jharkhand or should be ignored. The tribal paradigm constructed unchanging societies on the basis of a limited conception of culture. The positivistic tradition, which still sustains this paradigm, restricted culture solely to its material expressions and to external symbols of collective identification. It thus denied the *social* nature of culture as a synthesis of a people's social consciousness, operative in social practice. Paradoxically, given their concern with culture, the defenders of the 'tribe' in fact engaged in negating the living cultures of the populations called 'tribal'. The resulting picture has been one of people with a 'museum culture', uprooted from the *deep historical field*, devoid of dynamism and meaning.

The solidity that the myth of the tribe demonstrated during the colonial era is not surprising. This myth justified the colonizer's *mission civilisatrice*. The myth has not died and nowadays nurtures developmentalism and the recommendations made by applied anthropologists and administrators. Why has it preserved its vitality? In my view, this myth has been and remains an element which fosters the expansion of state hegemony over civil society through the distortion and/or nullification of the history and culture of the subordinated sectors, thus eroding the basis of their social consciousness.[2]

[2] Similarly, S. Varese states, regarding the situation of Peru's indigenous peoples: 'To abolish the history of a people, to suppress their collective memory, implies to veto the future, to disaggregate the consciousness of unity...to cut the roots of collective imagination' (1980: 10. My translation from Spanish).

In Jharkhand there exists, on the one hand, the ideology of tribe, and on the other, ethnic configurations grounded in specific socio–cultural styles expanding in the long time duration. This 'depth of the historical field' (see Abdel–Malek 1975), expressed in a consciousness of historical permanence, gives these ethnic configurations continuity and elements for the formulation of endogenous social projects through which to interpret and face concrete social realities.

The Voices of Culture

Culture is ethnicity's privileged field in two senses. First, culture expresses the collective identity and consciousness of a people, synthetized in a particular 'style' rooted in specific social and historical grounds. Second, through culture, a first level of social awareness develops, the one that sustains the political expressions of ethnicity: social contradictions and conflicts are 'handled in cultural terms'. Among subordinate ethnic groups, it is the cultural domain that provides the elements for a strategy of survival, for social reproduction and for strength to check and question the advance of an attempted hegemonic order. The cultural 'language' in which a particular ethnic identity is lived and expressed has codes and meanings that are significant only to those who create and share them. Therein lies the force of culture in situations of dominance–subordination: the preservation of coded spaces that can become *zones of resistance*.

In my treatment of the political manifestations of ethnicity in Jharkhand, I have attempted to bring together culture and politics, often divorced from each other in anthropological research. This issue has a place in structural Marxism (where culture is reduced to ideology), among the critics of Western-centric socio–anthropological perspectives (especially in the seminal works of Abdel–Malek 1963 and Said 1979) and in political anthropology. Most of the anthropological project, however, has come full swing to view culture in idealist/symbolic terms, separating culture and politics as if they were two mutually exclusive domains. This treatment of culture has ended up ignoring material and power issues. Geertzian cultural theory, very influential nowadays, is perhaps the clearest instance of the change operated in the conception of culture in anthropology. Geertz found inspiration in P. Ricoeur, but there was in Ricoeur a slight but significant difference in emphasis when he said '*like* a text, human action is an open work...' (1971: 201, italics added). Geertz translated this as 'culture...*is* an ensemble of texts' (1973: 452, italics added), written without considering questions of power and domination and separated from the material and historical processes that mark the creation of culture (see Roseberry 1982; Crapanzano 1986; Asad 1986). The stimulus for a necessary *volte face* in this state of affairs has come from the field of literary/cultural history through the works of Raymond Williams and through the writings of social historians like E.P. Thompson.

A Western-centric perspective, particularly in the political sciences, has tended to view the political manifestations of the subaltern sectors 'from above', when not ignoring them altogether. Several issues should be considered in this light with reference to culture and politics. The dynamics of ethnicity in Jharkhand invalidates the generalized dichotomy of resistance–acquiescence. Reality is more subtle. Everyday life surprises us with actions, gestures, words that may have more than one meaning and purpose. The voices of resistance and protest are often uttered in modes that may look non-political or with meanings that may appear only as marginal to explicit political discourses. The best examples of this are the different readings that can be made of peasant 'passivity' and 'endurance'.

A mechanicist interpretation has also vitiated the understanding of power relationships giving rise to the dichotomy—consensus-coercion. The complexities of the Jharkhand situation show that in reality there is a dialectical tension between forces of oppression and forces of resistance, between potential and achieved consensus and coercion. The perception of political phenomena radically changes when the *locus* of power is not sought in the apparatus of power but in the operation of forces that have to do with power. With this are related the value judgements through which 'failure' and 'success' in politics have been perceived. The dialectical tension in which dominance and subordination operate is more complex than what is reflected in electoral politics. As the *tradition of protest* among the adivasis of Jharkhand up to the present shows, the relations between processes of domination and subordination have given rise to *cultural formations of oppression and protest*. These two formations develop far beyond the formal scenario of politics. The 'success' of resistance and protest is better understood in terms of the gradual acquisition of experiences that can eventually translate into political actions (Devalle and Oberoi 1983).

Ethnicity: The Hidden Tropes

There is no absolute practice of ethnicity. The role played by the ethnic factor in politics will closely depend on the class situation and the interests of those sectors that resort to it to reinforce their ideological discourses and practical actions. The political formulation of ethnicity is not developed by the entire ethnic community/ group as a bloc, since this is not an homogeneous entity in class terms. The actions of the different sectors of the community are guided by different interests, based on the existence of structural class links that are present in the society as a whole. At the same time, it is only at certain points in the history of a society that ethnicity is asserted explicitly, although in practice it has been 'lived' and 'used' all the time. What are the conditions under which ethnicity emerges as a major element for political mobilization? In contemporary India and certainly in Jharkhand, ethnic-based political movements appear closely related to class interests and often to overt class conflicts. In Jharkhand, ethnicity and class are embedded in the same social formation and found in interaction.

Broadly, I am arguing that when class conflicts are diverted to confrontations at other levels (for instance, 'locals' *vs* 'outsiders'), or where the development of class-based movements encounters great obstacles, ethnicity may act as a factor of unity *at a certain moment* of political action. The issue remains as to when and under what circumstances class consciousness takes precedence over ethnic consciousness and becomes the leading force in popular movements. The JMM of the seventies did show this evolution but, at the same time, the eighties brought ethnicity back once more into the foreground in Jharkhand. This evolution is not complete and we will surely see more of it as changes continue to occur in the socio–political context of the region.

It is necessary to underline that to sharply separate the existence of an ethnic consciousness from the development of a class consciousness may be highly unproductive. When ethnic ascription and class situation correlate, as in the case of indigenous peasantries (and the majority of the adivasis in Jharkhand fall broadly into this category), both ethnic and class consciousness may develop in unison. This combined awareness is condensed in the expression 'Jharkhandi producer' that animated the grass-roots movement in Jharkhand.

Ethnicity as a process presents both continuities (what makes a particular ethnic/ethno-national style) and discontinuities (the different forms in which ethnicity is lived by different social sectors). The discontinuities in the process stem from the direct intervention of social and historical circumstances: the experience of conquest and colonialism, the advance of cultural hegemony, the process of class formation and the development of class conflicts. From the intersecting of the two constituent tendencies of ethnicity, permanence and dynamics, emerge different formulations of ethnicity. The various formulations of Jharkhandi identity discussed in this study show that while some key indicators remain constant in the definition of identity and of political aims, these are differently formulated in each of the movements according to their class bases.

Class consciousness develops out of the collectively experienced everyday reality. For those involved, class, more often than not, is not translated into abstract discourses. Class is lived as a process and 'handled in cultural terms' in many different ways (see Thompson 1968: 10–12; 1978: 149–50). Ethnicity can be partly seen as one of these ways, particularly in systems of inequality in which ethnic ascription and class situation tend to correspond. It can be considered to be a mode of social consciousness as well as a form of ordering social relationships. Oppression is not perceived in the abstract either. What flesh and bone people experience are concrete realities: land alienation, rural indebtedness, inadequate wages, oppressive time–work–discipline for the sake of increased production, discrimination, and the negation or distortion of their collective identity. Their demands globally express a defence of basic human needs and rights.

For oppositional grass-roots politics, ethnicity can provide a strategic axis for mobilization against inequality and domination, engineered towards aims that are not limited to the economic *alone*. They will instead attempt to embrace realms of the social reality which have been subordinated by the mechanisms of formal politics to economic imperatives and to the 'higher' goals of a sectorial 'national interest'. When appealing to their collective historico–cultural identity, the subaltern sectors are expressing their concerns and views on issues of culture and deculturation, self-respect, self-determination, the right to linguistic specificity, their views on the unequal nature of existing socio–economic relationships, and especially their right to participate actively in politics. This participation is often sought outside the existing structures (like established parties) through a process of redefinition of the contents of politics. The people take a stand against the inequalities present in the society, against the authoritarianism of the state, and against the hegemonic claims of the ruling sectors.

In this context, the coalescence of class and ethnic/national subordination has usually resulted in an explosive combination. In the era of national liberation movements and decolonization, collective identities—ethnicity amongst them—have played an important role in popular political mobilization, given the added meanings they provide to mass solidarity. In the course of these struggles, existing contradictions expressed in ethnic, regional and class antagonisms are acknowledged from a holistic perspective that embraces the social, economic and cultural domains. This holistic perspective may help the subaltern sectors to more successfully resist the social and moral hegemony of the dominant classes and to develop alternative views about the society at large and their future. These alternative views can come together into potentially radical *cultures of protest*.

To sum up, ethnic discourses are many and varied in nature. Leaving aside the expressions of ethnic assertion in the shape of ultra-nationalisms and community exclusivism, we can say that in the hands of the state and the dominant classes, ethnicity serves as an element to reproduce systems of social relationships, to validate structures of inequality and to support policies of social control. In this context, sectors of those groups in a situation of ethno–national subordination may act, on account of their class situation, as mediators between the structure of power and the subaltern sectors, performing a role similar to that of Mafeje's 'converts' (1971). This mediation, translated in reformist efforts, moves always within the parameters established by the structure of power, ultimately help-ing in its reproduction. In specific situations of subordination, on the other hand, ethnic consciousness may provide the foundations for the emergence of an oppositional consciousness, expressed in counter-hegemonic practices. This consciousness entails an acknowledgement of the nature of inter-ethnic relationships, often accompanied by an acute perception of class differences and antagonisms. At the practical level, ethnicity may provide the subaltern sectors with a strategy to combat inequality and to cancel forms of domination.

I have attempted to show in this book that the examination of social processes such as ethnicity calls for a change in the method-ology, the modes of inquiry and analysis in anthropological practice. The subject needs to be approached in terms different from those that originate in ethno-centric perceptions. A methodology that combines historical, sociological and anthropological analyses of social phenomena can transform the terms in which issues of domi-nance and subordination have been posed. Former 'objects' will be viewed as the social agents they are. The presence of Jharkhand adivasi societies as active social and historical agents challenges the existence of the 'illusory object' that anthropology has con-structed (in the guise of 'tribes', in this case) to conceptualize non-Western societies.

Glossary

Abwabs	miscellaneous cesses, imposts and charges levied by landlords and public officers
Adhi dharma	'a person whose *dharma* is the original one.' An adivasi who follows his/her own religion
Adivasi	from the Sanskrit: *adi* = original, *vasi* = inhabitant; the Indian native ethnic minorities
Akhra, akhara	village dancing ground. A space used for any communal activity
Anna	one-sixteenth of a rupee
A'sar	bow and arrow
Barkandaz	armed watchman
Begar	forced labour
Beth begari	bonded labour system
Bhuinhar	original clearers of land among the Oraons and the Mundas, with remnants of *khuntkatti* lands as privileged tenures (*bhuinhari* lands)
Bitlaha	temporal or permanent excommunication for breaching the social code of conduct (Santal)
Bonga	deity; god
Brahmottar	land granted rent-free to Brahmins
Chuar	'bandit'
Dacoity	brigandage
Daroga	head of a police, custom or excise station
Deswali lands	lands under the control of the religious chief (Munda)
Diku	a non-adivasi person alien to the area; 'alien–exploiter'
Disum	territory
Diwan	a minister, a chief officer of a state
Duk dukia(*dum-duggia*)	drum
Eta-haturenko	'men of other villages'
Ghatwal	village headman with a service tenure (Bhumij); constable in Jungle Mahals. Guardians of passes and wardens of marches
Gola	depot
Hatu	village (Mundari)

Hor, horo	'us, the people'; self-definitory term among adivasis of the Munda group
Hul	uprising. The Santal Movement of 1855
Jagarthan	sacred grove (Santal)
Jagir	a service tenure
Jagirdar	holder of a *jagir*
Johar	expression used by adivasis as a greeting; a salutation between equals
Junglee	'people of the jungle', 'primitive'
Kali paraja	from the Sanskrit *kali* = black, and *paraja* = born of another, alien, different. 'Black people'
Kamioti	bonded labour system
Khas	own cultivation
Khorposh	maintenance grants
Khorposhdar	maintenance grantee
Khunt	lineage
Khuntkatti lands	lands communally owned by the *Khuntkattidars*
Khuntkattidar	descendant of the village's founding lineage (Chotanagpur)
Kili	clan
Lathait	muscle-man trained in the use of batons
Lalkhand	red land
Lo Bir Sendra	Hunt council (santal)
Mahajan	moneylender
Mahato	village headman
Mahua	(*Bassia latifolia*). Fermented drink made out of its flowers
Manjhi	village headman
Manjiha lands	A landlord's privilege private lands (Chotanagpur)
Manki	leader of a confederacy of villages (Munda)
Marang Buru Bonga	the sacred Great Mountain
More hor	'group of five' similar to the *panchayat*; Santal village council
Munda	village headman (Munda)
Naia, nayaka, naeke	village religious chief (Santal)
Naib	deputy
Ojha or sokha	'witch finder'. Traditional healer
Pahan	village religious chief (Munda)
Paik	village watchman
Panchayat	a village 'council of five'. Consultative body
Paramanik	person in charge of matters regarding land and cultivation (Santal)
Pargana	confederacy of twelve villages (Santal). A revenue subdivision of a *tahsil* (subdivision of a district)
Parganait	Santal territorial chief
Parha	inter-village council
Parja-horoko	'men of other villages'
Patti	confederacy of villages (Munda)

Pradhani system	a system in which the landlord does not deal directly with the tenants but through the mediation of the village headman (Chotanagpur and Santal Parganas)
Raiyat, ryot	a cultivator, as distinct from labourer
Raj	kingdom/ruler
Raja	ruler
Rajha	'the share of the raja', the raja's rent-paying lands (Chotanagpur)
Sadan	Non-adivasi speaking Sadani
Sal	A tree of the species *Shorea robusta*
Sannyasi	a 'houseless devotee', wandering mendicant
Sardar	chieftain, village headman (Paharia)
Sardar ghatwal	chief of several twelve-village units (Bhumij)
Sarkar	government
Sarna	village sacred grove (Munda)
Sasan	burial ground
Sing Bonga	the solar deity in the Munda pantheon
Suzawal	a native collector of revenue
Tanbedar	watchman, a subordinate to the *ghatwal*
Tarai	belt of plains between Bihar and Nepal
Thakur	god
Thana	a police station or area under the jurisdiction of a local police station
Thika	permanent or temporary land lease
Thikadar	holder of a permanent or temporary lease
Tumduka	Santal drum
Ulgulan	uprising. The Birsaite Movement of 1895
Zamindar	landlord or landholder. Under British law: a person recognized as possessing proprietory rights over land
Zamindari	estate of a zamindar

Bibliography

ABDEL–MALEK, A. (1963) 'L' Orientalisme en Crise'. *Diogène*, 44: 109–42.
──────── (1975) *La Dialéctica Social. La Reestructuración de la Teoría Social y de Filosofía Política*. México–Madrid–Buenos Aires: Siglo XXI.
──────── (1981)*Social Dialectics* (Vols. 1 and 2). London: Macmillan Press.
ADAS, M. (1979) *Prophets of Rebellion. Millenarian Protest Movements Against the European Colonial Order*. Chapel Hill: The University of North Carolina Press.
AGUERO, C., S. DEVALLE and M. TANAKA (1981) 'Perspectives for the Study of the Peasantry and National Integration' in C. Agüero, S. Devalle and M. Tanaka (eds.), *Peasantry and National Integration*. México: El Colegio de México: 45–49.
AHMED, F. (1983) 'Ground into the Dust'. *India Today*, 31 August: 50–53.
──────── (1986) 'Jharkhand: Renewed Call'. *India Today*, 28 February: 3.
AMIN, S. (1974) *El Capitalismo Periférico*. México: Nuestro Tiempo.
ANDERSON, B. (1983) *Imagined Communities. Reflections on the Origin and Spread of Nationalism*. London: Verso.
ANTROBUS, H.A. (1957) *History of the Assam Company* 1839–1953. Edinburgh: Constable.
APTE, M.L. (1978) 'Region, Religion, and Language: Parameters of Identity in the Process of Acculturation' in R. Holloman and S., A. Arutionov (eds.), *Perspectives on Ethnicity*. The Hague-Paris: Mouton: 223–31.
ARCHER, W.G. (1945) 'Comment. A Rebellion Number'. *Man in India*, XXV(4): 205–07.
ARGYLE, W.J. (1969) 'European Nationalism and African Tribalism' in P.H. Gulliver (ed.), *Tradition and Transition in East Africa*. London: Routledge and Kegan Paul: 41–57.
ASAD, T. (1975a) 'Anthropological Texts and Ideological Problems: An Analysis of Cohen on Arab Villages in Israel'. *Review of Middle East Studies*, I: 1–40.
──────── (ed.) (1975b) *Anthropology and the Colonial Encounter*. Ithaca: Ithaca Press.
──────── (1986) 'The Concept of Cultural Translation in British Social Anthropology' in J. Clifford and G.E. Marcus (eds.), *Writing Culture. The Poetics and Politics of Ethnography*. Berkeley: University of California Press: 141–64.

ASPELIN, P. L. and S. COELHO DOS SANTOS (1981) *Indian Areas Threatened by Hydro–electric Projects in Brasil*. Copenhagen: IWGIA.

BAILEY, F.G. (1960) *Tribe, Caste and Nation. A study of Political Activity and Political Change in Highland Orissa*. Manchester: Manchester University Press.

——————— (1961) '"Tribe" and "Caste" In India'. *Contributions to Indian Sociology*, V: 7–19.

BALANDIER, G. (1955) *Sociologie Actuelle de l'Afrique Noire*. Paris: PUF.

BANTON, M. (1981) 'The Direction and Speed of Ethnic Change' in C.F. Keyes (ed.), *Ethnic Change*. Seattle: University of Washington Press: 32–52.

BARA, D. (1980) *Vikas Maitri. Annual Report, 1979*. Ranchi: Vikas Maitri.

BARBADOS SYMPOSIUM (1971) *Declaration of Barbados*. Copenhagen: IWGIA.

BARRERA, M. (1979) 'Colonial Labor Theories of Inequality: The Case of the International Harvester' R. Cohen, P.C.W. Gutkind and P. Brazier (eds.) *Peasants and Proletarians. The Struggle of Third World Workers*. London: Hutchinson: 331–52.

BARRIER, N.G. and V.A. DUSENBERY (eds.) (1989) *The Sikh Diaspora: Migration and the Experience Beyond Punjab*. Columbia: South Asia Publ.

BARTH, F. (ed.) (1970) *Ethnic Groups and Boundaries. The Social Organization of Culture Difference*. London: George Allen and Unwin.

BARTHES, R. (1984) *Mythologies*. London: Paladin.

BASU, K.K. (1934) 'The Sontal Outbreak in Bhagalpur'. *The Journal of the Bihar and Orissa Research Society, XX*: 186–224.

BENNETT, J.W. (ed.) (1975) *The New Ethnicity. Perspectives from Ethnology*. New York: West Publ.

BERNSTEIN, H. (1976) 'Underdevelopment and the Law of Value: a Critique of Kay'. *Review of African Political Economy*, 6: 51–64.

BETEILLE, A. (1974) *Studies in Agrarian Social Structure*. Delhi: Oxford University Press.

BETTELHEIM, C. (1972) 'Theoretical Comments' in A. Emmanuel (ed.) *Unequal Exchange: A Study of the Imperialism of Trade*. London–New York: Monthly Review Press: 271–322.

BHADURI, A. (1973) 'Agricultural Backwardness under Semi-feudalism'. *Economic Journal, 83*, (329).

BHATTACHARYA, S. (1982) *Modern Indian History*. Presidential Address, Indian History Congress. New Delhi: Jawaharlal Nehru University.

BOGAERT, M.V. d. (1980) 'To Sit Together and to Stand Together'. (Unpublished manuscript).

BOGAERT, M.V. d., A.K. SINHA, M. BHOWMIK and D. BARA (1980) *Training Village Guidelines for Development Workers*. Ranchi: Xavier Institute of Social Service.

BOGAERT, M.V. d., D. BARA and A.K. SINHA (n.d.) *Development of Village Entrepreneurs in a Tribal Area. A Case Description*. Ranchi: Bagla Press.

BOMPAS, C.H. (1909) *Folklore of the Santal Parganas*. London: David Nutt.

BONACICH, E. (1980) 'Class Approaches to Ethnicity and Race'. *The Insurgent Sociologist*, X(2): 9–23.

BONFIL BATALLA, G. (1972) 'El Concepto de Indio en América: Una Categoría de la Situación Colonial'. *Anales de Antropología*, IX: 105–24.

———— (1979) 'Las Nuevas Organizaciones Indigenas' in Documentos de la Segunda Reunión de Barbados, *Indianidad y Descolonización en América Latina*. Mexico: Nueva Imagen: 23–40.

———— (1981) *Utopía y Revolución: El Pensamiento Político Contemporáneo de los Indios América Latina*. Mexico: Nueva Imagen.

BOSE, N.K. (1964) 'Change in Tribal Cultures before and after Independence'. *Man in India*, 44 (1): 1–10.

BOSE, S.R. (1971) *Economy of Bihar*. Calcutta: Mukhopadhyay.

BRADBY, B. (1980) 'The Destruction of Natural Economy' in H. Wolpe (ed.), *The Articulation of Modes of Production*. London: Routledge & Kegan Paul: 93–127.

BRADLEY–BIRT, F.B. (1903) *Chota Nagpore. A Little-Known Province of the Empire*. London: Smith, Elder & Co.

BRASS, P.R. (1976) 'Ethnicity and Nationality Formation'. *Ethnicity*, 3: 225–41.

BRIDGES, L. (1973) 'Race Relations Research: from Colonialism to Neo-Colonialism? Some Random Thoughts'. *Race*, XVI(3): 331–41.

BUCI–GLUCKSMANN, C. (1982) 'Hegemony and Consent' in A. Showstack Sassoon (ed.) *Approaches to Gramsci*. London: Writers and Readers Publ. Coop.: 116–26.

BYRES, T.J. and H. MUKHIA (eds.) (1985) 'Feudalism and Non-European Societies'. Special Issue of *The Journal of Peasant Studies*, 12 (2–3).

CABRAL, A. (1973) *Return to the Sources. Selected Speeches by Amilcar Cabral*. New York and London: Monthly Review Press.

CAPLAN, L. (1970) *Land and Social Change in East Nepal*. Berkeley and Los Angeles: University of California Press.

CASIMIR, J. (1981) *La Cultura Oprimida*. Mexico: Nueva Imagen.

CASTELLS, M. (1979) 'Immigrant Workers and Class Struggles in Advanced Capitalism: The Western European Experience' in R. Cohen, P.C.W. Gutkind and P. Brazier (eds.) *Peasants and Proletarians. The Struggle of Third World Workers*. London: Hutchinson: 353–79.

CÉSAIRE, A. (1946) *Les Armeés Miraculeuses (Et Les Chiens se taisaint)*. Paris: Gallimard.

CHAKRABORTY, S. (1982) 'Jharkhand Movement and the Working Class'. *Frontier*: July 17: 3–5.

CHAUDHURI, M.R. (1978) *The Tea Industry in India. A Diagnostic Analysis of its Geo–economic Aspects*. Calcutta–New Delhi: Oxford University Press.

CHAUDHURY, S.B. (1955) *Civil Disturbances during the British Rule in India (1765–1857)*. Calcutta: Punthi Pustak.

CHESNEAUX, J. (1973) *Peasant Revolts in China. 1840–1949*. London: Thames and Hudson.

CLIFFE, L. (1976), 'Rural Political Economy of Africa' in P.C. Gutkind and I. Wallerstein (eds.) *The Political Economy of Contemporary Africa*. London: Sage: 112–30.

CLIFFORD, J. (1986a) 'Introduction: Partial Truths' in J. Clifford and G.E. Marcus (eds.) *Writing Culture. The Poetics and Politics of Ethnography*. Berkeley: University of California Press: 1–26.

CLIFFORD, J. (1986b) 'On Ethnographic Allegory' in J. Clifford and G.E. Marcus (eds.) *Writing Culture. The Poetics and Politics of Ethnography*. Berkeley: University of California Press: 98–121.

CLIFFORD, J. and G.E. MARCUS (eds.) (1986) *Writing Culture. The Poetics and Politics of Ethnography*. Berkeley: University of California Press.

COHEN, A. (1969) *Custom and Conflict in Urban Africa. A Study of Hausa Migrants in Yoruba Towns*. London: Routledge and Kegan Paul.

————— (1974a) 'The Lesson of Ethnicity' in A. Cohen (ed.) *Urban Ethnicity*, ASA Monograph 12. London: Tavistock: ix–xxiv.

————— (1974b) *Two–Dimensional Man*. London: Routledge and Kegan Paul.

————— (1981) 'Variables of Ethnicity' in C.F. Keyes (ed.) *Ethnic Change*. Seattle: University of Washington Press: 307–31.

COHEN, R. (1978) 'Ethnicity: Problem and Focus in Anthropology'. *Annual Review of Anthropology*, 7: 379–403.

COHN, N. (1962) 'Medieval Millenarism: its Bearing in the Comparative Study of Millenarian Movements' in S. Thrupp (ed.) *Millenial Dreams in Action. (Comparative Studies in Society and History Supplement 2)*. The Hague: Mouton: 31–43.

————— (1970) *The Pursuit of the Millennium*. New York: Paladin.

COMAROFF, J. (1985) *Body of Power, Spirit of Resistance. The Culture and History of a South African People*. Chicago and London: University of Chicago Press.

CONNOR, W. (1972) 'Nation–building or Nation-destroying?' *World Politics*, XXIV(3): 319–35.

COPANS, J. (1974) *Critiques et Politiques de l' Anthropologie*. Dossiers Africaines, Paris: Maspero.

————— (ed.) (1975) *Anthropologie et Imperialisme*. Paris: Maspero.

CORBRIDGE, S. (1982) 'Industrial Development in Tribal India. The Case of the Iron Ore Mining Industry in Singhbhum District, 1900–1960' in N. Sengupta (ed.) *Fourth World Dynamics: Jharkhand*. Delhi: Authors Guild Publ.: 40–62.

————— (1988) 'The Ideology of Tribal Economy and Society: Politics in the Jharkhand, 1950–1980'. *Modern Asian Studies* 22(I): 1–42.

COUPLAND, H. (1911) *Bengal District Gazetteers. Manbhum*. Calcutta: Bengal Secretariat Book Depot.

COX, O. C. (1970) *Caste, Class and Race. A Study in Social Dynamics*. London: Monthly Review Press.

CRAPANZANO, V. (1986) 'Hermes' Dilemma: The Masking of Subversion in Ethnographic Description' in J. Clifford and G. E. Marcus (eds.) *Writing Culture. The Poetics and Politics of Ethnography*. Berkeley: University of California Press: 51–76.

CULSHAW, W.J. (1949) *Tribal Heritage. A Study of the Santals*. London: Lutterworth Press.

CULSHAW, W.J. and W.G. ARCHER (1945) 'The Santal Rebellion'. *Man in India*, XXV(4): 218–39.

DALTON, E.T. (1872) *Descriptive Ethnology of Bengal*. Calcutta: Office of the Superintendent of Government Printing (Reprint of 1960).

DANDA, A.K. (1988) 'Tribes in India'. *Man in India*, 68(4): 313–34.

DAS, A.N. (1975) 'Bihar: The Struggle of Workers and Tribal Peasants in Chota-nagpur'. *Economic and Political Weekly*, X(9), 1 March: 384–86.

———————— (1983) *Agrarian Unrest and Socio–economic Change in Bihar, 1900–1980*. New Delhi: Manohar.

———————— (1984) 'Class in Itself, Caste for Itself: Social Articulation in Bihar'. *Economic and Political Weekly*, XIX(37): 1616–19.

———————— (1986) 'Bihar: Landowners' Armies Take Over "Law and Order"'. *Economic and Political Weekly*, XXI(1), 4 January: 15–17.

DAS, A.N. and V. NILAKANT (eds.) (1979) *Agrarian Relations in India*. New Delhi: Manohar.

DAS GUPTA, B. (1989) 'Anatomy of Jharkhand Movement'. *Mainstream*, 18 February: 7–8: 34.

DAS GUPTA, D. P. (1980a) 'After Gua'. *Frontier*, 13(2), 15 November: 7–8.

———————— (1980b) What Happened in Gua? *Frontier*, 13(5), 27 September: 3–4.

DAS GUPTA, J. (1975) 'Ethnicity, Language Demands, and National Develop-ment' in Glazer and Moynihan (eds.) *Ethnicity, Theory and Experience*. Cambridge: Harvard University Press: 466–88.

DAS, V. (1985) 'Introduction: Varieties of Life and the Word'. *Contributions to Indian Sociology* (N.S.), 19(1): 1–8.

DAS, Victor (1990)'Jharkhand Movement:From Realism to Mystification'. *Econo-mic and Political Weekly* XXV(30), 28 July: 1624–26.

DATTA, K.K. (1940) *The Santal Insurrection of 1855–1857*. Calcutta: Calcutta University Press.

———————— (1958) *History of the Freedom Movement in Bihar*, I and III. Patna: Government of Bihar.

DATTA-MAJUMDER, N. (1956) *The Santal. A Study in Culture-Change*. Delhi: Manager of Publications.

DAVIS, S.H. and R.O. MATHEWS (1976) *The Geological Imperative. Anthro-pology and Development in the Amazon Basin of South America*. Cambridge, Mass.: Anthropology Resources Center.

DE, N.R. (1979) 'India's Agrarian Situation: Some Aspects of Changing the Con-text' in A. N. Das and V. Nilakant (eds.) *Agrarian Relations in India*. New Delhi: Manohar: 231–61.

DEERE, C.D. (1979) 'Rural Women's Subsistence Production in the Capitalist Periphery' in R. Cohen, P.C.W. Gutkind and P. Brazier (eds.) *Peasants and Proletarians. The Struggle of World Workers*. London: Hutchinson: 133–48.

DE LEPERVANCHE, M. (1980) 'From Race to Ethnicity'. *The Australia and New Zealand Journal of Sociology*, 16(1): 24–37.

DENOON, D. (1985) 'Capitalism in Papua New Guinea'. *The Journal of Pacific History*, XX(3): 119–34.

DESAĪ, A.R. (1961) *Rural India in Transition*. Bombay: Popular Book Depôt.

DESPRES, L.A. (ed.) (1975) *Ethnicity and Resource Competition in Plural Societies*. The Hague–Paris: Mouton.

DEVALLE, S.B.C. (1977a) *La Palabra de la Tierra. Protesta Campesina en India, Siglo XIX*. Mexico: El Colegio de Mexico.

———————— (1977b) 'Un Poema. Una Industria'. *Estudios de Asia y Africa*. XII(1): 67–70.

———————— (1980) *Multiethnicity in India*. Copenhagen: IWGIA.

DEVALLE, S.B.C. (1981) 'Language and Culture: A Defining Axis of Ethnic Identity'. *Comunicación e Informática*, 2(1): 26–33.

───────── (1983) 'Antropología, Ideología, Colonialismo'. *Estudios de Asia y Africa*, XVIII(3): 337–68.

───────── (1985a) 'Clandestine Culture of Protest in Colonial Situations'. *Canberra Anthropology*, 8(1 & 2): 32–57.

───────── (1985b) 'India en 1984: el Colapso del Estado y el Comunalismo en Política'. *Estudios de Asia y Africa*, XX(4): 646–78.

───────── (ed.) (1989) *La Diversidad Prohibida. Resistencia Etnica y Poder de Estado*. Mexico: El Colegio de Mexico.

───────── (1990) 'Los Sikhs en Canadá: "Diaspora" O Migraciones?' *Estudios de Asia y Africa*, XXV (82): 209–49.

DEVALLE, S.B.C. and H.S. OBEROI (1983) 'Sacred Shrines, Secular Protest and Peasant Participation: the Babbar Akalis Reconsidered'. *Punjab Journal of Politics*, VII(2): 27–62.

DEVI, M. (1981a) 'Contract Labour or Bonded Labour?' *Economic and Political Weekly*, XVI(23), 6 June: 1010–13.

───────── (1981b) 'Witch-Sabbath at Singhbhum'. *Economic and Political Weekly*, XVI(40), 3 October: 1595–97.

───────── (1983) 'Singhbhum. A Countryside Slowly Dying'. *Economic and Political Weekly*, XVIII(10), 5 March: 329–30.

DHAN, R.O. (1977) 'Tribal Movements in Chotanagpur'. In S.C. Malik (ed.) *Dissent, Protest and Reform in Indian Civilization*. Simla: Indian Institute of Advanced Study: 199–209.

DHAR, H. (1980a) 'Bihar: A Strange Alliance'. *Frontier*, 14 June: 7–8.

───────── (1980b) 'Split in Jharkhand Mukti Morcha'. *Economic and Political Weekly*, XV(31), 2 August: 1299–300.

DHOQUOIS, G. (1976) 'La Formación Económico–social como Combinación de Modos de Producción' in Luporini, Sereni *et al. El Concepto de 'Formación Económico–social'*. Mexico: Siglo XXI: 185–89.

D.N. (1988) 'Factors in the Jharkhand Movement'. *Economic and Political Weekly*, 30 January: 185–87.

D.N. and G.K. (1989) 'Some Agrarian Questions in the Jharkhand Movement'. *Economic and Political Weekly*, XXIV(27), 8 July: 1505–10.

DOCUMENTOS DE LA SEGUNDA REUNION DE BARBADOS (1979) *Indianidad y Descolonización en América Latina*. Mexico: Nueva Imagen.

DUBE, S.C. (1960) 'Approaches to the Tribal Problem in India' in L.P. Vidyarthi (ed.) *Indian Anthropology in Action*. Ranchi: Ranchi University: 11–15.

───────── (1977) *Tribal Heritage of India. I: Ethnicity, Identity and Interaction*. New Delhi: Vikas.

DUMONT, J.P. (1986) 'Prologue to Ethnography or Prolegomena to Anthropography'. *Ethos* 14(4): 334–67.

ELIADE, M. (1954) *Traité d' Histoire des Religions*. Paris: Payot.

ELWIN, V. (1943) *The Aboriginals*. London: Oxford University Press.

───────── (1945) 'The Kol Insurrection'. *Man in India*, XXV(4): 258–60.

───────── (1960) 'Do We Really Want to Keep them in a Zoo?' in Government of India, *Adivasis*. Delhi: Publications Division.

ENLOE, C.H. (1973) *Ethnic Conflict and Political Development*. Boston: Little, Brown and Co.

EPSTEIN, A.L. (1969) 'The Network and Urban Social Organization' in J.C. Mitchell (ed.) *Social Networks in Urban Situations*. Manchester: Manchester University Press: 77–116.

———— (1973) *Politics in an Urban African Community*. Manchester: Manchester University Press.

ESSIEN–UDOM, E.U. (1975) 'Tribalism and Racism' in L. Kuper (ed.) *Race, Science and Society*. Paris–New York: UNESCO–Columbia University Press: 234–61.

EVANS–PRITCHARD, E.E. (1961) *Anthropology and History*. Manchester: Manchester University Press.

FANON, F. (1973) *Black Skin, White Masks*. St. Albans: Paladin.

———— (1983) *The Wretched of the Earth*. Bungay, Suffolk: Pelican.

FITZPATRICK, P. (1980) *Law and State in Papua New Guinea*. London: Academic Press.

FORREST, G.W. (ed.) (1910) *Selection from the State Papers of the Governors General of India*, II (Warren Hastings. Documents). Oxford–London: Blackwell–Constable.

FRANK, A.G. (1966) *Development of Underdevelopment*. New York: Monthly Review Press.

———— (1969) 'Sociology of Development and Underdevelopment of Sociology' in A.G. Frank *Latin America: Underdevelopment or Revolution*. New York: Monthly Review Press.

FRANKEL, F.R. (1971) *India's Green Revolution. Economic Gains and Political Costs*. Princeton: Princeton University Press.

FRIED, M.H. (1975) *The Notion of Tribe*. Menlo Park, Cal.: Cummings Publ. and Co.

FUCHS, S. (1965) *Rebellious Prophets. A Study of Messianic Movements in Indian Religion*. Bombay: Asia Publishing House.

GALEANO, M.J. (1984) 'El Animal y el Cazador'. *Casa del Tiempo*, IV(40), May: 32–33.

GANGULY, D.C. (ed.) (1958) *Select Documents of the British Period of Indian History*. Calcutta: Secretariat Press.

GANGULY, T. (1987) 'A Non-Violent Struggle'. *The Week*, 5(50), 29 November: 38–39.

GANGULY, T. and U. SINHA (1987) 'The Jharkhand Reawakening'. *The Week*, 5(50), 29 November: 38–39.

GAIT, E.A., C.G.H. ALLEN and H.F. HOWARD (1909) *Imperial Gazetteer of India. Provincial Series, Bengal*, I and X. Calcutta: Superintendent of Government Printing.

GAUTAM, M.K. (1977) *In Search of an Identity. A Case of the Santal in Northern India*. Leiden: Gautam.

———— (1978a) 'Are we doing Justice to the Tribal Studies in India? A Critical View about the Trends and Prospects' in R.R. Moser and M.K. Gautam (eds.) *Aspects of Tribal Life in South Asia I: Strategy and Survival*. Berne: University of Berne: 9–24.

———— (1978b) 'Tradition, Modernization and the Problem of Identity among the Santal' in R.R. Moser and M.K. Gautam (eds.) *Aspects of Tribal Life in South Asia I: Strategy and Survival*. Berne: University of Berne: 105–21.

GEERTZ, C. (1963) 'The Integrative Revolution: Primordial Sentiments and Civil Politics in the New States' in C. Geertz *Old Societies and New States*. New York: The Free Press: 105–57.

———— (1973) *Interpretation of Cultures*. New York: Basic Books.

GENOVESE, E.D. (1976) *Roll, Jordan, Roll. The World the Slaves Made*. New York: Vintage Books.

GHOSH, H.N. (1916) 'The Bhumij of Chota Nagpur'. *Journal of Bihar and Orissa Research Society*, 2: 265–82.

GHURYE, G.S. (1963) *The Scheduled Tribes*. Bombay: Popular Book Depôt.

GISMONDI, M.A. (1985) '"The Gift of Theory": A Critique of the Histoire des Mentalités'. *Social History*, 10 (2): 211–30.

GLAZER, N. and D.P. MOYNIHAN (1963) *Beyond the Melting Pot: the Negroes, Puerto Ricans, Jews, Italians and Irish of New York*. Cambridge: MIT Press (Revised ed. 1970).

———— (eds.) (1976) *Ethnicity, Theory and Experience*. Cambridge, Mass. and London: Harvard University Press.

GLUCKMAN, M. (1961) 'Anthropological Problems Arising from the African Industrial Revolution' in A. Southall (ed.) *Social Change in Modern Africa*. London: Oxford University Press: 67–82.

GODELIER, M. (1974) 'El Concepto de Tribu: Crisis de un Concepto o Crisis de los Fundamentos Empíricos de la Antropología?' in M. Godelier. *Economia, Fetichismo y Religión en las Sociedades Primitivas*. México, Siglo XXI: 198–222.

GONZALEZ CASANOVA, P. (1965) 'Internal Colonialism and National Development'. *Studies in Comparative International Development*, 1(4): 15–30.

GOPAL, S. (1949) *The Permanent Settlement in Bengal and its Results*. London: George Allen & Unwin.

GOUGH, K. (1968) 'New Proposals for Anthropologists'. *Current Anthropology*, 9: 403–07.

———— (1974) 'Indian Peasant Uprisings'. *Economic and Political Weekly*, IX(32–33 & 34): 1391–1412.

GRAMSCI, A. (1973) *Selections from the Prison Notebooks of Antonio Gramsci*. Hoare and G.N. Smith (eds.). London: Lawrence and Wishart.

———— (1975) *Los Intelectuales y la Organización de la Cultura*. Mexico: Juan Pablos Editor.

GRIERSON, G.A. (1967) *Linguistic Survey of India*. I: parts I and IV. New Delhi: Motilal Banarsidas (1st ed. 1904).

GRIGSON, W.V. (1946) 'The Aboriginal in the Future of India'. *Man in India*, XXVI(2): 81–96.

GUHA, R. (1981) *A Rule of Property for Bengal. An Essay on the Idea of Permanent Settlement*. New Delhi: Orient Longman.

———— (1983) *Elementary Aspects of Peasant Insurgency in Colonial India*. Delhi: Oxford University Press.

GUHA, RAMACHANDRA (1983) 'Foresty in British and Post-British India. A Historical Analysis'. *Economic and Political Weekly*, XVIII(44), 29 October: 1882–96.

GULLIVER, P.H. (ed.) (1969) *Tradition and Transition in East Africa. Studies of the Tribal Element in the Modern Era*. London: Routledge and Kegan Paul.

GUTKIND, P.C.W. and I. WALLERSTEIN (eds.) (1976) *The Political Economy of Contemporary Africa*. London–Berkeley: Sage.

GUZMAN–BOCKLER, C. (1975) *Colonialismo y Revolucion*. Mexico: Siglo XXI.

HABIB, I. (1963) *The Agrarian System of Mughal India*. Bombay: Asia Publishing House.

————— (1985) 'Classifying Pre-Colonial India'. *The Journal of Peasant Studies* 12(2 & 3): 44–53.

HALL, S. and P. WHANNEL (1965) *The Popular Arts*. New York: Pantham Books.

HALL, S. (1981) 'Notes on Deconstructing "the Popular"' in R. Samuel (ed.) *People's History and Socialist Theory*. London: Routledge and Kegan Paul: 227–40.

HALL, S., B. LUMLEY and G. Mc LENNAN (1978) 'Politics and Ideology: Gramsci' in Centre for Contemporary Cultural Studies, *On Ideology*. London: Hutchinson: 45–76.

HALLET, M.G. and T.S. MACPHERSON (1917) *Bihar District Gazetteers*. Ranchi–Patna: Secretariat Press.

HAMILTON, R.S. (ed.) (1990) *Creating a Paradigm and Research Agenda for Comparative Studies of the Worldwide Dispersion of African Peoples*, ADRP, Monograph 1, East Lansing: Michigan State University.

HEBER, R. (1861) *Narrative of a Journey Through the Upper Provinces of India from Calcutta to Bombay, 1824–25. An Account of a Journey to Madras and the Southern Provinces, 1826, and Letters Written in India* I & II (1856). London: John Murray.

HEUZE, G. (1989) *Ouvriers d' un Autre Monde. L' Example des Travailleurs de la Mine en Inde Contemporaine*. Paris: Maison des Sciences de L'Homme.

HILL, C. (1972) *The World Turned Upside Down*. London: Penguin.

HINTON, P. (1981) 'Where Have the New Ethnicists Gone Wrong?' *Australia and New Zealand Journal of Sociology*, 17(3): 14–19.

HOBSBAWM, E.J. (1963) *Primitive Rebels. Studies in Archaic Forms of Social Movements in the 19th and 20th Centuries*. New York: Norton.

————— (1965) 'Introduction' in K. Marx *Pre-Capitalist Economic Formations*. New York: International Publications: 9–65.

————— (1971) 'Class Consciousness in History' in I. Meszaros (ed.) *Aspects of History and Class Consciousness*. London: Routledge and Kegan Paul: 5–21.

————— (1976) *Bandidos*. Barcelona–Caracas–Mexico: Ariel.

————— (1983) 'Introduction: Inventing Traditions' in E.J. Hobsbawm and T.O. Ranger (eds.) *The Invention of Traditions*. Cambridge: Cambridge University Press: 1–14.

HOBSBAWM, E.J. and T.O. RANGER (eds.) (1983) *The Invention of Traditions*. Cambridge: Cambridge University Press.

HOFFMANN, J. (1961) 'Principles of Succession and Inheritance among the Mundas'. *Man in India*, 41(4): 324–38.

HOFFMANN, J. *et al.* (1936–50) *Encyclopaedia Mundarica*. Patna: Superintendent of Government Printing.

HRACH, H.G. (1978) 'From "Regulated Anarchy" to "Proto–nationalism": The Case of the Santals' in R.R. Moser and M.K. Gautam (eds.) *Aspects of Tribal Life in South Asia I: Strategy and Survival*. Berne: University of Berne: 93–104.

HUIZER, G. (1974) *El Potencial Revolucionario del Campesino en América Latina.* Mexico: Siglo XXI.

HUNTER, G. and A.F. BOTTRALL (1974) *Serving the Small Farmer: Policy Choices in Indian Agriculture.* London: Croom Helm and O.D.I.

HUNTER, W.W. (1868) *The Annals of Rural Bengal.* New York: Leypoldt and Holt.

——————— (1877) *A Statistical Account of Bengal,* XIV. London: Trübner & Co.

IYER, K.G. and R.N. MAHARAJ (1977) 'Agrarian Movement in Dhanbad'. New Delhi: National Labour Institute (mimeo).

JAY, E. (1961) 'Revitalization Movements in Tribal India' in L.P. Vidyarthi (ed.) *Aspects of Religion in Indian Society.* Meerut: Kedar Ram Nath: 282–315.

JAULIN, R. (1973) *La Paz Blanca. Introducción al Etnocidio.* Buenos Aires: Tiempo Contemporáneo.

——————— (ed.) (1976) *El Etnocidio a través de las Américas,* Mexico–Madrid–Buenos Aires: Siglo XXI.

——————— (ed.) (1979a) *La Des-civilización (Política y Práctica del Etnocidio).* Mexico: Nueva Imagen.

——————— (1979b) 'Del Folklore' in R. Jaulin (ed.), *La Des–civilización (Política y Práctica del Etnocidio.* Mexico: Nueva Imagen: 85–90.

JHA, C. and N. JHA (1964) 'Some Aspects of Bihar Politics'. *Indian Quarterly,* XX(3): 312–29.

JHA, J.C. (1963) 'Restoration of Indigenous Police in a Tribal Area of Bihar and Bengal, 1800'. *The Journal of the Bihar Research Society,* XLIX(I–IV): 265–75.

——————— (1967) *The Bhumij Revolt (1832–1833). Ganga Narain's Hangama or Turmoil.* Delhi: Munshiram Manoharlal.

——————— (1971) 'History of Land Revenue in Chotanagpur (c. 1770–1830 AD)' in R.S. Sharma (ed.) *Land Revenue in India. Historical Studies.* Delhi: Motilal Banarsidas: 71–79.

JHA, S. (1972) *Political Elite in Bihar.* Bombay: Vora and Co. Publ.

JIMENEZ TURON, S. (1979) 'Historia de la Dominación Europea en América, Escrita por un Dominado' in Documentos de la Segunda Reunion de Barbados *Indianidad y Descolonización en América Latina.* México: Nueva Imagen: 201–06.

JOJOGA, O.W. (1978) 'Some Suggestions for Promoting Equilibrium in South Pacific Research' in A. Mamak and G. Mc Call (eds.) *Paradise Postponed.* Rushcutters Bay: Pergamon Press: 90–94.

JONES, S. (1978) 'Tribal Underdevelopment in India'. *Development and Change,* 9: 41–70.

KAHN, J.S. (1981) 'Explaining Ethnicity: A Review Article'. *Critique of Anthropology,* 4 (16): 43–52.

KAMATH, M.V. (1981) 'Operation Gangajal'. *The Illustrated Weekly of India,* CII(2), 11–17 January: 6–23.

KANNAN, K.P. (1982) 'Forestry. Forest for Industry's Profit'. *Economic and Political Weekly,* XVII(23) 5 June: 936–37.

KESHARI, B.P. (1980) 'Jharkhand Movement'. *Frontier,* 26 April: 3–5.

——————— (1982) 'Problem and Prospects of Jharkhandi Languages' in N. Sengupta (ed.) *Fourth World Dynamics: Jharkhand.* Delhi: Authors Guild Publ.: 137–64.

KEYES, C.F. (ed.) (1981) *Ethnic Change.* Seattle: University of Washington Press.

KLEIN, M. (1960) 'Envidia y Gratitud' in M. Klein and J. Riviere *Las Emociones Basicas del Hombre*. Buenos Aires: Nova.

KOPPAR, D.H. (1976) 'Tribal Art and its Place in the Ethnological Museum'. *The Eastern Anthropologist*, 29(1): 91–99.

KULKARNI, S. (1982) 'Encroachment on Forests. Government versus People'. *Economic and Political Weekly*, XVII(3), 16 January: 55–59.

——— (1983) 'Towards a Social Forest Policy'. *Economic and Political Weekly*, 5 February: 191–96.

KUMAR, RADHA (1982) 'Will Feminist Standards Survive in Jharkhand?' in N. Sengupta (ed.) *Fourth World Dynamics: Jharkhand*. Delhi: Authors Guild Publ.: 203–09.

KUMAR, RAJIV (1981a and b) 'Nationalisation by Default: The Case of Coal in India'. *Economic and Political Weekly* Part I: XVI(17), 25 April: 757–68; Part II: XVI(18) 2 May: 824–30.

KUMAR, S. (1978) *Report of the Commissioner for Scheduled Castes and Scheduled Tribes 1977–1978*. Delhi: Government of India Press.

KUPER, L. (1971) 'Theories of Revolution and Race Relations'. *Comparative Studies in Society and History*, 13: 87–107.

——— (1974) *Race, Class and Power. Ideology and Revolutionary Change in Plural Societies*. London: Duckworth.

KUPER, L. and M.G. SMITH (eds.) (1969) *Pluralism in Africa*. Berkeley and Los Angeles: University of California Press.

LAIRD, M.A. (ed.) (1971) *Bishop Heber in Northern India. Selections from Heber's Journal*. Cambridge: Cambridge University Press.

LANGTON, M. (1981) 'Urbanizing Aborigines: the Social Scientists' Great Deception'. *Social Alternatives*, 2(2): 16–22.

——— (1984) '"Medicin Square": for the Recognition of Aboriginal Swearing and Fighting as Customary Law'. B.A. Honours thesis: Australian National University.

LANTERNARI, V. (1965) *The Religion of the Oppressed. A Study of Modern Messianic Cults*. New York: Mentor Books.

——— (1977) *Crisi e Ricerca d' Identitá. Folklore e Dinamica Culturale*. Naples: Liguori.

LECLERC, G. (1972) *Anthropologie et Colonialisme*. Paris: Arthème Fayard.

LEIRIS, M. (1976) 'Folklore y Cultura Viva' in R. Jaulin (ed.) *El Etnocidio a traves de las Americas*. Mexico–Madrid–Buenos Aires: Siglo XXI: 303–20.

LEWIS, I.M. (1986) *Religion in Context. Cults and Charisma*. London: Cambridge University Press.

LEWIS, O. (1980) *Anthropological Essays*. New York: Random House.

LIJPHART, A. (1968) *The Politics of Accommodation: Pluralism and Democracy in the Netherlands*. Berkeley: University of California Press.

LUCKACS, G. (1971) *History and Class Consciousness. Studies in Marxist Dialectics*. London: Merlin Press.

LUPORINI, C., E. SERENI *et al.* (1976) *El Concepto de 'Formación Económico-social'*. Mexico: Siglo XXI.

MAC DOUGALL, J. (1977) 'Agrarian Reform vs. Religious Revitalization: Collective Resistance to Peasantization among the Mundas, Oraons and Santals, 1858–1895'. *Contribution to Indian Sociology N.S.*, 11(2): 296–327.

Mc EACHERN, D. (1976) 'The Mode of Production in India'. *Journal of Contemporary Asia*, 6(4): 444–57.

MAFEJE, A. (1971) 'The Ideology of Tribalism'. *The Journal of Modern African Studies*, 9(2): 253–61.

———— (1976) 'The Problem of Anthropology in Historical Perspective: An Inquiry into the Growth of the Social Sciences'. *Canadian Journal of African Studies*, X(2): 307–33.

———— (1981) 'On the Articulation of Modes of Production: Review Article'. *Journal of Southern African Studies*, 8(1): 123–38.

MAGUBANE, B.M. (1976) 'The Evolution of the Class Structure in Africa' in P.C.W. Gutkind and I. Wallerstein (eds.) *The Political Economy of Contemporary Africa*. London–Berkeley: Sage: 169–97.

———— (1979) *The Political Economy of Race and Class in South Africa*. New York and London: Monthly Review Press.

MAHARAJ, R.N. and K.G. IYER (1982) 'Agrarian Movement in Dhanbad' in N. Sengupta (ed.) *Fourth World Dynamics: Jharkhand*. Delhi: Authors Guild Publ.: 165–200 (extended version in monograph of the National Labour Institute 1977).

MAHTO, S. (1971) *Hundred Years of Christian Missions in Chotanagpur since 1845*. Ranchi: G.E.L. Church Press.

MAIR, L. (1936) *Native Policies in Africa*. London: Routledge.

MALINOWSKI, B. (1967) *A Diary in the Strict Sense of the Term*. New York: Harcourt, Brace & World.

MAN, E.G. (n.d.) *Sonthalia and the Sonthals*. Calcutta: Geo. Wyman & Co. (Preface dated 1867).

MANDAL, B.B. (1975) 'Are Tribal Cultivators in Bihar to be called "Peasants"' *Man in India*, 55(4): 335–62.

MAQUET, J.J. (1964) 'Objectivity in Anthropology'. *Current Anthropology*, 5: 47–55.

MARCUS, G.E. and D. CUSHMAN (1982) 'Ethnographies as Texts'. *Annual Review of Anthropology*, 11: 25–69.

MARX, K. (1976) *Capital. A Critique of Political Economy*, I. London: Penguin New Left Review.

———— (1978) *Pre-Capitalist Economic Formations*. New York: International Publications.

MARX, K. and F. ENGELS (1968) 'The Eighteenth Brumaire of Louis Bonaparte' in K. Marx and F. Engels, *Selected Works*. London: Lawrence and Wishart.

———— (1965) *The German Ideology*. London: Lawrence and Wishart.

MATHUR, K.S. (1972) 'Tribe in India: a Problem of Identification and Integration' in K.S. Singh (ed.) *Tribal Situation in India*. Simla: Indian Institute of Advanced Studies: 457–61.

MATHUR, K.S. and B.C. AGRAWAL (1974) *Tribe, Caste and Peasantry*. Lucknow: Ethnographic and Folk Culture Society.

MATHUR, V.K. (1967) 'The Traditional–Modern Continuum. An Assumption in Tribal Development'. *Journal of Social Research*, X(2): 11–25.

MEDICK, H. (1982) 'Plebeian Culture in the Transition to Capitalism' in R. Samuel and G.S. Jones (eds.) *Culture, Ideology and Politics*. London: Routledge and Kegan Paul: 84–113.

MEDINA, A. (1983) 'Los Grupos Etnicos y los Sistemas Tradicionales de Poder en México'. *Nueva Antropología*, V(20): 5–29.

MEHTA, B.K. (1982) 'Hi.torical and Cultural Basis of Jharkhandi Nationality,' in N. Sengupta (ed.) *Fourth World Dynamics: Jharkhand*. Delhi: Authors Guild Publ.: 91–103.

MEILLASSOUX, C. (1972) 'From Reproduction to Production'. *Economy and Society*, 1(1):93–105.

———— (1978) '"The Economy" in Agricultural Self-Sustaining Societies: A Preliminary Analysis' in D. Seddon (ed.) *Relations of Production. Marxist Approaches to Economic Anthropology*. London: Frank Cass: 127–57.

MIES, M. (1976) 'The Shahada Movement: A Peasant Movement in Maharashtra (India). Its Development and its Perspectives'. *The Journal of Peasant Studies*, 3(4): 472–82.

———— (1982) 'Violence against Women'. Paper presented at the 'Women and Society' program, Goethe Institute. New Delhi (mimeo).

MILES, R. (1980) 'Class, Race and Ethnicity: A Critique of Cox's Theory'. *Ethnic and Racial Studies*, (3)2: 169–87.

MINTZ, N. (1979) 'Tribals are the Victims of Progress'. *The New Republic* (Ranchi): 14 August.

MISHRA, G. (1970) *History of Bihar, 1740–1772*. New Delhi: Munshiram Manoharlal.

MITCHELL, J.C. (1960) *Tribalism and the Plural Societies*. Oxford: Oxford University Press.

———— (1969) 'Theoretical Orientations in African Urban Studies: Methodological Approaches', in M. Banton (ed.) *The Social Anthropology of Complex Societies*. London: Tavistock: 37–68.

———— (1974) 'Perceptions of Ethnicity and Ethnic Behaviour. An Empirical Exploration' in A. Cohen, (ed.) *Urban Ethnicity*. London: Tavistock: 1–35.

MITRA, A. (ed.) (1954) *West Bengal District Records. N.S. Birbhum. 1786–1797 and 1855*. Calcutta: Secretariat Press.

MOHAPATRA, P. P. (1985) 'Coolies and Colliers: a Study of Labour Migration from Chotanagpur'. *Studies in History*. (N.S.), 1(2): 247–303.

MONCKTON JONES, M. E. (1918) *Warren Hastings in Bengal 1772–1774*, Vol. 9 of *Oxford Historical and Literary Studies*. Oxford: Clarendon Press.

MONSIVAIS, C. (1985) Interview. *Proceso* (Mexico), September.

MOSER, R. R. (1978) 'Movements versus Rebellions' in R.R. Moser and M.K. Gautam (eds.) *Aspects of Tribal Life in South Asia I: Strategy and Survival*. Berne: University of Berne: 123–34.

MUKHERJEA, C. L. (1943) *The Santals*. Calcutta: Mukherjee and Co.

MUKHERJEE, K. and M. KALA (1979) 'Bhojpur: the Long Struggle' in A. N. Das and V. Nilakant (eds.) *Agrarian Relations in India*. New Delhi: Manohar: 213–30.

MUKHERJEE, R. (1933) *Land Problems of India*. London: Longmans, Green & Co.

MUKHIA, H. (1981) 'Was there Feudalism in Indian History?' *The Journal of Peasant Studies*, 8(3): 273–310.

———— (1985) 'Peasant Production and Medieval Indian Society'. *The Journal of Peasant Studies*, 12(2 & 3): 228–51.

MUNDA, R. D. (1967) *Seled* (in Mundari, Hindi and Nagpuri). Ranchi: Sahkari Prakashan Samiti.

MUNDA, R. D. (1967) (ed.) *Hisir. Anthology of Twelve Munda Poets.* Ranchi: Sahkari Prakashan Samiti.

——————— (1988) 'The Jharkhand Movement: Retrospect and Prospect'. *Social Change*, 18(2): 28–42.

NAIRN, T. (1975) 'The Modern Janus'. *New Left Review*, 94: 3–29.

NARAYAN, H. (1978) 'Bihar. The Pupri Killings'. *Economic and Political Weekly*, XIII(37): 1580–81.

NARAYAN, S. (1984) 'Plan and Planned Development'. *Mainstream*, 4 August: 25–27.

NIKOLINAKOS, M. (1973) 'Notes on an Economic Theory of Racism'. *Race*, XIV(4): 365–81.

NUN, J. (1969) 'Superpoblación Relativa, Ejército Industrial de Reserva y Masa Marginal'. *Revista Lainoamericana de Sociología*, V(2): 178–236.

OBEROI, H.S. (1986) 'The "New" Old Trope: The Application of Psychohistory in the Study of Socio-Religious Movements in Colonial India'. *Sudies in History*, N. S., 2(2): 255–73.

O'MALLEY, L.S.S. (1910) *Bengal District Gazetteers. Santal Parganas.* Calcutta: The Bengal Secretariat Book Depôt.

——————— (1938) *Bihar District Gazetteers. Santal Parganas.* Patna: Superintendent of Government Printing.

OMVEDT, G. (1981) 'Steel Workers, Contract Labourers and Adivasis'. *Economic and Political Weekly*, XVI(30): 1227–29.

ONOGE, O. (1977) 'Revolutionary Imperatives in African Sociology' in P.C.W. Gutkind and P. Waterman (eds.) *African Social Studies.* London: Heinemann: 32–43.

——————— (1979) 'The Counter-revolutionary Tradition in African Studies: The Case of Applied Anthropology' in G. Huizer and B. Manheim (eds.) *From Colonialism and Sexism, Toward a View from Below.* The Hague: Mouton: 45–66.

ORANS, M. (1965) *The Santal. A Tribe in Search of a Great Tradition.* Detroit: Wayne State University Press.

ORTEGA HEGG, M., J. VELEZ and EckArt. BOEGE (1983) 'El Conflicto Etnia-Nación en Nicaragua'. *Nueva Antropología*, V(20): 53–66.

OWUSU, M. (1978) 'Ethnography of Africa: The Usefulness of the Useless'. *American Anthropologist*, 80: 310–34.

PANDE, B.M. (1968) 'Development Schemes as Factors of Change in Tribal Areas'. *Journal of Social Research*, XI(2): 33–57.

PANDEY, M.S. (1963) *The Historical Geography and Topography of Bihar.* Delhi–Patna–Varanasi: Motilal Banarasidas.

PARDESI, G. (1980) 'Gua Incident. Operation Annihilation?' *Mainstream*, XIX(11): 6–7.

PASOLINI, P.P. (1982) 'Gramsci's Language' in Showstack Sassoon (ed.) *Approaches to Gramsci.* London: Writers & Readers Publ. Coorp. Soc.: 180–87.

PATEL, M.L. (1974) *Changing Land Problems of Tribal India.* Bhopal: Progress Publications.

PATHY, J. (1982) 'An Outline of Modes of Production in "Tribal India"' in B. Chandhuri (ed.) *Tribal Development in India. Problems and Prospects.* Delhi: Inter–India Publ.: 23–48.

——————— (1984) *Tribal Peasantry.* New Delhi: Inter–India Publ.

PATHY, J. (1988) *Ethnic Minorities in the Process of Development*. Jaipur: Rawat.

PATHY, J., P. SUGUNA and M. BHASKAR (1976) 'Tribal Studies in India: an Appraisal'. *The Eastern Anthropologist*, 29(4): 399–417.

PATWARDHAN, R.P. (ed.) (1971) *Fort William–India House Correspondence and Other Contemporary Papers* (Indian Record Series, vol. VII, 1773–1776). Delhi: National Archives of India.

PEOPLE'S UNION FOR CIVIL LIBERTIES AND DEMOCRATIC RIGHTS (1979) *Repression in Singhbhum*. New Delhi: PUCL.

PELZER WHITE, C. (1986) 'Everyday Resistance, Socialist Revolution and Rural Development: the Vietnamese Case'. *The Journal of Peasant Studies*, 13(2): 49–63.

POLIER, N. and W. ROSEBERRY (1989) 'Tristes Tropes: Post-modern Anthropologists' Encounter the Other and Discover Themselves'. *Economy and Society*, 18(2), May: 245–64.

POST, K.W.J. (1979) 'The Alliance of Peasants and Workers: Some Problems Concerning the Articulation of Classes (Algeria and China)' in R. Cohen, P.C.W. Gutkind and P. Brazier (eds.) *Peasants and Proletarians. The Struggle of Third World Workers*. London: Hutchinson: 265–85.

PRASAD, B. (ed.) (1960) *Fort William–India House Correspondence and other Contemporary Papers Relating Thereto, VI (1770–1772)*. Delhi: Manager of Publication, Government of India.

PRASAD, P. (1974) 'Reactionary Role of Usurers' Capital in India'. *Economic and Political Weekly*, IX (32–34), August.

————— (1979) 'Semi-Feudalism: The Basic Constraints of Indian Agriculture' in A.N. Das and V. Nilakant (eds.) *Agrarian Relations in India*. New Delhi: Manohar: 33–49.

PRATT, M.L. (1986) 'Fieldwork in Common Places' in J. Clifford and G.E. Marcus (eds.) *Writing Culture. The Poetics and Politics of Ethnography*. Berkeley: University of California Press: 27–50.

RABINOW, P. (1986) 'Representations are Social Facts: Modernity and Postmodernity in Anthropology' in J. Clifford and G.E. Marcus (eds.) *Writing Culture*. Berkeley, Los Angeles, London: University of California Press: 234–61.

RAGHAVAIAH, V. (1971) *Tribal Revolts*. Nellore: Andhra Rashtra Adimajati Sevak Sangh.

RAMOS, A.R. and K.I. TAYLOR (1979) *The Yanoama in Brazil*. Copenhagen: IWGIA.

RANGER, T.O. (1983) 'The Invention of Tradition in Colonial Africa' in E. Hobsbawm and T.O. Ranger (eds.) *The Invention of Tradition*. Cambridge: Cambridge University Press: 211–62.

RANJAN, A. (1981) 'Illegal Coal Mining: Deadly but Paying'. *New Delhi*, 16–29 March: 19–21.

REBEL, H. (1989) 'Cultural Hegemony and Class Experience: A Critical Reading of Recent Ethnological–Historical Approaches'. *American Ethnologist* 16 (1 & 2): 117–36; 350–65.

REDFIELD, R. (1960) *The Little Community and Peasant Society and Culture*. Chicago: University of Chicago Press.

RIBEIRO, D. (1968) *The Civilizational Process*. Washington: Smithsonian Institute Press.

RIBEIRO, D. (1969) *Las Américas y la Civilización*. Buenos Aires: Ceal.
————— (1981) 'Ethnicity, Peasantry and National Integration' in Agüero, Devalle, Tanaka (eds.) *Peasantry and National Integration*. Mexico: El Colegio de Mexico: 83–94.
————— 1984 'La Civilización Emergente'. *Nueva Sociedad*, 73: 26–37.
RICHES, D. (ed.) (1986) *The Anthropology of Violence*. Oxford: Basil Blackwell.
RICOEUR, P. (1971) 'The Model of the Text: Meaningful Action Considered as a Text'. *Social Research*, 38: 185–218.
RISLEY, H. (1891) *The Tribes and Castes of Bengal*. Calcutta: Bengal Secretariat Press.
————— (1908) *The People of India*. London: Thacker Spink & Co.
ROBBINS, E. (1975) 'Ethnicity or Class? Social Relations in a Small Canadian Industrial Community' in J.W. Bennett (ed.) *The New Ethnicity. Perspectives from Ethnology*. Los Angeles–San Francisco: West: 285–304.
ROSEBERRY, W. (1982) 'Balinese Cockfights and the Seduction of Anthropology'. *Social Research*, 49: 1013–28.
ROY, A. (1981) 'Second Phase of Jharkhand Movement'. *Frontier*, 9 May: 2–3.
————— 1982 'Tribal Protest in Ranchi,' *Frontier*, 26 June: 2–3.
ROY, A.G. *et al.* (1964) *The Bihar Local Acts, 1793–1963*. Vol. III. Allahabad: Bharat Law House.
ROY, A.K. (1982a) 'Jharkhand: Internal Colonialism, I'. *Frontier*, 17 April: 4–7.
————— (1982b) 'Jharkhand: Internal Colonialism, II'. *Frontier*, 24 August: 8–10.
————— (1983) 'Caste, Class, Nationality...'. *Frontier*, 4 June: 5–8.
ROY BURMAN, B.K. (1960) 'Basic Concepts of Tribal Welfare and Tribal Integration' in L.P. Vidyarthi (ed.) *Indian Anthropology in Action*. Ranchi: Ranchi University: 16–24.
————— (1968) 'Some Dimensions of Transformation of Tribal Societies in India'. *Journal of Social Research* XI(1): 88–94.
————— (1983a) 'State and Tribals in India'. *Mainstream*, 26 November: 16–18.
————— (1983b) 'Transformation of Tribes and Analogous Social Formations'. *Economic and Political Weekly*, XVII(27), 2 July: 1172–74.
ROY CHAUDHURY, P.C. (1958) *Bihar District Gazetteers. Singhbhum*. Patna: Secretariat Press.
————— (1959) *1857 in Bihar*. Patna: Revenue Department, Bihar.
————— (1965a) *Bihar District Gazetteers. Santal Parganas*. Patna: Superintendent, Secretariat Press.
————— (1965b) *Temples and Legends of Bihar*. Bombay: Bharatiya Vidya Bhavan.
ROY, S.C. (1912) *The Mundas and their Country*. Calcutta: The City Book Society (2nd ed. of 1970 also used).
————— (1915) *The Oraons of Chota Nagpur. Their History, Economic Life, and Social Organization*. Calcutta: The Brahmo Mission Press.
————— (1961) 'The Administrative History and Land Tenures of the Ranchi District under British Rule'. *Man in India*, 41(4): 276–323. (1st. edition of 1914).
RUDE, G. (1980) *Ideology and Popular Protest*. New York: Pantheon Books.

RUDRA, A. (1978) 'Class Relations in Indian Agriculture, I'. *Economic and Political Weekly*, XII(22), 3 June: 916–23.

RUSSELL, R.V. (1916) *The Tribes and Castes of the Central Provinces of India*, IV. London: Macmillan & Co.

SABERWAL, S. (1979) 'Sociologists and Inequality in India. The Historical Context'. *Economic and Political Weekly*, XIV(7 & 8) February (Annual Number): 243–54.

SACHCHIDANANDA, (1955) 'Caste and Class in Tribal Bihar'. *Man in India*, 35(3): 195–202.

————— (1959) 'Political Consciousness in Tribal Bihar'. *Man in India*, 39(4): 301–08.

————— (1964) *Culture Change in Tribal Bihar. Munda and Oraon*. Calcutta: Bookland Private Ltd.

————— (1974) 'Bitlaha' in K.S. Mathur and B.C. Agrawal (eds.) *Tribe, Caste and Peasantry*. Lucknow: Ethnographic and Folk Culture Society: 48–53.

————— (1976) *The Tribal Voter in Bihar*. New Delhi: National Publishing House.

————— (1979) *The Changing Munda*. New Delhi: Concept Publishing Co.

SAID, E.W. (1979) *Orientalism*. New York: Vintage Books.

SAHAY, K.N. (1980) 'The Transformation Scene in Chotanagpur: Hindu Impact on the Tribals' in P. Dash Sharma (ed.) *The Passing Scene in Chotanagpur*. Ranchi: Maitryee Publications: 25–71.

SAHLINS, M. (1968) *Tribesmen*. Englewood Cliffs, N.J.: Prentice Hall.

SAMUEL, R. (ed.) (1981) *People's History and Socialist Theory*. London: Routledge and Kegan Paul.

SAUL, J. (1979) 'The Dialectics of Class and Tribe'. *Race and Class*, XX(4): 347–72.

SAXTON, A. (1979) 'Historical Explanations of Racial Inequality'. *Marxist Perspectives*, 2(2): 146–68.

SCHEMERHORN, R.A. (1978) *Ethnic Plurality in India*. Tucson: University of Arizona Press.

SCOOT, J. (1977) 'Hegemony and the Peasantry'. *Politics and Society*, 7(3): 267–96.

————— (1985) *Weapons of the Weak. Everyday Forms of Resistance*. New Haven and London: Yale University Press.

————— (1986) 'Political Analysis and the Hidden Transcript of Subordinate Groups'. Paper presented at the Department of Anthropology, RSSR, ANU, Canberra.

SEDDON, D. (ed.) (1978) *Relations of Production. Marxist Approaches to Economic Anthropology*. London: Frank Cass.

SELBOURNE, D. (1979) 'State and Ideology in India'. *Monthly Review*, 31(7): 25–37.

SEN, J. (1972) 'The Jharkhand Movement' in K.S. Singh (ed.) *Tribal Situation in India*. Simla: Indian Institute of Advanced Study: 432–37.

SENGUPTA, N. (1979) *The Destitute and Development: A Study of the Bauri Community in Bokaro Steel City Region*. New Delhi: Concept Publishing Co.

————— (1980) 'Class and Tribe in Jharkhand'. *Economic and Political Weekly*, XV(14), 5 April: 664–71.

SENGUPTA, N. (ed.) (1982a) *Fourth World Dynamics: Jharkhand.* Delhi: Authors Guild Publ.

————— (1982b) 'Native Situation in India and Appraisal of Policies'. Mexico, CEESTEM (mimeo).

————— (1982c) 'Agrarian Movement in Bihar'. *The Journal of Peasant Studies,* 9(3): 15–39.

————— (1983) 'Beyond Marx's Capital: "Sons of the Soil" in Particular, Ethnic Upsurges in General' in A.N. Das, V. Nilakant and P.S. Dube (eds.) *The Worker and the Working Class: A Labour Studies Anthology.* New Delhi: PECCE.

————— (1984) 'From Peasant to Tribe. Peasant Movements in Chotanagpur'. Paper presented at the Seminar on Peasants and Peasant Resistance in Eastern India. Shillong: North Eastern Hill University (mimeo).

————— (1985) 'Irrigation: Traditional and Modern'. *Economic and Political Weekly,* XX (45, 46 & 47), November: 1919–38.

————— (1986) 'The March of an Idea: Evolution and Impact of the Dychotomy Tribe–Mainstream'. Mids Offprint 9. Madras: Madras Institute of Development Studies.

SENGUPTA, U. (1984) 'Koel–Karo: A Project Doomed'. *The Telegraph,* 28 June: 7.

SHANIN, T. (1972) *The Awkward Class. Political Sociology of Peasantry in a Developing Society: Russia 1910–1925.* Oxford: Clarendon Press.

SHARMA, A.P. (1988) 'The Jharkhand Movement. A Critique'. *Social Change,* 18(2): 60–82.

SHARMA, R.S. (1965) *Indian Feudalism c. 300–1200.* Calcutta: Calcutta University.

————— (ed.) (1971) *Land Revenue in India. Historical Studies.* Delhi: Motilal Banarsidas.

————— (1985) 'How Feudal was Indian Feudalism?' *The Journal of Peasant Studies,* 12(2–3): 19–45.

SHOWSTACK SASSOON, A. (1982) 'Hegemony, War of Position and Political Intervention' in A. Showstack Sassoon (ed.) *Approaches to Gramsci.* London: Writers and Readers Publ. Coop.: 94–115.

SILVERMAN, S. (1976) 'Ethnicity as Adaptation: Strategies and Systems'. *Reviews in Anthropology* (Nov–Dec): 626–36

SIMEON, D. (1982) 'Jharkhand. Community or Proletariat?' in N. Sengupta (ed.) *Fourth World Dynamics: Jharkhand.* Delhi: Authors Guild Publ.: 210–30.

SINGH, J. (1981) 'Illegal Mining Only Livelihood'. *The Times of India,* 23 March: 19.

SINGH, K.S. (1963) 'The Haribaba Movement in Chotanagpur, 1931–1932'. *The Journal of the Bihar Research Society,* XLIX (I–IV): 284–96.

————— (1966) *The Dust-Storm and the Hanging Mist. A Study of Birsa Munda and his Movement in Chotanagpur (1874–1901).* Calcutta: Mukhopadhyay (reprinted by Oxford University Press, Delhi).

————— (1971a) 'The Munda Land System and Revenue Reforms in Chotanagpur during 1869–1908' in R.S. Sharma (ed.) *Land Revenue in India. Historical Studies.* Delhi: Motilal Banarsidas: 80–107.

SINGH, K.S. (1971b) 'State-formation in Tribal Society: Some Preliminary Observations'. *Journal of the Indian Anthropological Society*, 6(2): 161–81.

—————— (1972a) 'Agrarian Issues in Chotanagpur' in K.S. Singh (ed.) *Tribal Situation in India*. Simla: Institute for Advanced Study: 374–87.

—————— (ed.) (1972b) *Tribal Situation in India*. Simla: Indian Institute of Advanced Study.

—————— (1977) 'From Ethnicity to Regionalism: A Study in Tribal Politics and Movements in Chotanagpur from 1900 to 1975' in S.C. Malik (ed.) *Dissent, Protest and Reform in Indian Civilization*. Simla: Indian Institute of Advanced Study: 317–43.

—————— (1982) 'Transformation of Tribal Society. Integration vs. Assimilation'. *Economic and Political Weekly*, XVII(33), 14 August: 1318–25.

—————— (1985) *Tribal Society in India*. New Delhi: Manohar.

SINHA, A. (1978a) 'Class War in Bhojpur'. *Economic and Political Weekly*, XIII(1) 7 January: 10–11.

—————— (1978b) 'Bihar. The Bishrampur Carnage'. *Economic and Political Weekly*, XIII(13), 1 April: 568–69.

—————— (1978c) 'Development *versus* People'. *Economic and Political Weekly*, XIII(18), 6 May: 750–51.

—————— (1978d) 'Resurgent Adivasis'. *Economic and Political Weekly*, XIII(36), 9 September: 1544–46.

—————— (1980) 'Bihar: Who Destroys the Forests?' *The New Republic*, 14 October: 2.

—————— (1982a) 'Struggles against Bureaucratic Capitalism' in N. Sengupta (ed.) *Fourth World Dynamics: Jharkhand*. Delhi: Authors Guild Publ.: 111–34.

—————— (1982b) 'Class War, not "Atrocities against Harijans"'. *The Journal of Peasant Studies*, 9(3): 148–52.

SINHA, B.B. (1979) *Socio–Economic Life in Chota Nagpur, 1858–1935*. Delhi: B.R. Publishing Corporation.

SINHA, D.P. (1972) 'Tribalism, Pluralism and Nationalism: Levels of Cultural Identity in Banari' in K.S. Singh (ed.) *Tribal Situation in India*. Simla: Indian Institute of Advanced Study: 494–501.

SINHA, N.K. (1962) *The Economic History of Bengal*, Vol. II. Calcutta: Mukhopadhyay.

SINHA, R.N. (1968) *Bihar Tenantry, 1783–1833*. Bombay: People's Publishing House.

SINHA, S. (1953) 'Some Aspects of Change in Bhumij Religion in South Manbhum, Bihar'. *Man in India*, 33(2): 148–64.

—————— (1962) 'State Formation and Rajput Myth in Tribal Central India'. *Man in India*, 42(1): 35–80.

—————— (1965) 'Tribe–Caste and Tribe–Peasant Continua in Central India'. *Man in India*. 45(1): 57–83.

—————— (1974) 'Levels of Economic Initiative and Ethnic Groups in Paragana Barabhum' in K.S. Mathur and B.C. Agrawal (eds) *Tribe, Caste and Peasantry*. Lucknow: Ethnographic and Folk Culture Society: 54–63.

—————— (1982) 'Re-thinking about Tribes and Indian Civilization' in B. Chaudhuri (ed.) *Tribal Development in India*. Delhi: Inter–India Publ.: 3–13.

SINHA, S.P. (1959) 'The First Birsa Rising (1895)'. *The Journal of the Bihar Research Society*, XLV(I–IV): 391–403.

————— (1964) *Life and Times of Birsa Bhagwan*. Ranchi: Bihar Tribal Research Institute.

————— (1972) 'Some Typical British Experiments in Administration in Tribal Areas'. *Journal of Administrative Training Institute*, August. Ranchi: Government of Bihar: 12–20.

SINHA, U. (1985) 'Bihar. Teaching the Santhals a Lesson'. *Economic and Political Weekly*, XX(24): 15 June: 1028–29.

————— (1987a) 'Thinning Patience'. *The Week*, 5(50), 29 November: 37.

————— (1987b) 'A Rite of Death'. *The Week*, 5(50), 29 November: 40.

SIVERTS, H. (1970) 'Ethnic Stability and Boundary Dynamics in Southern Mexico' in F. Barth (ed.) *Ethnic Groups and Boundaries*. London: George Allen and Unwin: 101–16.

SKLAR, R.L. (1967) 'Political Science and National Integration. A Radical Approach'. *The Journal of Modern African Studies*, 5(1): 1–11.

SLOAN, W.N. (1979) 'Ethnicity or Imperialism? A Review Article'. *Comparative Studies in Society and History*, 21: 113–25.

SMITH, M.G. (1965) *The Plural Society in the British West Indies*. Los Angeles and Berkeley: University of California Press.

SOMERS, G.E. (1977) *The Dynamics of Santal Traditions in a Peasant Society*. New Delhi: Abhinav.

SOUTHALL, A. (1961) 'Social Change, Demography and Extrinsic Factors' in A. Southall (ed.) *Social Change in Modern Africa*. London: Oxford University Press: 1–13.

————— (1970) 'The Illusion of Tribe'. *Journal of Asian and African Studies*, V(1 & 2): 28–50.

SRINIVAS, M.N. (1966) *Social Change in Modern India*. Berkeley: University of California Press.

SRIVASTAVA, A. (1979a) 'Bihar. New Trends in Rural Violence'. *Frontier*, 5 March: 2–4.

————— (1979b) 'Bihar: "Trade Union" Murders in Dhanbad'. *Economic and Political Weekly*, XIV(10), 10 March: 550.

————— (1980a) 'RSS in Adivasi Belt'. *Frontier*, 19 January: 6–7.

————— (1980b) '"Encounters" in Bhojpur'. *Frontier*, 13 December: 6–7.

————— (1981a) 'Formation of a Morcha'. *Frontier*, 24 January: 3–4.

————— (1981b) 'Christian Missionaries in Tribal Belt (I)' *Frontier*, 21 February: 4–6 and (II) 7 March: 8–11.

SRIVASTAVA, L.R.N. *et al.* (1971) *Education and Economic Condition and Employment Position of 18 Tribes*. Delhi: National Council of Educational Research and Training.

STAVENHAGEN, R. (1968) 'Seven Fallacies about Latin America' in J. Petras and M. Zeitlin (eds.) *Latin America: Reform or Revolution*. Greenwich: Fawcett: 14–31.

————— (1973) 'The Future of Latin America: Between Underdevelopment and Revolution'. *Latin American Perspectives*: 124–48.

————— (1975) *Las Clases Sociales en las Sociedades Agrarias*. Mexico: Siglo XXI.

STAVENHAGEN, R. (1981) 'Decolonizing the Applied Social Sciences' in R. Stavenhagen *Between Underdevelopment and Revolution: a Latin American Perspective*. New Delhi: Abhinav.
————— (1982) 'Indian Ethnic Movements and State Policies in Latin America'. Paper presented at the Symposium on Ethnic Minorities and National States, México: CEESTEM.
————— (1984a) 'Las Minorías Culturales y los Derechos Humanos en América Latina'. Mexico: El Colegio de Mexico and The United Nations University.
————— (1984b) 'Los Movimientos Etnicos Indígenas y el Estado Nacional en América Latina'. *Civilización*, 2: 181–204.
————— (1985) 'The Indigenous Problematique'. *Ifda Dossier*, 50: 3–14.
STEIN, B. (1985) 'Politics, Peasants and the Deconstruction of Feudalism in Medieval India'. *The Journal of Peasant Studies*, 12(2 & 3): 54–86.
TATZ, C. (1982) *Aborigines and Uranium and Other Essays*. Richmond: Heineman Educational Australia.
TEXIER, J. (1976) 'Desacuerdos sobre la Definición de los Conceptos' in Luporini, Sereni *et al. El Concepto de 'Formación Económicó–Social'*. Mexico: Siglo XXI: 190–95.
THAPAR, R. (1966) *A History of India*. Vol. 1. Middlesex: Penguin.
THAPAR, ROMESH (1980) 'Blind, Blind, Blind...'. *Economic and Political Weekly*, XV(52), 27 December: 21–67.
THAPAR, R. and M.H. SIDDIQI (1979) 'Chota Nagpur: the Precolonial and Colonial Situation'. *Trends in Ethnic Groups Relations in Asia and Oceania*. Paris: UNESCO—Series Race and Society: 19–64.
THOMAS, K. (1963) 'History and Anthropology'. *Past and Present*, 24 April: 3–24.
THOMAS, M.M. and R.W. TAYLOR (eds.) (1965) *Tribal Awakening. A group Study*. Bangalore: Christian Institute for the Study of Religion and Society.
THOMPSON, E.P. (1967) 'Time, Work-discipline and Industrial Capitalism'. *Past and Present* , (38): 56–97.
————— (1968) *The Making of the English Working Class*. Middlesex: Penguin.
————— (1972) 'Anthropology and the Discipline of Historical Context'. *Midland History*, I(3): 41–55.
————— (1974) 'Patrician Society, Plebeian Culture'. *Journal of Social History*, 7(4): 382–405.
————— (1977) 'Folklore, Anthropology and Social History'. *Indian Historical Review*, 3(2): 247–66.
————— (1978) 'Eighteenth–Century English Society: Class Struggle without Class?' *Social History*, 3(3): 133–65.
————— (1980) *The Poverty of Theory and Other Essays*. London: Merlin Press.
————— (1981) 'The Politics of Theory' in R. Samuel (ed.) *People's History and Socialist Theory*. London: Routledge and Kegan Paul: 396–408.
THORNER, A. (1982) Semi-Feudalism or Capitalism? Contemporary Debate on Classes and Modes of Production in India. *Economic and Political Weekly*, XVII (49, 50 and 51).
THORNER, D. and A. THORNER (1965) *Land and Labour in India*. Lucknow and Bombay: Asia Publishing House.
TOMASSON JANNUZI, F. (1974) *Agrarian Crisis in India. The Case of Bihar*. Austin and London: University of Texas Press.
TURNER, V. (1969) *The Ritual Process. Structure and Anti-Structure*. Middlesex: Penguin.

TURNER, V. (1974) *Dramas, Fields and Metaphors. Symbolic Action in Human Society*. Ithaca and London: Cornell University Press.

——— (1982) *From Ritual to Theatre. The Human Seriousness of Play*. New York: Performing Arts Journal Publications.

TURTON, A. (1984) 'Limits of Ideological Domination and the Formation of Social Consciousness' in A. Turton and Shigeharu Tanabe (eds.) *History and Peasant Consciousness in South East Asia*. Osaka: National Museum of Ethnography: 19–73.

TYLER, S. (1986) 'Post-Modern Ethnography: From Document of the Occult to Occult Document' in J. Clifford and G.E. Marcus (eds.) *Writing Culture*. Berkeley, Los Angeles, London: University of California Press: 122–40.

UPADHYAYA, A. (1979) 'Peasant Movements in Western India. A Tentative Hypothesis' in A.N. Das and V. Nilakant *Agrarian Relations in India*. Delhi: Manohar: 169–87.

VAN DER BERGHE, P.L. (1976) 'Ethnic Pluralism in Industrial Societies. A Special Case?' *Ethnicity*, 3: 242–55.

VAN DER LEEUW, G. (1964) *Fenomenología de la Religión*. Mexico: F.C.E.

VAN EXEM, A. (1973) *Basic Socio–Economic Attitudes of Chotanagpur Tribals*. Ranchi: The Catholic Cooperative Society.

——— (1975) *Evangelization Today. A Local Church Reflects*. Ranchi: Ranchi Jesuit Society.

VARESE, S. (1975) 'Etnología de Urgencia, Conciencia Etnica y Participación Social en el Perú'. *América Indígena*, XXXV(2): 251–63.

——— (1978) 'El Falso Estado: Hipótesis sobre la Multietnicidad en Peru y México'. Oaxaca, Mexico: Instituto Nacional de Antropologia e Historia (mimeo).

——— (1979) 'Estrategia Etnica o Estrategia de Clase?' in Documentos de la Segunda Reunión de Barbados, *Indianidad y Descolonización en América Latina*. Mexico: Nueva Imagen: 357–72.

——— (1980) 'El Rey Despedazado: Resistencia Cultural y Movimientos Etnopolitícos de Liberación India'. Mexico: SEP (mimeo).

——— (1981) 'The Difficult Pluralism: Multi-ethnicity and National Revolution in Peru' in Aguero, Devalle, Tanaka (eds.) *Peasantry and National Integration*. Mexico: El Colegio de Mexico: 99–111.

——— (1989) 'Movimientos Indios de Liberación Estado Nacional' in S. Devalle (ed.) *La Diversidad Prohibida. Resistencia Etnica y Poder de Estado*. Mexico: El Colegio de Mexico.

VIDYARTHI, L.P. (1960) 'Anthropology and Tribal Policy: A Case Study among the Maler Paharia: Some Preliminary Thoughts' in L.P. Vidyarthi (ed.) *Indian Anthropology in Action*. Ranchi: Ranchi University.

——— (1967a) 'Some Preliminary Observations on Inter-Group Conflicts in India: Tribal, Rural and Industrial'. *Journal of Social Research*, X(2): 1–10.

——— (1967b) 'Aspects of Tribal Leadership in Chota Nagpur' in L.P. Vidyarthi (ed.) *Leadership in India*. Bombay: Asia Publishing House: 127–44.

——— (1969) *Cultural Configuration of Ranchi. Survey of an Emerging Industrial City of Tribal India (1960–1962)*. Calcutta: Punthi Pustak.

——— (1970) *Socio–Cultural Implications of Industrialization in India. A Case Study of Tribal Bihar*. Delhi: Research Programmes Committee, Planning Commission.

VIDYARTHI, L.P. and K.N. SAHAY (1976) *The Dynamics of Tribal Leadership in Bihar*. Allahabad: Kitab Mahal.

VIKAS MAITRI (1970) *The Silent Revolution. A Report of the Second All–Chotanagpur Seminar*. Ranchi: The Printer.

VOLKEN, H. (1979) *Vikas Maitri: A People's Organization in Chotanagpur*. Ranchi: Sudarshan Press.

VOVELLE, M. (1982) 'Ideologies and Mentalities' in R. Samuel and G.S. Jones (eds.) *Culture, Ideology and Politics*. London: Routledge and Kegan Paul: 84–113.

WEINER, M., M. FAINSOD KATZENSTEIN and NARAYAMA RAO (1981) *India's Preferential Policies. Migrants, Middle Classes and Ethnic Equality*. Chicago and London: University of Chicago Press.

WILLIAMS, R. (1976) *Culture and Society, 1780–1950*. Middlesex: Penguin.

————— (1978) *Marxism and Literature*. Oxford: Oxford University Press.

————— (1982) *The Sociology of Culture*. New York: Schocken Books.

WOLF, E.R. (1975) 'On Peasant Rebellions' in T. Shanin (ed.) *Peasants and Peasant Societies*. Middlesex: Penguin: 264–74.

WOLPE, H. (1971) 'The Theory of Internal Colonialism: The South African Case' in I. Oxaal, T. Barnett and D. Booth (eds.) *Beyond the Sociology of Development*. London–Boston–Henley: Routledge and Kegan Paul: 229–52.

————— (1972) 'Capitalism and Cheap Labour-Power in South Africa: from Segregation to Apartheid'. *Economy and Society*, 1 (4): 425–56.

————— (ed.) (1980) *The Articulation of the Modes of Production*. London: Routledge and Kegan Paul.

WORSLEY, P. (1970) *The Trumpet Shall Sound: A Study of 'Cargo' Cults in Melanesia*. New York: Schocken Books.

XAVIER INSTITUTE OF SOCIAL SERVICE (XISS) (Ranchi) (1980) *Development from Below. Notes for Workers Engaged in Rural Development and Adult Education*. Ranchi: Bagla Press.

ZIDE, N.H. (1971) 'Some Munda Etymological Notes on Names in the Ramayana'. *The Journal of Ganganath Jha Kendriya Vidyapeeth* (Allahabad), XXVII: 747–63.

ZIDE, N.H. and R.D. MUNDA (1969) 'Revolutionary Birsa and the Songs related to him'. *Journal of Social Research*, XII(2): 37–60.

Government Publications

GOVERNMENT OF BIHAR and ORISSA, Legislative Department (1931) *The Chota Nagpur Tenancy Act, 1908*. Patna: Superintendent of Government Printing.

GOVERNMENT OF INDIA (1952) *Report of the Scheduled Castes and Tribes Commission*. New Delhi: Government of India Press.

————(1961) *Report of the Scheduled Castes and Scheduled Tribes Commission, 1 (1960–1961)*. New Delhi: Government of India Press.

————(1962) *Report of the Scheduled Castes and Scheduled Tribes Commission*, U.N. Dhebar (Chairman). New Delhi: Government of India Press.

GOVERNMENT OF INDIA (1962) *Census of India 1961*. Bihar, Ranchi, 15. Delhi: Manager of Publications.

————— (1967) *Report of the Commissioner for Scheduled Castes and Scheduled Tribes*, (1946–1965). Delhi: Manager of Publications.

————— (1968) *Census Atlas of Bihar*. (Census of India, 1961), IV (Bihar), IX. Patna: Bihar Secretariat Press.

————— (1976) *Report of the National Commission on Agriculture*, IX: Forestry. New Delhi: Ministry of Agriculture and Irrigation.

————— (1980) *Census of India 1971*. Bihar, series 4, IV–A. Delhi: Manager of Publications.

————— (1982) *Statistical Abstract, India, 1980*, New Series (25). New Delhi: Government of India Press.

————— (1983) *Census of India 1981. Primary Census Abstract. Scheduled Tribes*. Delhi: Controller of Publications.

DEPARTMENT OF ECONOMIC & STATISTICS, Ministry of Food and Agriculture (1956) *Agricultural Legislation in India*, VI ('Land Reforms. Reforms in Tenancy'). Delhi: Manager of Publications.

INDUSTRIAL DEVELOPMENT BANK OF INDIA (1971) *Industrial Potential Survey. Bihar. Report of a Study Team*. Bombay: Industrial Bank of India.

Documents

Declaration of Barbados (1971). Copenhangen: IWGIA.

Diary of R. I. Richardson, Bhagalpur Collector. In A. Mitra (ed.) *West Bengal District Records, N.S. Birbhum*, 1786–1797 and 1855. Calcutta: 1954.

Document of the Judicial Department, No. 42 of 1856, from W.H. Tykes and other directors to the Governor–General, dated London 10 October 1856. In R.C. Roy Chaudhuri, *1857 in Bihar*. Patna, 1959: Revenue Department, Bihar: 21: 30.

Document No. 3254, Home (Judicial) Department Proceedings, dated 11 July 1871, from Sir C. Bayley, Secretary of the Bengal Government, Judicial Department, to the Secretary of the Indian Government, Ministry of the Interior. In P.C. Roy Chaudhury, *Bihar District Gazetteers. Santal Parganas*. Patna: Superintendent, Secretariat Press.

Document relating to 22 convicts sentenced by the Birbhum Judge on 3 December, 1855. In A. Mitra (ed.) *West Bengal District Records, N.S. Birbhum, 1786–1797 and 1855*. Calcutta, 1954.

J.C.C. Draft Declaration of the Jharkhand Co-ordination Committee. *For a New Democracy*, August–December: 32–34.

Letters from several Bhagalpur Planters to W. Theobald, Secretary of the Indigo Planters Association, dated 31-1-1856, received in Fort William on 28-1-1856, *Bengal Judicial Proceedings*, 33, 1856.

Letter from W. Theobald, Secretary, Indigo Planters Association to Grey, Secretary of the Bengal Government, dated 2-2-1856. 6, received in Fort William on 28-2-1856. *Bengal Judicial Proceedings*. 33, 1856.

Letter from A. Cleveland to W. Hastings, dated November 1779. In L.S.S. O'Malley, *Bengal District Gazetteers. Santal Parganas*. Calcutta, 1910: The Bengal Secretariat Book Depot.

Letter from A. Cleveland to the Honourable Board of Directors, dated February 1783. In L.S.S. O'Malley, *Bengal District Gazetteers. Santal Parganas*. Calcuta, 1910: The Bengal Secretariat Book Depôt.

Letter from G. Loch, Collector at Bhagalpur, to G.F. Brown, Commissioner of Revenue at Bhagalpur, dated 18 September 1850. In P.C. Roy Chaudhury, *1857 in Bihar*. Patna, 1959: Revenue Department, Bihar.

Letter from the Secretary of the Governor of Bengal to A.C. Bidwell, dated 6 August 1855 (No. 1808). In A. Mitra (ed.) *West Bengal District Records, N.S. Birbhum, 1786–1797 and 1855*. Calcutta, 1954.

Letter from J.R. Ward, Special Commissioner, to the Suri Collector, dated 9 September 1855. In A. Mitra (ed.) *West Bengal District Records, N. S. Birbhum, 1786–1797 and 1855*. Calcutta, 1954.

Letter from R.I. Richardson, Bhagalpur Collector, to Brigadier Bird, dated 13 September 1855. In A. Mitra (ed.) *West Bengal District Records, N.S. Birbhum, 1786–1797 and 1855*. Calcutta, 1954.

Letter from R.I. Richardson, Bhagalpur Collector to Colonel Burney, dated 21 September 1855. In A. Mitra (ed.) *West Bengal District Records, N.S. Birbhum, 1786–1797 and 1855*. Calcutta, 1954.

Letter from Mr. Pontet to the Collector at Bhagalpur, dated 1 January 1857. *Bengal Judicial Records*.

Letter from Mr. Pontet, Superintendent of the Damini-i-Koh to Mr. H.J. James, Acting Collector at Bhagalpur, dated 17 July 1823. In P. C. Roy Chaudhuri, *1857 in Bihar*. Patna, 1959: Revenue Department, Bihar: 3.

Petition from Seedoo and Kanoo Manjhis to the inhabitants of Rajmahal, included in a letter from A.C. Bidwell to Mr. Grey, the Secretary of the Governor of Bengal, dated 14 February 1856 (No. 157). *Bengal Judicial Records*.

Petition from Nursingh Manjhi and Kudru Manjhi to the Commissioner at Bhagalpur dated 29 August 1854, included in a letter for A. C. Bidwell to Mr. Grey, the Secretary of the Governor of Bengal, dated 14 February 1856 (No. 157). *Bengal Judicial Records*.

Report from Mr. Pontet, Superintendent of the Damin-i-Koh, to the Commissioner at Bhagalpur, dated August 1848, quoted in a letter from A. C. Bidwell to Mr. Grey, the Secretary of the Governor of Bengal, dated 1 February 1857 (No. 157). *Bengal Judicial Records*.

Report from Mr. Pontet to the Commissoner at Bhagalpur, dated May 1851, quoted in a letter from A. C. Bidwell to Mr. Grey, the Secretary of the Governor of Bengal, dated 17 February 1856 (No. 157), *Bengal Judicial Records*.

Santal Communiqués included in a letter from several Bhagalpur Planters to W. Theobald, Secretary of the Indigo Planters Association, dated 31 January 1856 and received at Fort William on 28 February 1856.

Newspapers and Periodicals

CALCUTTA REVIEW 'The Sonthal Rebellion' (1855), 'The Friends of India' (1856), XXVI, (LI), March: 233–64.

ECONOMIC AND POLITICAL WEEKLY (1975) 'Bihar. Material Base of Santal Movement' X(11), 15 March: 464–65.

———————— (1979a) 'Containing the Jharkhand Movement' XIV(14), 7 April: 648–50.

———————— (1979b) 'Singhbhum. Exploitation, Protest and Repression' XIV (22), 2 June: 940–43.

———————— (1979c) 'Bihar. Dhanbad's Dispossessed Peasants' XIV(33), 18 August: 1411–12.

———————— (1980a) 'Class and Caste in Parasbigha Massacre' XV(8) 23 February: 421.

———————— (1980b) 'A Culture of Torture' XV (48), 29 November: 1993–94.

———————— (1980c) 'Dhanbad: New Aspects of Coalfield Politics' XV (49), 6 December: 2046.

———————— (1981) 'Bihar. Illegal Plunder of Mines and Tribals of Kolhan' XVI(38), 19 September: 1525.

———————— (1982a) 'Coal Mines. Slaughter of Mines and Miners' XVII(40), 9 October: 1641–42.

———————— (1982b) 'When the Forest Disappear, We Will Also Disappear', XVII (48), 27 November: 1901–02.

———————— (1986) 'Bihar: Landowners' Armies Take Over "Law and Order"', XXI (1) 4 January: 15–18.

FRONTIER (1979a) 'Arms to Harijans', 17 March: 7–8.

———————— (1979b) 'Bihar Incidents', 10 November: 4.

———————— (1980a) 'Another Santal Rebellion?' 26 April: 7–8.

———————— (1980b) 'The Mineworkers of Singhbhum', 12(51), 16 August: 2–7.

———————— (1980c) 'More About Gua', 13(5), 27 September: 4–5.

———————— (1981a) 'A Gua Report', 14, 21 March: 7–8.

———————— (1981b) 'Jharkhandi Justice', 16 May: 5–6.

———————— (1983) 'Forest Policy and Tribal Problem', 15 January: 9–10.

———————— (1983) 'Ground into the Dust', 31 August: 50–53.

INDIA TODAY (1986a) 'Jharkhand. Renewed Call', 26 February: 3.

———————— (1986b) 'Bihar. Area of Darkness', 31 December: 40–43.

LINK (1971) 'Issue', 5 December: 25–26.

———————— (1978) 'Children of the Forests', 6 August: 21–23.

———————— (1981) 'Arms and the Man. The Gun has a Caste', 6 December: 16–17.

———————— (1982a) 'Before Drought Turns Famine', 25(12), 31 October: 9, 11–12.

———————— (1982b) 'Santhals. Victims of Double Cheat', 25(13), 7 November: 10–11.

———————— (1982c) 'Adivasis Feel Bitter', 25(13), 7 November: 11–12.

———————— (1983) 'Forward Caste: Criminal Acts', 16 January: 9–10.

NEWSWEEK (1987) 'A Grim Journey to the "Other India"', 15 June: 20–21.

PATRIOT (1980) 'Steps to Prevent Harvesting Clashes', 25 November: 4.

PIONEER (1984) 'Jharkhand Party no more a Challenge', 14 December.

THE BENGALEE (1886) 'Slavery in British Dominion', XXVII (39), 25 September: (40), 2 October; (41), 23 October; 'Child Life in Tea Gardens' (42), 30 October; (43), 6 November; (49), 19 December; 1887 XVIII (4), 22 January.

THE HINDUSTAN TIMES (1981) 'Coal Belt Land Acquisition Challenged', 20 January.

——————— (1986) 'Who Will Save Belchchi?' 7 September: 6–7.

THE ILLUSTRATED WEEKLY OF INDIA (1981) CII(2), 11–17 January: 6–23.

THE INDIAN EXPRESS (1980a) 'Supreme Court has a Look at Blinded Victims. Let this not Happen to Others', 3 December: front page.

——————— (1980b) 'Minister Was Aware of Blinding Campaign', 12 December, front page.

——————— (1980c) 'New Body Formed to Fight Oppression', 17 December.

THE NEW REPUBLIC (Ranchi) (1980a) 'Unchain Birsa', 23 February: Letters to the editor section.

——————— (1980b) 'Confrontation in Tata and CCL Collieries. Whom to Absorb "Sons" or "Sons of the Soil"?', 19 July: 3.

——————— (1980c) 'Indiscriminated Felling of Trees to Stop, Assures Shibu Soren', 1 November: 3.

——————— (1980d) 'Justin Richards Castigates Processes of "Detribalization"', 1 November: front page.

——————— (1980e) 'Police Open Fire Near Chakradharpur', 29 November: front page.

——————— (1980f) 'Paltry Compensation Irks Singhbhum Villages', 6 December: 3.

——————— (1980g) 'Ban on Bows and Arrows Withdrawn', 6 December: front page.

THE STATESMAN (1980a) 'Harvesting Clash: One Killed', 4 December.

——————— (1980b) 'Santhal Group Tear-gassed', 12 December.

——————— (1980c) 'The Sound of Defiance in Tribal Areas', 13 December: 5.

——————— (1983) 'Tribals in Bihar Agitated', 9 March: 5.

——————— (1984a) 'Singhbhum Courts Asked to Release Adivasi Prisoners', 26 September: 3.

——————— (1984b) 'Minicement Plant in Orissa Tribal Village', 17 November.

THE TELEGRAPH (1984) 'Bihar. Koel–Karo: A Project Doomed', 28 June: 7.

THE TIMES OF INDIA (1978a) 'Adivasis Stop Work on Hydel Projects', 7 May.

——————— (1978b) 'Tribal Agitators Destroy Trees', 13 December.

——————— (1981a) 'Tribes Hopes of Jobs Belied', 15 February.

——————— (1981b) 'Bihar no Different After Bhagalpur', 12 March: 3.

——————— (1981c) '4 Killed by Adivasis in Purnea', 10 March: 5.

——————— (1981d) '$32 m Saudi Loan for Bihar Project', 15 April.

THE WEEK (1987) 5 (50), 29 November, 34–40.

Index

Jannuzi, T., 75
Jaulin, 41
Jay, E., 111
Jha, J.C., 66
Jha, Sadananda, 142, 184
Jharkhand, 13, 14; community, 49, 153–60, 166; Divas, 219–20; incorporation into colonial system, 69–75; identity, 165; movement, 136, 219; socio-economic profile of, 79–89; State, demand for, 103, 104, 143–44
Jharkhand Co-ordination Committee (JCC), 155
Jharkhand Mukti Morch (JMM), 91, 141, 142, 155, 157, 165, 167, 169, 170, 176, 181, 182, 184, 186, 188, 189, 201, 219, 237; agrarian protests and 185–87; MCC coalition, 181
Jharkhand Party, 54, 95, 103, 104, 110, 135, 139–40, 167
Johar, 176
Jones, M., 56
Jones, S., 44, 96, 98, 102
jungle kato movement, 104
Jungle Mahals, resistance to Colonial conquests in, 146–49
Jungleterry, 58, 59
justice, 217–18

kamioti, 68, 119–22
Kannan, K. P., 86
Kasipur, 148
Keyes, C.F., 43
Kherwar Movement, 118n, 125–26
Khuntkatti system, 62, 70. 103
Khuntkattidars, 62, 63
Kimioti system, 70
Klein. 208
Koel Karo project, opposition to, 102
Koilapal, 147
Kolhan, 69
Kol Movement, 118n
Koppar, 41
Kulkarni, S., 86, 87
Kumar, S., 82, 96

Kuper, L., 41
Kurmi peasants. 142

labour, aristocracy, 93, 172; as commodity, 95; market, 15, 93; reserve, 73, 79, 94–99; segmentation of, 91–94
labouring community, 170, 172
Lalkhand, 165, 166, 169–70, 219–20
land, alienation, 68, 70, 75, 83, 127, 137, 185; grants, 63, 64; ownership, 60, 62, 170; rights, 140; tenure system, 64; and territory, 134; transfers, 68, 70, 75; usufrust of, 60, 62
landlords, 67, 68, 70, 185–86, 187, 212
Langton, M., 37
languages, adivasi, 17, 175, 177, 223, 227, 235; identity, 188
Laternari, V., 133
Latin America, 45
laughing, as expression of resistance, 214
Leiris, M., 41
legalist actions, 116–17
leisure, 226
liberation movements, 45–46
· liquor consumption issue, 188
locals, and migrants, 87–89
Lutherans, 164

Mafeje, A., 27, 30, 31, 36, 98, 154, 239
Maharaj, R.N., 85, 165, 185, 187, 220
Mahato, Binod Bihari, 142, 143
Mahila Shilpa Kala Kendra, 189
Mair, L., 30, 39
Man, E.G., 119
Manbhaum, 148
Mandal, B.B., 35
Manjhi, D., 165–66
manjhis, 58, 59, 63
Maquet, J.J., 15
Marxist perspective, 26
Marxist tradition, 37
massacre, 131
Mathur, K.S., 33, 35